AFRICAN ISSUES

Disability Rights and Inclusiveness in Africa

AFRICAN ISSUES

AFRICAN ISSUES

Disability Rights and Inclusiveness in Africa

The Convention on the Rights of Persons with Disabilities, challenges and change

Edited by

Jeff D. Grischow and Magnus Mfoafo-M'Carthy

JAMES CURREY

James Currey
is an imprint of Boydell & Brewer Ltd
PO Box 9, Woodbridge
Suffolk IP12 3DF (GB)
www.jamescurrey.com
and of
Boydell & Brewer Inc.
668 Mt Hope Avenue
Rochester, NY 14620–2731 (US)
www.boydellandbrewer.com

First published 2022

British Library Cataloguing in Publication Data
A catalogue record of this publication is available from the British Library

ISBN 978-1-84701-291-3 (James Currey paperback)

CONTENTS

ILLUSTRATIONS

Figures

Tables

Full credit details are provided in the captions to the images in the text. The editors, contributors and publisher are grateful to all the institutions and persons for permission to reproduce the materials in which they hold copyright. Every effort has been made to trace the copyright holders; apologies are offered for any omission, and the publisher will be pleased to add any necessary acknowledgement in subsequent editions.

NOTES ON CONTRIBUTORS

Mikyas Abera is an assistant professor of sociology at the University of Gondar. His research interests include education, urbanization, psychosocial rehabilitation, and gender, among others. Currently, Dr Abera manages the Mastercard Foundation Scholars Program at the University of Gondar, a scholarship programme for talented East African youth with disabilities.

Charlotte Capri is a clinical psychologist and researcher in intellectual disability. She holds a PhD in Clinical Psychology (Intellectual Disability) and a DPhil in Political Science. Her current interests include ethics of care and psychiatric and behavioural health in intellectual disability.

Tsitsi Chataika is a disability studies and inclusive education associate professor and consultant. She is the chairperson of the Educational Foundations Department, University of Zimbabwe. She has written several publications including the 2019 Outstanding Taylor and Francis (Routledge) Handbook Award Winner in the Social Sciences, *The Routledge Handbook of Disability Activism.*

Juventus Duorinaah is the executive director of the Ghana National Association of the Deaf. He holds a Bachelor of Arts degree from the University of Ghana and a Master of Law degree from Cardiff School of Law and Politics and is currently pursuing a Bachelor of Law degree at the University of Ghana.

Jeff D. Grischow is an associate professor of history at Wilfrid Laurier University in Ontario, Canada. His research interests include the idea and practice of development in Africa and the history and experience of disability and disability rights in Ghana. His current research includes three projects with Magnus Mfoafo-M'Carthy supported by the Social Sciences and Humanities Research Council of Canada, which focus on disability rights and inclusive education in Ghana.

Lincoln Hlatywayo is a disability studies and inclusive education associate professor at Zimbabwe Open University. He is also a specialist in sign language training and development and a disability consultant and has been engaged by various organizations and ministries in Zimbabwe.

Bonny Ibhawoh is professor and Senator William McMaster Chair in Global Human Rights at McMaster University, Canada. He is the director of the McMaster Centre for Human Rights and Restorative Justice. He also chairs the United Nations Expert Mechanism on the Right to Development. He is the author of the books *Imperial Justice: African in Empire's Court* and *Human Rights in Africa*.

Elvis Imafidon lectures at the Department of Religions and Philosophies, School of History, Religions and Philosophies at the School of Oriental and African Studies, University of London. He is the author of *African Philosophy and the Otherness of Albinism* (Routledge, 2019).

Magnus Mfoafo-M'Carthy is an associate professor at the Lyle S. Hallman Faculty of Social Work, Wilfrid Laurier University, and a former Carnegie Diasporan Fellow at the University of Ghana. He has published articles in journals including the *International Journal for Equity in Health* and the *International Journal of Mental Health*.

Wisdom Kwadwo Mprah is a senior lecturer at the Centre for Disability and Rehabilitation Studies, Department of Health Promotion and Disability Studies, School of Public Health, Kwame Nkrumah University of Science and Technology, Kumasi, Ghana. He holds a Diploma in Education, Bachelor of Arts (Geography), and MPhil (Geography) from the University of Cape Coast, Ghana, and a PhD (Disability Studies) from the University of Illinois at Chicago, USA.

Herbert Muyinda is a senior lecturer at the Child Health and Development Centre, Makerere University. Muyinda's research centres on disability, mental illness, HIV and AIDS, and tuberculosis. He is currently involved in exploring, developing, and testing culturally safe, strengths-based, trauma-informed, and technology-enhanced interventions in war-affected (disabled) populations in Northern Uganda.

Augustina Naami is a senior lecturer at the University of Ghana. She holds a Bachelor of Arts in Economics from the University of Ghana, and a master's degree and PhD in Social Work from the Universities of Chicago and Utah, respectively. Her research interests include disability and the intersection of vulnerabilities and social policy.

Joana Okine is a graduate assistant at the Department of Social Work, University of Ghana. She holds a Bachelor of Arts in Social Work with Sociology and an MPhil in Social Work, both from the University of Ghana. Her research interests are disability and health-related issues.

Maxwell Peprah Opoku is currently an Assistant Professor in Special Education at the United Arab Emirates University (UAEU). He holds a PhD in Education from the University of Tasmania, Australia. Before Joining UAEU, he worked as a casual academic, teaching undergraduate and graduate courses at the Faculty of Education, University of Tasmania, Australia.

Billian Otundo is currently a postdoctoral researcher at the University of Bayreuth, Germany. She is also a lecturer at Moi University in Kenya and holds a PhD in English Linguistics from the University of Bayreuth. In 2019, she completed her first postdoctoral fellowship as a collaborative researcher of Moi University, Kenya and Radboud University and Leiden University of the Netherlands.

Bernard Nsaidzedze Sakah is a Cameroonian who holds a PhD and MSc in Governance and Regional Integration from the Pan African University, Cameroon. He also holds a Bachelor of Science in Sociology and Anthropology from the University of Buea, also in Cameroon. His research interests include governance, education, human rights, and education. He has served as a volunteer with many non-governmental organizations and is currently the managing director of Big Steps Outreach Network – Cameroon.

Susan Reynolds Whyte is a professor at the Department of Anthropology, University of Copenhagen, who carries out research in East Africa on efforts to secure well-being. Her publications deal with the management of misfortune, gender, generation, changing healthcare systems, disability, social lives of medicines, legacies of violence, HIV, and other chronic conditions.

ACKNOWLEDGEMENTS

We would like to thank the authors in this volume for their hard work and profound insights into disability rights in Africa. We owe a great debt to James Currey for taking on this project and, in particular, to Commissioning Editor Jaqueline Mitchell, whose steadfast commitment to the manuscript and insightful editorial suggestions were deeply appreciated. The book also benefited greatly from detailed comments and suggestions by an anonymous reviewer, as well as excellent copy editing by Karen Francis and indexing by Cheryl Lemmens. Thanks also to Emily Champion at Boydell and Brewer for managing the proofreading process thoroughly and efficiently. On a personal level, Magnus Mfoafo-M'Carthy would like to thank his partner, Stella, and daughters, Daisy and Michelle, for their support, patience, and encouragement during the course of this project. Jeff Grischow would like to thank his partner Yvette for her unwavering support of his work on disability in Africa, and Sydney and Theo for their encouragement and curiosity. Together, we would also like to thank the Social Sciences and Humanities Research Council of Canada for funding, as well as the facilitators at Wilfrid Laurier University's Office of Research Services.

ABBREVIATIONS

ADA	Americans with Disabilities Act
AfriNEAD	African Network for Evidence-to-Action in Disability
AHC	Ad Hoc Committee
ANRS	Amhara National Regional State
AT	Assistive technology
BoLSA	Bureau of Labor and Social Affairs
CBC	Competency-based curriculum
CBID	Community-based inclusive development
CBR	Community-based rehabilitation
CHRAJ	Commission on Human Rights and Administrative Justice
CSO	Civil Society Organization
CoRPD	Committee on the Rights of Persons with Disabilities
CRPD	Convention on the Rights of Persons with Disabilities 2006
CwDs	Children with Disabilities
DPI	Disabled Peoples' International
DPO	Disabled People's Organization
DRDP	Declaration on the Rights of Disabled Persons
DRMRP	Declaration on the Rights of Mentally Retarded Persons
EARCs	Education assessment and resource centres
ECDD	Ethiopian Centre for Disability and Development
ECDE	Early childhood development and education
ERI	Early reading initiative
FASD	Foetal alcohol spectrum disorders
FGD	Focus group discussion
FPE	Free primary education
GEM	Global Education Monitoring
GMR	Global Monitoring Report
GNAD	Ghana National Association of the Deaf
GSL	Ghana Sign Language
HEI	Higher educational institution
HIV	Human immunodeficiency viruses
ICCPR	International Covenant on Civil and Political Rights

ICESCR	International Covenant on Economic, Social and Cultural Rights
ID	Intellectual disability
IE	Inclusive education
IGAs	Income-generating activities
ILO	International Labour Organization
INWWD	International Network of Women with Disabilities
IYDP	International Year of Disabled Persons
KISE	Kenya Institute of Special Education
KNCHR	Kenya National Commission on Human Rights
KNSPWD	Kenya National Survey for Persons with Disabilities
LDs	Learning disabilities
LCDZ	Leonard Cheshire Disability Zimbabwe
LwDs	Learners with disabilities
MoEST	Ministry of Education, Science and Technology
MoPSE	Ministry of Primary and Secondary Education
NCCE	National Commission on Civic Education
NCPWD	National Council for Persons with Disabilities
NESC	National Economic and Social Council
NGEC	National Gender and Equality Commission
NGO	Non-governmental organization
NRM	National Resistance Movement
NUDIPU	National Union of Disabled Persons of Uganda
PLAP	Performance lag address programme
PPIPMI	Principles on the Protection and Integrity of People with Mental Illness and the Improvement of Mental Health Care
PwD	Persons with disabilities
PwDA	Persons with Disability Act (Ghana)
PwIDs	Persons with intellectual disability
RI	Rehabilitation International
RSA	Republic of South Africa
SREOPD	Standard Rules on the Equalization of Opportunities for Persons with Disabilities
SSA	Statistics South Africa
SDG	Sustainable Development Goals
SIG	Special interest groups
SNE	Special needs education
SRH	Sexual and reproductive health
TAF	The Albino Foundation
TRC	Truth and Reconciliation Commission

TVETs	Technical and vocational education and training institutes
UDHR	Universal Declaration of Human Rights
UoG-CBR	The University of Gondar's Community-Based Rehabilitation
UN	United Nations
UNCRC	United Nations Convention on the Rights of the Child
UNDP	United Nations Development Programme
UNICEF	United Nations Children's Fund
UNESCO	United Nations Educational, Scientific and Cultural Organization
VRC	Vocational rehabilitation centre
WB	World Bank
WGwDs	Women and girls with disabilities
WHO	World Health Organization
YwDs	Youth with disabilities

Introduction

JEFF D. GRISCHOW & MAGNUS MFOAFO-M'CARTHY

Disability rights have risen to global prominence since the introduction of the United Nations (UN) Convention on the Rights of Persons with Disabilities (CRPD) in 2006. The CRPD represented the culmination of 'the last civil rights movement' for disability rights, which can be traced back to the early 1980s and the founding of Disabled Peoples' International (DPI), an organization dedicated to advancing human rights for persons with disabilities (PwDs) on a global level (Driedger, 1989). The relative lateness of the global campaign for disability rights occurred despite the fact that disability has been part of the human condition since time immemorial, in the sense that all human beings will experience it in some form, even if only from ageing. The historical factors leading up to the CRPD will be discussed below; its current relevance is borne out by the estimate that 15% of the world's population – one billion people – 'experience some form of disability', and that between 190 and 200 million people are severely disabled (World Bank [WB], 2021). As such, PwDs represent 'the largest minority group' on a global scale (Lindsay, Hartman, and Fellin, 2015). However, the need for global disability rights arises from not only the sheer number of people who experience disability globally, but also the fact that PwDs are among the most marginalized populations worldwide.

Disabled persons are more likely to be poor (International Labour Organization, UN Development Programme, and World Health Organization [ILO, UNDP, and WHO], 2004). They experience widespread stigma and discrimination, poor healthcare, comparatively low literacy rates, and high levels of unemployment or menial, precarious, low-paying work. PwDs are more susceptible to social isolation and marginalization (WHO and World Bank [WB], 2011). These issues and challenges can be especially severe among certain social groups. Disabled youth are particularly badly affected by unemployment and are more prone to work in precarious, informal sector positions than disabled adults (Lindsay, Hartman, and Fellin, 2015). Disabled women, minorities and children face even more severe challenges: their employment rates, wages and formal sector employment tend to be lower than those of their male counterparts (WHO, 2011). These issues and challenges are especially serious in the Global South, which is home to 80% of the world's population of PwDs (Trani and Loeb, 2012; Cramm, Lorenzo, and Nieboer, 2014; Échevin, 2013). Of these, it is estimated that 300 million persons with disabilities (PwDs) live in Africa.[1]

Despite the large population of Africans with disabilities, relatively few academic studies have been published specifically on disability rights in African contexts. Indeed, until recently, most work on disability rights has focused on the West. For Africa, Driedger's history of international disability rights briefly mentions Zimbabwe and French West Africa (Driedger, 1989), and some research has explored Southern Africa after 1980 (Malinga, 1999; Howell, Chalklen, and Alberts, 2006). More recently, Gebrekidan (2012) investigated the history of disability rights in Kenya. Grischow (2011, 2015), Geurts (2015), Geurts and Komabu-Pomeyie (2019), and Mfoafo-M'Carthy and Grischow (2017, 2020) have examined the history and experience of disability rights in Ghana. South Africa has received perhaps the most attention from scholars focusing on disability rights. Some of the most notable publications include Rowland (2004) and Howell, Chalklen, and Alberts (2006) on the history of the South African disability rights movement, Black and Matos-Ala (2016) on disability rights and inclusion, Kamga (2016) on disability rights and legislation, and Capri *et al.* (2018) on intellectual disability (ID) rights.

Beyond individual articles scattered across the literature, there are very few single volumes dedicated to disability rights in the Global South and Africa. Two notable exceptions are a special volume of the journal *Disability and Rehabilitation* on the rights of PwDs in Africa (2009) and the annual *African Disability Rights Yearbook*, which began publication in 2013. The special issue of *Disability and Rehabilitation* contains an excellent overview

[1] According to the African Studies Centre Leiden. Available at <https://www.ascleiden.nl/content/webdossiers/disability-africa> [accessed 11 March 2022].

of the CRPD in Africa, including its relationship to the African Network for Evidence-to-Action in Disability (AfriNEAD), an organization devoted to achieving disability rights across the continent. However, all but one of the articles focus on South Africa, which unfortunately limits the scope significantly. This leaves the *African Disability Rights Yearbook* as the only substantial publication on African disability rights between 2013 and the present. Fortunately, it is an excellent resource, providing an annual compendium of original research articles, country updates, and book reviews. It is here that we find some of the best writing on disability rights in Africa, although only fourteen contributions have focused specifically on the CRPD since 2013. Still, the contributions are notable, especially Lord and Stein's (2013) seminal article surveying the prospects and challenges of the Convention for Africa as a whole. While recognizing the CRPD as a defining moment for disability rights in Africa, Lord and Stein argue that the biggest challenges will fall on Civil Society Organizations (CSOs) as they attempt to hold African governments accountable for implementing and monitoring the Convention's provisions. This is one, but not the only, challenge that the contributors to this volume will highlight.

Apart from specific studies of disability rights in Africa, two recent collections on disability in the Global South deserve mention, because they engage with themes covered by the contributors in this book: Grech and Soldatic's *Disability in the Global South* (2016) and Watermeyer *et al.*'s The *Palgrave Handbook of Disability and Citizenship in the Global South* (2019). While not concerned specifically with the CRPD in Africa, both volumes adopt perspectives and themes that have informed our book, and both offer individual chapters relevant to disability rights in Africa. For example, in *Disability in the Global South*, Eide and Loeb highlight the importance of using disability statistics as a foundation for ensuring the disability rights embedded in the CRPD and monitoring its implementation (Eide and Loeb, 2016). Several chapters explore the economic rights enshrined in the CRPD. Hanass-Hancock and Mitra use the concept of livelihoods as a means of attaining the economic rights of the Convention (Hanass-Hancock and Mitra, 2016); Ferrante and Joly examine the CRPD as a vehicle to address the problem of begging in the Global South, from the perspective of Latin America (Ferrante and Joly, 2016); Grech assesses the CRPD as a tool for addressing poverty generally in the Global

South (Grech, 2016). One chapter focuses on the Convention and the right to education in Ethiopia (Katsui *et al.*, 2016), and another focuses on India and South Africa (Singal and Nithi Muthukrishna, 2016). Price and Goyal (2016) provide an analysis of the CRPD and gender in the Global South.

The *Palgrave Handbook of Disability and Citizenship* also contains chapters connected to the themes in this book. Garland-Thomson's (2019) analysis of Kazuo Ishiguro's *Never Let Me Go* views the novel from the perspectives of the CRPD, personhood and inclusion. Kahonde and McKenzie (2019) discuss the Convention in relation to ID, sexuality, citizenship, and family caregiving, with a particular focus on a feminist ethics of care that is a cultural norm in the South African context. In a separate chapter, Capri (2019) addresses a similar theme, including personhood and an ethics of care relating to intellectual development. McConkey (2019) extends the discussion of ID to the question of citizenship rights in the Global South. Horton and Shakespeare (2019) focus on the Convention's Articles on healthcare and employment in Kenya, Uganda, and Zambia, arguing that progress has been very slow despite all three countries having ratified the CRPD. Wood *et al.* (2019) assess the CRPD's potential impact on education for children with intellectual disabilities in South Africa. Claassens, Shaikh, and Swartz (2019) tackle the issue of religion as a force to engage with in implementing the CRPD in the Global South, with a focus on Southern Africa, including possibilities for using religious beliefs as a basis for social inclusion. Lorenzo and Coleridge (2019) argue that disability rights will not flow automatically from the CRPD; instead, achieving the Convention's rights will require proactive advocacy and action by PwDs in partnership with people without disabilities. Roulstone (2019) addresses the CRPD provisions for freedom from harm and inequity, including protection from violence and hate crimes. Many of the contributions in *Disability in the Global South* and The *Palgrave Handbook of Disability and Citizenship in the Global South* relate to the themes addressed by our contributors, although neither book focuses specifically on the CRPD. This volume is therefore unique in its contribution to the literature on disability rights in Africa. As a foundation for what follows, we will now turn to an overview of the Convention as it applies to the themes discussed by our contributors.

United Nations Convention on the Rights of PwDs

Opened for ratification in 2006, the CRPD brought the world's attention to the need for human rights for PwDs around the world. Currently ratified by 186 countries as well as the European Union, the CRPD aims to 'promote, protect and ensure the full and equal enjoyment of all human rights and fundamental freedoms by all PwDs, and to promote respect for their inherent dignity'. In contrast to previous UN instruments on disability, the CRPD integrates the social model of disability into its framework.

The Convention was a very important addition to the canon of UN rights Declarations and Conventions, which stretched back to the Universal Declaration of Human Rights (UDHR) of 1948, created in response to the Holocaust and designed to protect citizens against predatory behaviour and atrocities by their own States. This provided the foundation for subsequent UN Conventions on human rights (excluding the CRPD for the moment), including: the International Convention on the Elimination of All Forms of Racial Discrimination (1965); the International Covenant on Civil and Political Rights (ICCPR; 1966); the International Covenant on Economic, Social and Cultural Rights (ICESCR; 1966); the Convention on the Elimination of All Forms of Discrimination against Women (1979); the Convention against Torture and Other Cruel, Inhuman or Degrading Treatment or Punishment (1984); the Convention on the Rights of the Child (UNCRC; 1989); the International Convention on the Protection of the Rights of All Migrant Workers and Members of their Families (1990); and the International Convention for the Protection of All Persons from Enforced Disappearance (2006). None of these Conventions mentioned PwDs except for the Convention of the Rights of the Child (Kanter, 2015).

The UN did produce other instruments on disability rights, although none of them carried the weight of the formal Conventions. The first two of these, which appeared in the 1970s, were the Declaration on the Rights of Mentally Retarded Persons (DRMRP; UN, 1971) and the Declaration on the Rights of Disabled Persons (DRDP; UN, 1975). The UN followed up the Declarations of the 1970s with two documents in the 1990s: the Principles on the Protection and Integrity of People with Mental Illness and the Improvement of Mental Health Care (PPIPMI; UN, 1991) and the Standard Rules on the Equalization of Opportunities for Persons with Disabilities (SREOPD; UN, 1993). Taken together, these four initiatives established some rights for PwDs, including economic security, medical care, and protection against exploitation. However, they were limited in significant ways. The DRMRP of 1971 and DRDP of 1975 adopted the language of the prevailing 'medical model' of disability, which portrayed disability as an individual problem arising from physical or mental impairment and requiring medical fixes designed to return the person to 'normal'. As such, human rights for PwDs in the 1970s tended to be limited to supporting individual rehabilitation and the 'normalization' of disabled bodies (Grischow, 2019). Moreover, the DRMRP and DRDP provided for a few specific rights, rather than a complete package of unequivocal rights. The PPIPMI and SREOPD adopted more universal rights language. For example, the PPIPMI includes the provision that persons with mental illness 'shall have the right to exercise all civil, political, economic, social and cultural rights' contained in other UN documents (UN, 1991: Provision 1[5]). The SREOPD established a set of guiding rules for enforcing disability rights in order 'to ensure that girls, boys, women and men with disabilities, as members of their societies, may exercise the same rights and obligations as others' (UN, 1993: Introduction, Article 15). These documents signalled a major step forward towards universal rights for PwDs. However, as with the declarations of the 1970s, neither of them was 'binding and legally enforceable', and therefore they fell short of providing full, equal, and unequivocal rights for PwDs (Kanter, 2015: 6).

Meanwhile, there were other global developments during the 1970s and 1980s that fed into the growth of the international disability rights movement and would become a driving force behind the CRPD. First, the UN developed 'third generation' human rights, focused on specific groups (e.g. women, children, and PwDs, as described above) rather than individuals as undifferentiated citizens. Second, disability activists began to challenge the ableist attitudes that kept disability off the human rights agenda at the UN (Kanter, 2015). Their sustained efforts laid the foundation for the emergence of a key disability rights initiative at the UN (Heyer, 2015).

A major turning point for global disability activism happened in Winnipeg, Canada, at the annual conference of Rehabilitation International (RI) in 1980. Fed up with the exclusion of PwDs from RI's board, the conference's disabled delegates demanded majority control over the organization. When RI flatly rejected the petition, the disabled delegates withdrew and formed their own organization, DPI (Driedger, 1989). DPI connected disabled activists to each other and empowered them to create national disability organizations controlled by PwDs themselves. African initiatives were led by Joshua Malinga from the Zimbabwean Movement of Disabled Persons, who transformed Zimbabwe's disability movement by forming the rights-focused National Council of Disabled Persons of Zimbabwe and played a leading role in the development of Disabled People South Africa (Charlton, 1998; Howell, Chalklen, and Alberts, 2006). Meanwhile, the UN declared 1981 the International Year of Disabled Persons (IYDP), and then declared 1983–92 the International Decade of Disabled Persons. In 1983–84 the UN also appointed two Special Rapporteurs on global disability issues, Leandro Despouy and Erica-Irene Daes. Their reports documented widespread human rights abuses, which supported the calls of the international disability movement for action on disability rights (Kanter, 2014). In the United States, the disability rights movement achieved an important victory with the passage of the Americans with Disabilities Act (ADA) of 1990, which 'catapulted the United States into an unaccustomed position of leadership in the human rights community and played a central role in a global 'paradigm shift' in thinking about disability as a rights issue' (Heyer, 2015: 2–3). The ADA's example prompted more discussions of disability rights at the UN, which culminated in Leandro Despouy's report, *Human Rights and Disabled Persons*, in 1993. Despouy's report led to the adoption of the UN's Standard Rules on the Equalization of Opportunities for Disabled Persons in late 1993, which was 'the most progressive non-binding international standards-setting document to have been adopted prior to the CRPD' (Guernsey, Nicoli, and Ninio, 2007: 1, fn. 2).

The next major step towards the CRPD occurred in 2001, when the Mexican members of the UN General Assembly, supported mainly by States in the Global South, sponsored a General Assembly Resolution calling for an Ad Hoc Committee (AHC) to consider an international Convention on disability rights (Guernsey, Nicoli, and Ninio, 2007). The resulting AHC, which was tasked with drafting the CRPD, included representation from seven African countries: Cameroon, Comoros, Mali, Morocco, Sierra Leone, South Africa, and Uganda. African States were also represented on the Working Group on National Human Rights Institutions and the UN's Committee on the Rights of Persons with Disabilities (CoRPD) (Lord and Stein, 2013: 98).

After four years of work, the AHC forwarded the CRPD to the General Assembly, where it was adopted on 13 December 2006 (Guernsey, Nicoli, and Ninio, 2007). Not only was it the most quickly negotiated human rights treaty in the history of the UN (2015), but the CRPD also established systematic disability rights for the first time on a global scale. In the words of Don McKay, who chaired the AHC responsible for negotiating the draft of the CRPD 'What the Convention endeavours to do is to elaborate in detail the rights of PwDs and set out a code of implementation' (UN, 2020). In doing so, the CRPD is notable in establishing a set of legally binding disability rights and duties in which States who have ratified the Convention are obligated to implement and uphold its provisions. The CRPD is also noteworthy because it sets out a comprehensive range of civil, political, economic, cultural, and social rights which are 'indivisible, interrelated and interconnected' (UN General Assembly, 1993).

The CRPD: Rights and Duties

The contributions in this volume speak to the CRPD's provision of rights for PwDs, as well as the establishment of duties for States Parties.[2] Each of these will be discussed in turn below, but first it is necessary to present the Convention's definition of disability. It is important to note that the approach adopted by the CRPD is consistent with the social model of disability; this rejects the medical model, which equates disability with individual impairments and calls for expert medical 'fixes'. In contrast, the social model defines disability as the outcome of disabling conditions, such as inaccessible physical structures, and negative societal attitudes, which create barriers for disabled persons and thus limit their potential to participate in their communities (Oliver and Barnes, 1998; Palacios, 2015). The human rights approach adopted by the CRPD is also a departure from the charity model and views PwDs as subjects who have rights instead of objects of charity (Katsui, 2008; Silecchia,

[2] The full text of the CRPD can be found on the website of the Disability section of the UN's department of economic and social affairs: <https://www.un.org/development/desa/disabilities/convention-on-the-rights-of-persons-with-disabilities/the-convention-in-brief.html> [accessed 11 March 2022].

2013). These aspects of the Convention's definition of disability are contained in Article 1, which defines PwDs as including

> those who have long-term physical, mental, intellectual or sensory impairments which in interaction with various barriers may hinder their full and effective participation in society on an equal basis with others (UN, 2006).

This affirms the social construction of disability, whereby limitations/hindrances arise in a person's interactions with environmental barriers rather than as the consequence of an individualized impairment or inherent limitation. Keeping this definition in mind, we shall now move on to the rights and duties embedded in the CRPD.

Rights of PwDs

The Articles of the CRPD cover a wide range of rights. General rights include the inherent rights to life, liberty, property, and inheritance (Articles 10, 12, and 14); equality before the law, equal legal protection, and access to justice (Articles 5 and 13); equal access to cultural, social, and political activities (Articles 29 and 30); access to information in accessible formats (Article 21); and the right to privacy (Article 22). The Convention also enshrines the rights of PwDs to live independently and to have access to accessible built environments and services and the information to make this possible (Articles 9, 19, and 20), and to enjoy an equal standard of living and social protections (Article 28).

More specific provisions include equal rights to education and training (Article 24), rehabilitation (Article 26), healthcare (Article 25), employment including self-employment and entrepreneurship, and equal treatment in the workplace (Article 27). Specific provisions are also made for guaranteeing the rights of children (Articles 7 and 23) and women and girls (Article 6). Regarding the latter, the CRPD recognizes that women with disabilities (WwDs) face multiple levels of discrimination (Article 6, Section 1), which has been highlighted in the literature on gender and disability (Heymann, Stein, and Moreno, 2014; Mizunoya and Mitra, 2013; Mitra and Sambamoorthi, 2014; Mitra, Posarac, and Vick, 2011; Naami, 2014; WHO, 2011). They are reinforced by the subsequent Sustainable Development Goals (SDGs) of the UN, such as Goal 5, which seeks to 'achieve gender equality and empower all women and girls' (UN, 2015).

Three Articles deal either directly or indirectly with mental health: 12, 14, and 17. Article 12, which sets out the right of PwDs to play an active role in decisions affecting their well-being, allows for 'supported decision-making', in which a PwD voluntarily permits someone else to make decisions on their behalf. However, the Article is strongly opposed to 'substitute decision-making', which removes the requirement for voluntary consent by PwDs. To ensure equity and fairness, the CRPD's provision for supported decision-making allows for assistance based on the will of the disabled person (Capri and Swartz, 2018). Article 14 also guarantees equality of liberty and security, including protection from arbitrary detention (although it permits preventive detention on some other grounds). Article 17 sets out the right to 'physical and psychological integrity', which includes protection from compulsory medical treatment (Wildeman, 2013; Bartlett, 2012).

Duties of States Parties

In addition to establishing rights, the CRPD also sets out duties for States Parties to follow in the process of guaranteeing rights for PwDs. The chapters in this volume discuss a number of the duties enshrined in the Convention. General obligations are presented in Article 4, including the adoption of legal, policymaking, and administrative measures necessary for achieving economic, social, and cultural rights, as well as the abolition of laws inconsistent with human rights. The Article also mandates States to act in accordance with the CRPD's provisions and to ensure that public authorities uphold the Convention in implementing policies and programmes (UN, 2006). In addition, Article 4(3) calls on States to consult with disability associations in developing and implementing laws and policies consistent with the Convention. Other Articles also stipulate duties required to achieve specific rights, including facilitating access to justice and legal proceedings (Article 13), abolishing discrimination in general and with respect to marriage and family life (Articles 4 and 23), combatting prejudice, stigma, violence, abuse, and exploitation (Articles 8 and 16), guaranteeing physical and mental integrity (Article 17), and protecting PwDs from torture and inhumane treatment (Article 15).

The CRPD also includes duties relating to civil and political society, development assistance, and institutional support for disability rights. Article 28 calls on States to support the right of

PwDs to create and join Disabled People's Organizations (DPOs) in order to represent themselves 'at international, national, regional and local levels' (Article 29[b.ii]). Article 29 mandates States Parties to ensure full and equal participation in political and public life, including voting in democratic elections. Article 32 calls on governments to provide development assistance for disability programmes and to support partnerships with international and local partners, and grassroots participation and mobilization, in implementing this provision. This duty includes providing accessible information about assistive technologies (ATs), as well as other forms of assistance, support services, and facilities. Article 33 calls for the creation of national institutions and mechanisms – including central government bodies – responsible specifically for the promotion and achievement of disability rights. This Article also mandates States to involve PwDs themselves in monitoring the implementation of their rights (UN, 2006).

Grassroots Perspectives on the CRPD

Many scholars have been optimistic about the potential of the CRPD as a tool for achieving disability rights globally, including in the Global South and Africa. The Convention, they claim, has ushered in 'a paradigm shift in political conceptions of disability' (Mannan, MacLachlan, and McVeigh, 2012: 172). It has created a new disability discourse that will empower civil society (Harpur, 2017) and it will become a central tool for removing the 'societal barriers that create and reinforce disability' (Cobley, 2013: 453). In the opinion of Stein and Lord (2009: 32), two of the most important scholars of the CRPD, the Convention will make it possible to 'legislate a belief change regarding persons with disabilities'. Following up on this claim, in 2013 they reviewed the CRPD's potential for Africa by presenting 'successful CRPD-based responses' in a number of African countries – including South Africa, Uganda and Ghana, which are covered in this book – 'that have facilitated domestic-level human rights implementation' (Lord and Stein, 2013: 102). These actions include advocacy campaigns by DPOs to combat abuses of persons with mental illness (including in South Africa, Uganda, and Ghana), humanitarian assistance to persons disabled by war, work on HIV issues, and campaigns to increase legal capacity and access to justice. The authors end on a very hopeful note, writing that:

> The progressive developments recorded in this article constitute a viable and altogether hopeful set of interventions that can be built upon in order to further advance an emerging and uniquely African disability rights narrative. Ratification of the CRPD across the continent and the impetus that it has created for domestic law and policy change offers Africans with disabilities and their allies the promise of rights realization (Lord and Stein, 2013: 112).

With the exception of Cobley, the optimists discussed above based their conclusions on surveys of existing literature rather than original research conducted on the ground. The chapters in this volume use a grassroots approach to challenge their rather uncritical praise of the CRPD by presenting the findings of African-based researchers working in Ghana, Cameroon, Nigeria, Ethiopia, Uganda, Zimbabwe, and South Africa. Thematically, the authors consider many Articles of the CRPD, including education, employment, healthcare, justice, mental health, and information/advocacy. While many of the authors present positive developments that have come out of the CRPD, the main lesson of the book is that there are serious barriers inhibiting the Convention from being implemented in a way that actually achieves full and equal rights for PwDs in Africa. On balance, this volume offers many trenchant critiques of the CRPD in Africa and as such rejects the uncritical praise of the optimists described above. But many of the authors also see grounds for hope, and one of the goals of this collection is to provide ideas for removing the barriers preventing the implementation of the Convention's Articles in (and hopefully beyond) the African countries covered in the book.

The contributions identify barriers to the CRPD's successful implementation in Africa at the international, national, and local levels. Internationally, there are inherent problems with a global Convention as a tool for national and local-level rights. Some of this book's authors (e.g. Mprah and Duorinaah, Chapter 7) argue that even though representatives from the Global South were important actors in developing the CRPD, the Convention applies more to the Global North and is unsuited to African cultural contexts. Other authors express concern with the vagueness of the Convention's prescriptions as a 'one size fits all' instrument (see Capri, Chapter 1). There is also the problem of enforceability. Although the signatories promise to uphold the CRPD, it is up to individual governments to implement its Articles. This brings us to implementation barriers at the national level, which Capri (Chapter 1) describes as the problem of 'domesticating' the CRPD. At the highest level, this process requires that African States implement disability legislation and policies. Among our case studies, countries such as Uganda (Chapter 5) and South Africa (Chapter 2) have deeply rooted and longstanding constitutional/legal provisions for disability rights, while others such as Cameroon (Chapter 9) have not. Other countries, including Ghana (Chapters 7 and 8) and Zimbabwe (Chapter 3), came late to the table but passed national laws over the past five years. However, even where disability laws exist, they are not always entirely consistent with the CRPD, as in the case of laws relating to gender and disability in Ghana (Chapter 6).

Furthermore, assuming that progressive laws and policies can be implemented, most of the authors in this collection point to additional barriers to implementation, including a lack of political will/accountability to enforce legislation and implement policy, an absence of adequate resources, poor and inaccessible infrastructure, and gaps in social services (including education and healthcare). Politicians and civil servants also often lack adequate knowledge and training, so that they do not understand disability issues or stigmatize and discriminate PwDs. Several chapters also show that the leaders of national DPOs often lack adequate training, skills, and resources to implement and manage programmes (Chapters 5, 6, and 7). Even if they have good training and skills, DPO leaders are often excluded from participating in policymaking at the national level, as is the case in Cameroon (Chapter 9). At the other end of the spectrum, in Uganda DPO leaders have been captured and co-opted by predatory and clientelist States, which not only lends itself to corruption but also makes it very difficult for lower-level DPO leaders and rank-and-file members to criticize national disability politics and programmes. Muyinda and Whyte call this phenomenon 'disabolitics' (Chapter 5). Even if all of the above measures can be put in place and PwDs have a full voice at the national level, poverty at the State level makes it very difficult for governments to sustain policies and programmes without the perpetual support of foreign donors (Chapters 5 and 6).

Significant barriers to disability rights also exist at the regional and local levels in many African countries. Stigma and discrimination are widespread at the community level and among many family members. PwDs are stripped of their humanity and personhood, which leads to social exclusion and denials of legal capacity and other forms of agency such as power over decision-making (Chapters 1, 7, and 8). Combined with poverty and a general lack of social services and infrastructure, stigma and discrimination mean that PwDs are excluded from education and adequate healthcare and justice. Where facilities do exist, poverty and the lack of accessible built environments make it very difficult for PwDs to travel to school, clinics/ hospitals, and courts. Regional and local DPOs try their best to respond to these challenges, but in many cases their leaders lack training and resources and their organizations are chronically underfunded and unsupported, except perhaps by foreign non-governmental organizations (NGOs). To complicate the picture, evidence from Ethiopia suggests that where programmes focus on grassroots on initiatives like CBR, governments might hesitate to provide central funding for national-level disability programmes (Chapter 4).

Ways Forward?

The chapters in this volume largely reject the optimists who argue that the existence of the CRPD in itself will produce a revolution in disability rights in Africa. The view from the ground shows that even where governments have developed progressive laws, policies, and programmes, there are significant obstacles to implementing the CRPD in Africa. Even where laws are good (e.g. in South Africa) or where disability legislation is deeply embedded (Uganda), or where there is a thriving and well-informed DPO leadership class (Cameroon), in many (if not most) cases the CRPD's provisions have not reached PwDs at the local level in the African countries represented in this book. However, this is not to say that there is no hope. Despite major obstacles and challenges, our authors offer some very interesting and useful ideas for moving forward and translating the CRPD's provisions into action. At the most general level, there is a need in many African countries to pass adequate legislation and laws that are consistent with the Convention's provisions. There is also a need for governments to develop policies and programmes tied to disability rights, including inclusive education (IE), employment and training, healthcare and rehabilitation, and anti-stigma campaigns. To support these programmes, government should develop and fund training sessions for regional and local-level DPO leaders, as well as national advocacy and information campaigns to educate citizens on disability issues. For this to happen, stakeholders will have to find ways to build political will among government officials and civil servants. This could be attempted through external/ international support and funding for disability initiatives, as well as support for media coverage of States' actions towards PwDs, including shaming if necessary. It is also important to tailor disability programmes to local socio-economic, political, and cultural contexts. While there are similar challenges across Africa, our chapters show that specific country and regional/ local contexts are extremely important. To this end, local-level research and analysis of the achievements, needs, and challenges of different African countries should be supported, especially by Africa-based researchers. These projects should pay attention to the specific needs of different disability types such as deafness (Chapter 5) and albinism (Chapter 8) and different social groups such as women and girls with disabilities (WGwDs) (Chapter 6). Finally, for the CRPD to become a reality in Africa, the participation of PwDs is essential, from research to policy development to the implementation of disability rights programmes.

Bibliography

Bartlett, P. 2012. 'The United Nations Convention on the Rights of PwDs and Mental Health Law', *Modern Law Review* 75(5): 752–78.

Black, D.R., and Matos-Ala, J. 2016. 'Building a More Inclusive South Africa: Progress and Pitfalls in Disability Rights and Inclusion', *Third World Thematics* 1(3): 335–52.

Capri, C., and Swartz, L. 2018. 'The Right to be Freepeople: Relational Voluntary-assisted-Advocacy as a Psychological and Ethical Resource for Decolonizing Intellectual Disability', *Journal of Social and Political Psychology* 6(2): 556–74.

Capri, C., Abrahams, L., McKenzie, J., Coetzee, O., Mkabile, S., Saptouw, M., Hooper, A., Smith, P., Adnams, C., and Swartz, L. 2018. 'Intellectual Disability Rights and Inclusive Citizenship in South

Africa: What Can a Scoping Review Tell Us?' *African Journal of Disability* 25(7): a396.

Charlton, J.I. 1998. *Nothing About Us without Us: Disability Oppression and Empowerment.* Berkeley: University of California Press.

Claassens, L.J., Shaikh, S., and Swartz, L. 2019. 'Engaging Disability and Religion in the Global South'. In: B. Watermeyer, J. McKenzie, and L. Swartz. Eds. *The Palgrave Handbook of Disability and Citizenship in the Global South* (pp. 147–64). Cham: Palgrave Macmillan.

Cobley, D.S. 2013. 'Towards Economic Participation: Examining the Impact of the Convention on the Rights of Persons with Disabilities in India', *Disability and Society* 28(4): 441–55.

Cramm, J.M., Lorenzo, T., and Nieboer, A.P. 2014. 'Comparing Education, Employment, Social Support and Well-being among Youth with Disabilities and Their Peers in South Africa', *Applied Research Quality Life* 9: 517–24.

Driedger, D. 1989. *The Last Civil Rights Movement: Disabled Peoples' International.* New York: St Martin's Press.

Durojaye, E., and Agaba, D.K. 2018. 'Contribution of the Health Ombud to Accountability: The Life Esidimeni Tragedy in South Africa', *Health and Human Rights,* 20(2): 161–68.

Échevin, D. 2013. 'Employment and Education Discrimination against Disabled People in Cape Verde', *Applied Economics* 45: 857–75.

Eide, A.H., and Loeb, M. 2016. 'Counting Disabled People: Historical Perspectives and the Challenges of Disability Statistics'. In: S. Grech and K. Soldatic, *Disability in the Global South: The Critical Handbook* (pp. 51–68). Cham: Springer Nature.

Ferrante, C. and Joly, E. 2016. 'Begging and Disability: A Paradigmatic Way to Earn One's Living'. In: S. Grech and K. Soldatic, *Disability in the Global South: The Critical Handbook* (pp. 155–66). Cham: Springer Nature.

Garland-Thomson, R. 2019. 'World Building, Citizenship, and Disability: The Strange World of Kazuo Ishiguro's *Never Let Me Go*'. In: B. Watermeyer, J. McKenzie, and L. Swartz. Eds. *The Palgrave Handbook of Disability and Citizenship in the Global South* (pp. 27–43). Cham: Palgrave Macmillan.

Gebrekidan, F.N. 2012. 'Disability Rights Activism in Kenya, 1959–1964: History from Below', *African Studies Review* 55(3): 103–22.

Geurts, K. 2015. 'On the Worlding of Accra's Rehabilitation Training Centre'. *Somatosphere* <https://www.somatosphere.net/2015/04/on-the-worlding-of-accras-rehabilitation-training-centre.html> [accessed 10 April 2021].

Geurts, K.L., and Komabu-Pomeyie, S.G.M.A. 2019. 'From "Sensing Disability" to Seselelame: Non-dualistic Activist Orientations in Twenty-First-Century Accra'. In: S. Grech and K. Soldatic, *Disability in the Global South: The Critical Handbook* (pp. 85–98). Cham: Springer Nature.

Grech, S. 2016. 'Disability and Poverty: Complex Interactions and Critical Reframings'. In: S. Grech and K. Soldatic, *Disability in the Global South: The Critical Handbook* (pp. 217–35). Cham: Springer Nature.

Grech, S., and Soldatic, K. 2016. *Disability in the Global South: The Critical Handbook.* Cham: Springer Nature.

Grischow, J.D. 2011. 'Kwame Nkrumah, Disability and Rehabilitation in Ghana, 1957–66', *Journal of African History* 52(2): 179–99.

Grischow, J.D. 2015. 'I Nearly Lost My Work: Chance Encounters, Legal Empowerment and the Struggle for Disability Rights in Ghana', *Disability and Society* 30(1): 101–13.

Guernsey, K., Nicoli, M., and Ninio, A. 2007. *Convention on the Rights of Persons with Disabilities: Its Implementation and Relevance for the World Bank.* Social Protection Discussion Paper No. 0712. Washington, DC: World Bank.

Hanass-Hancock, J., and Mitra, S. 2016. 'Livelihoods and Disability: The Complexities of Work in the Global South'. In: S. Grech and K. Soldatic, *Disability in the Global South: The Critical Handbook* (pp. 133–49). Cham: Springer Nature.

Harpur, P. 2017. 'Embracing the New Disability Rights Paradigm: The Importance of the Convention on the Rights of PwDs', *Disability and Society* 27(1): 1–14.

Heymann, J., Stein, M., and Moreno, G. Eds. 2014. *Disability and Equality at Work.* New York: Oxford University Press.

Horton. A., and Shakespeare, T. 2019. 'In and Out of the Mainstream: Disability, Education and Employment in African Contexts'. In: B. Watermeyer, J. McKenzie, and L. Swartz. Eds. *The Palgrave Handbook of Disability and Citizenship in the Global South* (pp. 119–34). Cham: Palgrave Macmillan.

Howell, C., Chalklen, S., and Alberts, T. 2006. 'A History of the Disability Rights Movement in South Africa'. In: B. Watermeyer, L. Swartz, T. Lorenzo, M. Schneider, and M. Priestley. Eds. *Disability and Social Change: A South African Agenda* (pp. 46–84). Cape Town: HSRC Press.

International Labour Organization, United Nations Development Programme, and World Health Organization (ILO, UNDP, and WHO). 2004. *CBR – A Strategy for Rehabilitation, Equalization of Opportunities, Poverty Reduction and Social Inclusion of People with Disabilities.* Joint Position Paper 2004. Geneva: World Health Organization.

Kahonde, C., and McKenzie, J. 2019. 'Sexuality and Citizenship for People with Intellectual Disabilities in Lifelong Family Care: Reflections from a South African Setting'. In: B. Watermeyer, J. McKenzie, and L. Swartz. Eds. *The Palgrave Handbook of Disability and Citizenship in the Global South* (pp. 105–18). Cham: Palgrave Macmillan.

Kamga, S.D. 2016. 'Disability Rights in South Africa: Prospects for Their Realisation under the White Paper on the Rights of Persons with Disabilities', *South African Journal on Human Rights* 32(3): 569–80.

Katsui, H. 2008. 'Downside of the Human Rights-Based Approach to Disability in Development'. Working Paper 2/2008, Institute of Development Studies Helsinki University, Finland <https://www.sylff.org/wp-content/uploads/2008/12/downside_of_hrba_katsui_hisayo.pdf> [accessed 1 April 2021].

Katsui, H., Lehtomäki, E., Malle, A.Y., and Chalklen, S. 2016. 'Questioning Human Rights: The Case of Education for Children and Youth with Disabilities in Ethiopia'. In: S. Grech and K. Soldatic, *Disability in the Global South: The Critical Handbook* (pp. 187–98). Cham: Springer Nature.

Lindsay, S., Hartman, L.R., and Fellin, M. 2015. 'A Systematic Review of Mentorship Programs to Facilitate Transition to Post-Secondary Education and Employment for Youth and Young Adults with Disabilities', *Disability and Rehabilitation* 38(14): 1329–49.

Lord, J.E., and Stein, M.A. 2013. 'Prospects and Practices for CRPD Implementation in Africa', *African Disability Rights Yearbook* 1: 97–114.

Lorenzo, T., and Coleridge, P. 2019. 'Working Together: Making Inclusive Development a Reality'. In: B. Watermeyer, J. McKenzie, and L. Swartz. Eds. *The Palgrave Handbook of Disability and Citizenship in the Global South* (pp. 233–47). Cham: Palgrave Macmillan.

Malinga, J.T. 1999. 'The Pan-African Movement of People with Disabilities'. In: B. Holzer, A. Vreede, and G. Weigt. Eds. *Disability in Different Cultures: Reflections on Local Concepts* (pp. 274–276). New Brunswick, NJ: Transaction Books.

McConkey, R. 2019. 'Citizenship and People with Intellectual Disabilities: An International Imperative?' In: B. Watermeyer, J. McKenzie, and L. Swartz. Eds. *The Palgrave Handbook of Disability and Citizenship in the Global South*. Cham: Palgrave Macmillan.

Mannan, H., MacLachlan, M., and McVeigh, J. 2012. 'Core Concepts of Human Rights and Inclusion of Vulnerable Groups in the United Nations Convention on the Rights of PwDs', *ALTER – European Journal of Disability Research* 6(3): 159–77.

Mfoafo-M'Carthy, M., and Grischow, J.D. 2017. 'Mental Illness, Stigma and Disability Rights in Ghana', *African Disability Rights Yearbook* 5: 84–100.

Mfoafo-M'Carthy, M., and Grischow, J.D. 2020. '"Being Heard": The Socio-economic Impact of Psychiatric Care on People Diagnosed with Mental Illness and Their Caregivers in Ghana', *International Social Work* OnlineFirst, October 9 <https://journals.sagepub.com/doi/10.1177/0020872820962177> [accessed 10 April 2021].

Mitra, S., and Sambamoorthi, U. 2014. *Disability Prevalence among Adults: Estimates for 54 Countries and Progress Toward a Global*

Estimate. Department of Economics Discussion Paper Series. New York: University of Fordham.

Mitra, S., Posarac, A., and Vick, B. 2011. *Disability and Poverty in Developing Countries: A Snapshot from the World Health Survey*. Discussion Paper Series. Social Protection and Labor: World Bank <https://openknowledge.worldbank.org/handle/10986/27369> [accessed 25 March 2021].

Mizunoya, S., and Mitra, S. 2013. 'Is There a Disability Gap in Employment Rates in Developing Countries?' *World Development* 42: 28–43.

Naami, A. 2014. 'Breaking the Barrier: Ghanaians Perceptions about the Social Model', *Disability, CBR and Inclusive Development* 25(1): 21–39.

Oliver, M., and Barnes, C. 1998. *Disabled People and Social Policy: From Exclusion to Inclusion*. London: Longman.

Palacios, A. 2015. 'The Social Model in the International Convention on the Rights of PwDs', *The Age of Human Rights Journal* 4 (June 2015): 91–110. <https://ri.conicet.gov.ar/bitstream/handle/11336/55775/CONICET_Digital_Nro.47d56aa0-70b3-40de-9d40-cbf145a03774_A.pdf?sequence=2> [accessed 10 March 2021].

Price, J., and Goyal, N. 2016. 'The Fluid Connections and Uncertain Spaces of Women with Disabilities: Making Links Across and Beyond the Global South'. In: S. Grech and K. Soldatic, *Disability in the Global South: The Critical Handbook* (pp. 303–21). Cham: Springer Nature.

Roulstone, A. 2019. 'Disabled People, Hate Crime and Citizenship'. In: B. Watermeyer, J. McKenzie, and L. Swartz. Eds. *The Palgrave Handbook of Disability and Citizenship in the Global South* (pp. 339–57). Cham: Palgrave Macmillan.

Rowland, W. 2014. *Nothing About Us without Us: Inside the Disability Rights Movement of South Africa*. Pretoria: UNISA Press.

Silecchia. L.A. 2013. 'The Convention on the Rights of Persons with Disabilities: Reflections on Four Flaws that Tarnish its Promise', *Journal of Contemporary Health Law and Policy* 30: 96–130.

Singal, N., and Muthukrishna, N. 2016. 'Reflexive Re-storying of Inclusive Education: Evidence from India and South Africa'. In: S. Grech and K. Soldatic, *Disability in the Global South: The Critical Handbook* (pp. 199–216). Cham: Springer Nature.

Stein, M.A. and Lord, J.E. 2009. 'Future Prospects for the United Nations Convention on the Rights of PwDs'. In: M.A. Oddný and G. Quinn. Eds. *The UN Convention on the Rights of PwDs: European and Scandinavian Perspectives* (pp. 17–40). Leiden: Martinus Nijhoff Publishers.

Trani, J.F., and Loeb, M. 2012. 'Poverty and Disability: A Vicious Circle? Evidence from Afghanistan and Zambia', *Journal of International Development* 12(S1): S19–S52.

United Nations (UN). 2006. *Convention on the Rights of PwDs* <https://www.un.org/development/desa/disabilities/convention-on-the-rights-of-persons-with-disabilities/convention-on-the-rights-of-persons-with-disabilities-2.html> [accessed 11 April 2021].

United Nations (UN). 2015. 'Sustainable Development Goal 5: Gender Equality' <https://sdgs.un.org/goals/goal5> [accessed 10 April 2021].

United Nations (UN). 2020. 'The Convention in Brief', *United Nations Department of Economic and Social Affairs – Disability* <https://www.un.org/development/desa/disabilities/convention-on-the rights-of-persons-with-disabilities/the-convention-in-brief.html> [accessed 10 March 2022].

Watermeyer, B., McKenzie, J., and Swartz, L. 2019. *The Palgrave Handbook of Disability and Citizenship in the Global South.* Cham, Switzerland: Palgrave Macmillan.

Wildeman, S. 2013. 'Protecting Rights and Building Capacities: Challenges to Global Mental Health Policy in Light of the Convention on the Rights of PwDs', *Journal of Law, Medicine and Ethics* 41(1): 48–73.

Wood, T., Essop, F., Watermeyer, B., and McKenzie, J. 2019. 'Access to Education for Children with Severe to Profound Intellectual Disability in South Africa: The Potential and Limits of Social Action'. In: B. Watermeyer, J. McKenzie, and L. Swartz. Eds. *The Palgrave Handbook of Disability and Citizenship in the Global South* (pp. 135–45). Cham: Palgrave Macmillan.

World Bank (WB). 2021. '*Disability Inclusion*' <https://www.worldbank.org/en/topic/disability> [accessed 12 April 2021].

World Health Organization (WHO) and World Bank (WB). 2011. *World Report on Disability.* Geneva: World Health Organization.

1

Framing Disability Rights within African Human Rights Movements

BONNY IBHAWOH

Introduction

The adoption of the UN Convention on the Rights of Persons with Disabilities (CRPD) signalled a paradigm shift in international human rights. Apart from marking a shift from the medical and welfare approach to the social and rights approach to disability, the convention reframed disability as a human rights issue within international law and grassroots advocacy movements. It marked the global recognition of the importance of advancing the human rights of persons with disabilities (PwDs). In Africa, these shifts have influenced national and regional initiatives aimed at protecting disability rights and prompted broader debates about human rights. However, the key developments in disability rights have been limited to advocacy and policymaking. Gaps remain in implementation, and disability rights remain disconnected from other human rights and development interventions. Although the CRPD takes a holistic approach, disability rights continue to be framed mainly in social welfare terms rather than as economic, civil, and political rights entitlements. This framing impedes the mainstreaming of disability rights within the broader human rights movement.

This chapter locates disability rights within the broader trajectory of human rights discourses and movements. The disability rights movement represents the latest phase in longstanding struggles for human rights inclusion and expansion. Locating the disability rights movement within this historical and discursive context, I argue that the CRPD disability rights framework addresses three central tensions in human rights discourse and practice. The first tension is that between rights inclusion and exclusion, between rights expansion and restriction. This relates to the debate over whether the international human rights system should be expanded to include new provisions for 'specialized rights'. While the CRPD emerged from a global consensus on the need for a specialized covenant to protect PwDs, questions persist about 'rights inflation' and the rationale for crafting a new covenant for persons already covered by extant human rights instruments. The second tension that the CRPD framework addresses is that between civil and political rights, on one hand, and economic and social rights, on the other. In adopting a holistic approach that links all these rights, the CRPD affirms the indivisibility and interdependence of human rights. In so doing, it offers a useful framework for addressing the challenge of human rights prioritization in resource-constrained African contexts. Finally, the CRPD framework addresses the tensions between domestic and international obligations for human rights protection by focusing on both the duty of States and the role of international cooperation in supporting implementation.

The CRPD disability rights framework provides a space for reaffirming the universality and interdependence of human rights in the African context. In the debates over rights expansion and restriction, it pivots towards rights inclusion and expansion. In the tension between civil/political and social/economic rights, it offers a holistic perspective that reinforces the indivisibility of human rights. I conclude, therefore, that the CRPD-based approach offers a model for addressing, at both conceptual and practical levels, some of the key tensions within the international human rights system.

The Disability Rights Framework

With the adoption of the CRPD by the UN General Assembly in 2006, States Parties to the Convention committed to promote, protect, and ensure the full enjoyment of human rights by PwDs and to ensure that they enjoy full equality under the law. Since its adoption, the CRPD has catalysed a global disability rights movement, enabling a shift from the charity, welfare, and medical approaches to disability to a social and rights-based approach. The social and rights-based model views disability not simply as an impairment of the person but as an *evolving concept* that is socially constructed, involving interaction between impairments and social and environmental conditions. The shift to the social model of disability, along with the international recognition that disability is an evolving concept, has helped to reclassify disability as a human rights issue under international law (Corsi, 2021: 143).

The social model of disability recognizes that PwDs should determine the course of their lives to the same extent as other members of society and 'paves the way for social action by PwDs challenging barriers to participation, as well as exclusionary practices' (UN, 2016b: 4). As several commentators have noted, this approach to disability is potentially transformative, because it places the problem of disability not on the individual, but on the State and society whose responsibility it is to remove structural, socio-economic, environmental, and attitudinal barriers that *disable* certain people from interacting with society on an equal basis with others (Kanter, 2014: 8). Specifically, the rights-based model, as reflected in the CRPD, places disability within a framework of rights and responsibilities. PwDs are identified as rights holders and subjects of human rights law on an equal basis with other persons.

The CRPD understands disability as long-term physical, mental, intellectual, or sensory impairments which, in interaction with various barriers, may hinder people's full and effective participation in society on an equal basis with others. It addresses disability-specific prejudices and places the responsibility for ensuring the protection and promotion of the rights of PwDs on governments and society (UN, 2016b: 4). Since its adoption, the CRPD has galvanized a global disability rights movement and has become a benchmark document that 'works to ensure the enjoyment of human rights and fundamental freedoms by PwDs' (UN, 2016a). Along with other international human rights instruments, it establishes a comprehensive international framework that guides policymaking and legislation for protecting disability rights and fostering disability inclusive development.

The CRPD is the culmination of decades of efforts by Civil Society Organizations (CSOs) and Disabled People's Organizations (DPOs), at the UN and other forums, to frame the welfare and protection of PwDs within the international human rights agenda. Some of these earlier efforts resulted in the Declaration on the Rights of Mentally Retarded Persons adopted by the UN General Assembly 1971, the Declaration on the Rights of Disabled Persons adopted in 1975, and the UN's proclamation of 1983–92 as the 'Decade of Disabled Persons'. Viewed within the context of the historical development of international human rights, the CRPD is significant for several reasons. Apart from being the first UN human rights treaty of the twenty-first century, the CRPD was, at the time of its adoption, one of the most swiftly ratified international treaties, with strong support from all regional groups. One hundred and sixty States signed the Convention upon its opening in 2007, and 126 States ratified the Convention within its first five years (UN, 2016a). It became the first legally binding UN human rights treaty to comprehensively address the equal rights of individuals with respect to disability status specifically.

The CRPD is also the first human rights treaty to explicitly recognize *intersectional discrimination*. It recognizes that PwDs are subject to 'multiple or aggravated forms of discrimination on the basis of race, colour, sex, language, religion, political or other opinion, national, ethnic, indigenous or social origin, property, birth, age or other status' (UN, 2006: Preamble). Finally, the CRPD is the first UN convention to include a specific article focused on the role of international cooperation in supporting implementation (UN, 2016b: 4). While other UN instruments such as the Declaration on the Right to Development allude to the role of international cooperation in human rights fulfilment, the CRPD affirms this principle in international human rights law. This takes duty-bearer obligations for rights protection beyond individual States.

The swift ratification of the CRPD and the ensuing developments in disability rights protection is largely attributable to the advocacy roles of international CSOs and grassroots DPOs. Organizations such as Rehabilitation International (RI), the International Disability Alliance (IDA), and Disabled Peoples' International (DPI) have played pivotal roles in the drafting process and in mobilizing consensus on the convention. This also accounts for the comprehensive, holistic, and intersectional approach of the convention.

Disability Rights and Human Rights Expansion

The history of the international human rights movement has been defined by the struggle for progressive rights inclusion. Social movements for rights inclusion have involved groups working to ensure that universal protection of human rights and fundamental freedoms are available to *all* members of the human community, not just some. The great strides that have been made in human rights protection have historically been in response to abuses arising from gross violations or the discriminatory treatment of certain groups of peoples. Such discriminatory attitudes and treatments that exclude certain people from the circle of rights protection are often linked to discrimination based on race, gender, ethnicity, religion, class, or other differences. From the anti-slavery and women's franchise movements to anti-colonial and anti-apartheid struggles, key movements for rights inclusion have challenged the exclusionary and discriminatory status quo by demanding more inclusiveness in the enjoyment of social and political entitlements (Ibhawoh, 2014: 4).

Universal human rights challenge these forms of subjugation, prejudices, and exclusions. The adoption of the Universal Declaration of Human Rights (UDHR) in 1948 in the aftermath of the atrocities of the Second World War marked the international recognition of certain fundamental liberties as inalienable universal values to which all persons are entitled simply by virtue of their humanity. This all-inclusive notion of universal human rights is foregrounded in the principle of non-discrimination. Article 2 of the UDHR sets out a non-exhaustive list of prohibited grounds of discrimination which includes race or colour, sex, language, religion, political opinion, national or social origin, property, birth, or other status. The same list is included in Article 2 of both the International Covenant on Civil and Political Rights (ICCPR) and the International Covenant on Economic, Social and Cultural Rights (ICESCR). Subsequent treaties have expanded the list further. Of these, three are specifically aimed at eliminating specific forms of discrimination: racial discrimination, discrimination against women, and discrimination against PwDs.

By extending the non-discrimination principle to PwDs specifically, the CRPD framework includes them in the sphere of legally binding international human rights protection. Thus, in the tension between human rights expansion and restriction, the CRPD represents the impetus towards rights inclusion and expansion in a way that is significant and should not be taken for granted. Although the CRPD was swiftly adopted by several States, there was some opposition to the idea of a legally binding international covenant on disability rights. In the early UN Working Group debates on the draft CRPD, the most common argument against the Convention, a position held by some government representatives, was that it was a duplication. These representatives considered existing human rights documents and their provisions against non-discrimination of *all persons* sufficient for protecting PwDs. It was also suggested that if States reported to the existing UN treaty bodies with specific reference to disability, this should be sufficient. Several States expressed the need to avoid imposing onerous additional reporting requirements on States Parties. Australia, Canada, and Japan expressed concern over potential duplication of the work already done by other treaty bodies. The Russian Federation stated that the inclusion of disability in periodic reporting under the existing treaty bodies would be sufficient and that there was no need for a separate body to monitor implementation of a new convention (Combrinck, 2018: 1064).

Also raised in these debates were familiar arguments about rights inflation and the perils of the endless creation of new human rights instruments. If every entitlement claim is framed as a human right, critics argue, the human rights doctrine will ultimately lose its normative power. To have too many rights would trivialize the concept, and frivolous rights claims would undermine their authority. There was also the concern that the rights expansion would create unrealizable demands which could weaken the stature of human rights. Critics of rights expansion therefore caution against a tendency to frame every human and social problem in terms of human rights. They see the rights-based approach as having been applied to too many areas of human endeavour lately in ways that might ultimately undermine its effectiveness.

To be sure, these arguments for rights restriction or constriction have been well repudiated by several commentators. For one, the rights inflation argument largely mischaracterizes the interpretive process through which official bodies organically extend human rights protections. In focusing on the apparent extension of rights protection to more groups, critics of rights expansion tend to ignore the more pressing question of why new struggles seize the language of human rights. The obvious answer is that the human rights framework continues to prove appealing to new struggles for justice because, several decades after the proclamation of the UDHR, many people are still excluded from the circle of human rights protection. Thus, 'rights inflation' is not a sign of a movement going off-track, but rather a sign of its continuing relevance and attraction (Petrasek, 2020).

The CRPD framework marks an important intervention in these debates over rights expansion and restriction. Its swift adoption at the UN and its holistic approach to human rights represent a promising impetus towards continued rights expansion and inclusion. As the CRPD states, despite various existing instruments and undertakings, 'PwDs continue to face barriers in their participation as equal members of society and violations of their human rights in all parts of the world' (UN, 2006: Preamble). In effect, the CRPD ensures the principle of non-discrimination applies to persons with disabilities because extant international human rights mechanisms have not provided them with sufficient protection. It stresses the commitment of States Parties to raise awareness and foster respect for rights and dignity to counter disability discrimination (UN, 2006: Article 8). Thus, although the CRPD does not create new rights under international law, it includes new interpretations and applications of existing rights as well as new approaches to human rights treaty enforcement. It is therefore significant not only to people with disabilities but also to the development of international human rights generally (Kanter, 2014: 5).

Affirming the Interdependency of Rights

International human rights are premised on the indivisibility and interdependency of rights. This is the recognition that one set of rights cannot be enjoyed fully without the other. The Vienna Declaration adopted at the 1993 World Conference on Human Rights provides that human rights are 'universal, indivisible and interdependent and interrelated' and that States have a duty 'to promote and protect all human rights and fundamental freedoms' (Boutros-Ghali, 1993). Despite this claim to indivisibility, however, the tension between civil/political rights and economic/social rights has defined international human rights. This is evident in the generations of rights schema where civil and political rights are characterized as first-generation 'negative' rights, while social, economic, and cultural rights are considered second-generation 'positive' rights. The divide is also evident in the international human rights instruments which traditionally addressed either civil and political rights (i.e. the ICCPR) or social, economic, and cultural rights (i.e. the International Covenant on Economic, Social and Cultural Rights).

This tension is also evident in the history of human rights in Africa. Since independence in the 1960s, many African leaders have rhetorically prioritized social cohesion and economic development over civil and political rights. As post-colonial African leaders grappled with the challenges of forging viable States out of the fragile and fractured colonial entities that they inherited at independence, many began to emphasize economic development and social rights at the expense of individual civil and political rights. State policies were cast in terms of the paramountcy of collective economic rights of the people over the civic rights of individual citizens. Leaders such as Julius Nyerere of Tanzania, Modibo Keita of Mali, Léopold Senghor of Senegal and Kwame Nkrumah of Ghana espoused African socialism in terms of the collective social and economic rights of the people in ways that tended to undermine individual civil liberties. These leaders ranked the right to self-determination and collective sovereignty as 'lexically prior to individual human rights' (Getachew, 2020: 93).

Against the background of this historic tension between civil/political rights and economic/social rights, the CRPD framework asserts the interdependency of civil and political rights in relation to social, cultural, and economic rights. Although other covenants such as the Convention on the Elimination of All Forms of Discrimination against Women and the Convention on the Rights of the Child (UNCRC) include reference to political and civil rights as well as social, economic, and cultural rights, neither of those treaties makes explicit the important relationship between these various rights. In the CRPD, the right to equality and non-discrimination of PwDs is presented as dependent on civil and political rights (such as the right to political participation and access to justice), as well as economic and social rights (such as the right to education, healthcare, and accessible infrastructure). By linking civil and political rights with economic and social rights, the CRPD also bridges the distinction between positive and negative rights. Negative rights, such as the freedom of expression and association, impose a duty which calls only for inaction on the part of the duty-bearer. In contrast, positive rights, such as the right to education or health, impose a correlative duty which requires action on the part of the State as primary duty-bearer.

Among the civil and political rights outlined in the CRPD are non-discrimination, respect for inherent dignity, participation in political and public life, access to justice, full and effective inclusion in society, equality of opportunity, respect for difference, and participation in public life. Participation in public life provisions specifically require States Parties to protect 'the right of PwDs to vote by secret ballot in elections and public referendums' (UN, 2006: Article 29). The right to civil liberties for PwDs includes their right to be free from involuntary institutionalization because of their disability. It also includes their right to access to justice, which can be realized only if spaces for exercising franchise and assessing justice such as voting locations and courthouses are accessible to them.

These civil and political rights provisions are linked to economic and social rights similar to those outlined in the ICESCR, which impose a positive duty of fulfilment on the State. Central to these provisions are independence, autonomy, and accessibility for persons with disabilities. Persons with disabilities have the right to live independently and be included in the community, to personal mobility and rehabilitation, and to accessible information technology and infrastructure such as roads and buildings. In addition, the CRPD provides that PwDs should be guaranteed the right to health and inclusive education (IE) at all levels (UN, 2006: Articles 8 and 9). The CRPD also frames disability as a development issue because of the bidirectional links between poverty and disability. Disability can cause poverty by preventing full participation by PwDs in the economic and social life of their communities, particularly where appropriate support is lacking or unavailable. Poverty can also cause disability through malnutrition, poor healthcare, and precarious living conditions (UN, 2006).

Progressive Realization and International Cooperation

Overall, the social rights provisions in the CRPD require that States Parties recognize the right of PwDs to an adequate standard of living for themselves and their families. This reflects the recognition that human rights are interdependent, and that civil and political rights cannot be realized unless and until related social, economic, and cultural rights are also ensured. In the context of the CRPD, political rights would have been meaningless without social and economic support, and provisions for economic and social rights would have been redundant without provision for civil rights and political participation. Indeed, several studies have highlighted this intersection between political exclusion and socio-economic marginalization in Africa (Falola and Hamel, 2021; Chataika, 2019). For this reason, DPOs across Africa have adopted an intersectional approach by simultaneously advocating for political inclusion and economic empowerment.

While some rights provisions in the CRPD, such as prohibiting disability discrimination, are relatively cost-free, other rights entitlements carry cost implications. In affirming the interdependence of rights, the CRPD recognizes both rights that are subject to immediate implementation (civil and political rights) and those that are to be realized progressively (economic and social rights). Given their cost and resource implications, States are allowed to realize socio-economic rights progressively, with a view to achieving their full realization over time (UN, 2006: Article 4[2]).

The principle of progressive realization enshrined in the CRPD has been described as a practical device that acknowledges real-world challenges and helps to avoid overburdening States, employers, and other duty-bearers (Broderick, 2018: 131). Progressive realization recognizes that States have different economic capacities to implement economic and social rights fully within a given timeframe. Progressive realization therefore allows States to take steps towards their end goals to an extent that is in line with their available resources. This does not mean that implementation can be delayed, however; instead, 'It means that implementation can occur over time based on the available resources' (UN, 2016b: 13). The principle of progressive realization is particularly relevant in African contexts, where the lack of resources is often advanced by States as a reason for the non-implementation of their economic and social rights obligations.

Another innovation of the CRPD related to this can be seen in the links it makes between the obligations of States and the international community in fulfilling disability rights. The protection of human rights is essentially a State obligation, and most human rights instruments take a State-centric approach, which positions States as the primary duty-bearers. However, governments working at the international level have long recognized that it is impossible to achieve development goals without the inclusion and integration of the rights, well-being, and perspectives of PwDs in development efforts at national, regional, and international levels (UN, 2016b: 4). The CRPD was also the first convention to include a specific article focused on the role of international cooperation in supporting rights implementation. This includes ensuring that international cooperation, including international development programmes, is inclusive of and accessible to PwD (UN, 2006: Article 32). By affirming the *interdependence of rights* within a framework of *progressive realization* that recognizes the role of *international cooperation* in human rights protection, the CRPD offers new interpretations of international human rights principles on dignity, liberty, and human security.

Culture and Disability Rights in Africa

It is estimated that 15% of the world's population live with some form of disability, making PwDs the 'world's largest minority' (UN, 2016b). In Africa, this figure translates to about eighty million people. Although several initiatives have been taken at national and regional levels to improve the conditions of PwDs such as the declaration of the African Decade of Disabled Persons in 2002, most Africans with disabilities are still excluded from education and work opportunities, making them susceptible to poverty, abuse, malnutrition and disease, environmental hazards, natural disasters, and armed conflicts (Disability News, 2018). Opportunities for PwDs to participate in society are further constrained by harmful cultural attitudes, myths, and stereotypes regarding disability which reinforce discrimination.

Assessments of the impact of the CRPD in Africa have been mixed. While some scholars take an optimistic view, highlighting successful CRPD-based policy interventions, others take a more cautious and critical view. Critics point to the numerous barriers to CRPD implementation and enforcement across the continent, from the absence of political will to infrastructural limitations and the lack of resources. However, the past few decades have witnessed some promising policy interventions in disability rights protection in Africa, even though problems with implementation and enforcement remain. At a national level, governments have drawn on the CRPD framework to establish institutions and initiate national policies that address disability issues.

The rights and welfare of PwDs are increasingly seen as an integral part of national development planning, and disability issues are now part of the budgeting process in many countries (Kwenda, 2010). In Namibia, for example, all government ministries are required to integrate disability issues into their work, while in South Africa the Ministry of Women, Children and People with Disabilities takes up disability concerns nationally. In Zimbabwe, the Ministry of Public Service, Labour and Social Welfare is responsible for the needs of PwDs. In 2006 Ghana's parliament passed the Disability Act, which offers a legal framework for protecting the rights of PwDs. Across the continent, these advances have come about largely due to the efforts of CSOs dedicated to the welfare of PwDs with specific needs, such as the blind, deaf, paralysed, or mentally ill. Such organizations include the National Union of Disabled Persons of Uganda (NUDIPU), Ghana's Disabled People's Organization and Zimbabwe's National Association of Societies for the Care of the Handicapped.

At the continental level, the African Union (AU: formerly the Organisation of African Unity) developed a Plan of Action for Disabled People, which recognizes the need to integrate PwDs into society and to empower and involve them in the formulation and implementation of social and economic development policies. The plan proclaimed 2000–9 the African Decade of Disabled Persons, with the aim of promoting awareness and commitment to full participation, equality, and empowerment of PwDs in Africa. But while these initiatives set a roadmap for disability rights, many African governments continue to cite financial constraints as an impediment to promoting the rights of the disabled (Kwenda, 2010).

Recent studies of disability in Africa have argued that indigenous cultural and spiritual dimensions are crucial to understanding disability in Africa. Such research calls for new methodologies that combine the subaltern and indigenous approaches of African Studies with Disability Studies' focus on access, embodiment, and rehabilitation (Falola and Hamel, 2021). This is necessary because the specific historical and economic conditions that define the lived realities of most Africans with disabilities demand alternative approaches to those typically practiced in the Global North. Even though representatives from the Global South were involved in developing the CRPD, the Convention applies more to the Global North and is unsuited to African cultural contexts (see Mprah and Duorinaah, Chapter 7).

Uniquely African circumstances complicate the experiences of PwDs across the continent, including challenges related to cultural attitudes, poverty, geography, and global politics. One study shows, for example, that the most frequently stated causes of having a disabled child in Africa include 'witchcraft, a curse or punishment from God, anger of ancestral spirits, bad omens, reincarnation, heredity, incestuous relationships and the misdemeanors of the mother' (McKenzie and Chataika, 2018: 318). To be sure, these attitudes towards disability are not unique to African societies. They have prevailed historically and in contemporary forms in many societies around the world. However, there is merit in the calls for disability rights interventions explicitly framed by African worldviews. The emergent international disability rights movement needs to pay more attention to indigenous African definitions and conceptual understandings of disability and impairment, including their linguistic, spiritual, and communitarian dimensions (Falola and Hamel, 2021).

What is required is a holistic approach that grounds a rights-based model of disability within an indigenous cultural framework. Indigenous culture-based approaches to disability in Africa are essential, because the social and economic conditions of PwDs are often linked to harmful cultural attitudes and practices. In many parts of Africa, traditional approaches to disability give rise to stigmatization and discrimination against PwDs. Perhaps the most visible example of this is the well-publicized ritual murders of persons with albinism in some parts of Africa, and especially in Tanzania and Malawi. In 2015, over 200 'witchdoctors' and traditional healers were arrested in Tanzania in a crackdown on the murder of persons with albinism (BBC, 2015). These attacks and murders are fuelled by superstitious beliefs that persons with albinism have supernatural powers that bring bad or good luck. Such beliefs make them susceptible to accusations of witchcraft and ritual attacks (Imafidon, Chapter 10; UN, 2020a: 12). These serious crimes violate the right to life and create an environment that infringes on the most fundamental right to liberty and security of the person.

Successive reports of the UN Independent Expert on the Enjoyment of Human Rights by Persons with Albinism highlight how cultural beliefs foster wide-ranging human rights abuses of people with albinism (UN, 2018). At the Pan-African conference on 'Overcoming Harmful Traditional Practices' held in Addis Ababa in 2011, delegates discussed aspects of African culture, customs, and traditions which hinder development in general and impede the advancement of women, children, and PwDs in particular. The main outcome document of the conference was 'A Commitment for Action to the Elimination of Harmful Traditional Practices', in which participants called for holistic and integrated strategies founded on a recognition of the social and economic determinants of harmful traditional practices (AU, 2011).

The recognition that culture-based problems require culture-based solutions has prompted calls for indigenous cultural approaches to disability in Africa. Human rights-affirming aspects of culture can be invoked and deployed to counteract exclusionary and oppressive aspects of the same culture. In these conversations, the communal ethos of *ubuntu* has been dominant. Several African disability scholars have suggested mobilizing this traditional South African concept; a Bantu word, it indicates an ethics of community and humanity which was popularized by the work of the South African Truth and Reconciliation Commission (TRC). *Ubuntu*, as defined by its chief proponent Archbishop Desmond Tutu, who headed the TRC, encapsulates the notion of an interdependent humanity that is central to indigenous African cosmology. The humanness of the person who has *ubuntu* comes from knowing that the fate of each person is inextricably intertwined with their relationship with others (Tutu, 2000: 31). It is a distinctly African take on the golden rule or law of reciprocity that is evident in many religions and cultures. Many African communities have a communitarian and humanistic philosophical ethos similar to *ubuntu*.

Ubuntu has gained a prominent place in African disability studies because it suggests the symbiosis between the well-being of the individual and the integrity of the social whole and is underpinned by the notion that 'a person is a person through other persons'. *Ubuntu* represents a spiritual interconnectedness, interdependence, and reciprocal responsibility towards everyone. As a model of social ethics, *ubuntu* mobilizes against social injustices such as those PwDs face and works towards restoring humanity and the upholding of individual life and well-being. This approach both offers specifically African perspectives on disability and connects disability activism with other established forms of Pan African cooperation. An *ubuntu* approach to disability includes the social construction claims of traditional disability studies but also goes further, to create communities activated towards collective well-being (Falola and Hamel, 2021).

Although traditional approaches to disability have given rise to stigmatization and discrimination against PwDs, drawing on a rights-affirming indigenous ethos such as *ubuntu* also has the potential to address the challenges. For example, in Mozambique, the Ministry of Health has established a traditional medicine department which works with medical practitioners and traditional healers to ensure they are aware of the needs of persons with albinism and demystify harmful myths associated with them (UN, 2020a: 12). In Mali, a project on protection of human rights and the promotion of economic empowerment of persons with albinism centres on engagement with various religious leaders and traditional healers supported by the Ministries of Justice and Health and the police force (UN, 2020b: 17).

In embracing the benefits of the indigenous cultural approach to disability, however, there is a risk of developing an uncritical understanding of how culture intersects with disability. We must pay attention to how impairment is discursively formed and ascribed a positive or negative value, and how this is linked to understanding local cultures and global morality (Berghs, 2021). Whatever epistemological value they may have in academic circles, cultural studies of African disability worldviews are subservient to socio-economic imperatives (Gebrekidan, 2021). It has been suggested that in the post-industrial Global North, the social and rights-based model of disability has become prevalent because of the various legal and technological advances generated by surplus wealth. In contrast, disability realities in the Global South are shaped by distinct preindustrial modes of production. Just as the medical model has gone out of vogue in Western disability studies, so should the cultural model in African disability studies give way to socio-economic prerogatives. Critical African disability discourse should therefore be framed around the overarching themes of economy, technology, and environment and their concomitant impact on marginalization, agency, and activism rather than culture (Gebrekidan, 2021). While it is useful to centre African disability discourse around substantive political, social, and economic issues, culture and indigeneity remain important aspects of the lived experiences of PwDs and are likely to remain crucial to debates about disability rights as they have within the broader discourse of human rights in Africa.

There is a need for more empirical studies on the comparative benefits of an indigenous cultural model of disability inclusion in relation to a CRPD-based framework. For example, does the level of public awareness of, and access to, human rights law correlate with improvements in the human rights conditions of PwDs? Anecdotal evidence suggest that international human rights can provide protection to PwDs when States are either unwilling or unable to do so. Some optimistic assessments point to successful CRPD-based responses in several African countries that have facilitated domestic-level human rights implementation (Lord and Stein, 2013). CRPD mechanisms have also had impact on Africa. The appointment of an African person with albinism as the first Independent Expert on the Enjoyment of Human Rights by Persons with Albinism in 2015 resulted in increased awareness and National Policy interventions aimed at protecting the rights of persons with albinism. Similarly, the Optional Protocol to the CRPD which allows the CoRPD to consider complaints from individuals has proved to be a useful mechanism for African PwDs to seek redress from the UN.

In the case of X v. Tanzania, a Tanzanian citizen with albinism who had had an arm cut off submitted a complaint to the Committee on the grounds of the State's failure to investigate the violation or prosecute the perpetrators. The claimant stated that as a victim of a violation of his rights under the Convention, the State Party has failed to take effective measures to protect him from the targeted physical, emotional, and mental abuse by non-State actors. After investigations, the UN Committee concluded that Tanzania had indeed failed to fulfil its obligations under the Convention and recommended, among other things, that the Tanzanian government provide the claimant with an effective remedy, including compensation, redress for the abuses suffered, and the support that is necessary to enable the author to live independently again (UN, 2014). Although cases like these have been few and far between, they have high symbolic value in that they bring attention to national and international obligations under the CRPD.

Conclusion

The disability rights movement and the CRPD framework represent a relatively new phase in the struggles by marginalized groups against their political marginalization and socio-economic exclusion. While there are new ways of looking at the causes of PwDs, the same exclusionary socio-cultural and political forces at play in earlier rights struggles also stand in the way of fulfilling disability rights. To advance disability rights, we need to understand the dynamics of these exclusionary impulses and emphasize the discursive connections between disability rights and other human rights struggles. We also need to locate disability rights within the broader tensions that underlie international human rights.

By addressing the central tensions in international human rights, the CRPD framework offers a discursive space for reaffirming rights inclusion and reasserting the universality and interdependence of human rights. In the debate over rights expansion or restriction, it pivots towards rights inclusion and expansion; in the tension between civil/political and social/economic rights, it offers a holistic perspective that reinforces the indivisibility and interdependence of human rights. It therefore offers a model for addressing, at both conceptual and practical levels, some of the key tensions within the international human rights system.

In the African context, however, there is a need to combine a CRPD-based approach with more culturally grounded, indigenous approaches. As the other chapters in this volume show, even where governments have drawn on the CRPD framework to develop laws, policies, and programmes, there remain significant obstacles to implementing the CRPD in Africa. The barriers range from a lack of political will to implement policies and enforce legislation, to inaccessible infrastructure, gaps in social services, and a lack of adequate resources. Addressing these myriad challenges and deficits requires holistic and multipronged approaches to disability. These approaches should tailor disability programmes to suit local socio-economic, political, and cultural contexts. The cultural dimension remains crucial to addressing the challenges faced by PwDs in Africa. Although traditional approaches to disability have given rise to stigmatization and discrimination against PwDs, humanistic indigenous philosophies such as *ubuntu*, as well as rights-affirming cultural and traditional practices, also have the potential to address these challenges. There are therefore benefits to bridging the gap between the CRPD rights-based modes that have inspired several National Policy interventions and a more indigenous cultural approach advocated by scholars and grassroots activists.

Bibliography

African Union (AU). 2011. *Report of The Pan-African Conference on Celebrating Courage and Overcoming Harmful Traditional Practices in Africa.* Addis Ababa.

Berghs, E. 2021. 'An African Ethics of Social Wellbeing: Understanding Disability and Public Health'. In: T. Falola and N. Hamel, *Disability in Africa: Inclusion, Care, and the Ethics of Humanity* (pp. 75–90). Rochester: University of Rochester Press.

Boutros-Ghali, B. 1993. 'World Conference on Human Rights: the Vienna Declaration and Programme of Action, June 1993'. New York: United Nations Dept of Public Information.

British Broadcasting Corporation (BBC). 2015. 'Tanzania Albino Murders: "More than 200 Witchdoctors" Arrested', 12 March 2015 <www.bbc.com/news/world-africa-31849531> [accessed 5 April 2021].

Broderick, A. 2018. 'Article 4: General Obligation'. In: I. Bantekas, M.A. Stein, and D. Anastasiou, *The UN Convention on the Rights of PwDs: A Commentary* (pp. 106–139). Oxford: Oxford University Press.

Chataika, T. 2019. *The Routledge Handbook of Disability in Southern Africa.* New York: Routledge.

Combrinck, H. 2018. 'Article 36: Consideration of Reports 1060'. In: I. Bantekas, M.A. Stein, and D. Anastasiou, *The UN Convention on the Rights of PwDs: A Commentary* (pp. 1060–1083). Oxford: Oxford University Press.

Corsi, J.L. 2021. 'Article 5: Equality and Non-Discrimination'. In: I. Bantekas, M.A. Stein, and D. Anastasiou, *The UN Convention on the Rights of PwDs: A Commentary* (pp. 140–170). Oxford: Oxford University Press.

Disability News. 2018. 'Africa' <www.disabled-world.com/news/africa> [accessed 6 April 2021].

Falola, T., and Hamel, N. 2021. *Disability in Africa: Inclusion, Care, and the Ethics of Humanity.* Rochester: University of Rochester Press.

Gebrekidan, F. 2021. 'Rethinking African Disability History: From the Cultural Model to a Socio-Economic Perspective'. In: T. Falola and N. Hamel. *Disability in Africa: Inclusion, Care, and the Ethics of Humanity* (pp. 91–114). Rochester: University of Rochester Press.

Getachew, A. 2020. *Worldmaking after Empire: The Rise and Fall of Self-Determination.* Princeton: Princeton University Press.

Ibhawoh, B. 2014. 'Human Rights for Some: Universal Human Rights, Sexual Minorities and the Exclusionary Impulse', *International Journal: Canada's Journal of Global Policy Analysis* 69(4): 612–22.

Kanter, A.S. 2014. *The Development of Disability Rights Under International Law: From Charity to Human Rights.* London: Routledge.

Kwenda, S. 2010. 'Africa's Disabled Will Not Be Forgotten: People with Disabilities Fight for Services, Rights, Dignity', *Africa Renewal* <www.

un.org/africarenewal/magazine/april-2010/africa%E2%80%99s-disabled-will-not-be-forgotten> [accessed 11 April 2021].

McKenzie, J., and Chataika, T. 2018. 'Supporting Families in Raising Disabled Children to Enhance African Child Development'. In: K. Runswick-Cole, T. Curran, and K. Liddiard. Eds. *The Palgrave Handbook of Disabled Children's Childhood Studies* (pp. 315–32). London: Palgrave Macmillan.

Petrasek, D. 2020. 'Human Rights "Inflation": What's the Problem?' 23 February 2020. Centre for International Policy Studies <https://www.cips-cepi.ca/2020/02/23/human-rights-inflation-whats-the-problem/> [accessed 10 March 2022].

Tutu, D. 2000. *No Future without Forgiveness.* New York: Doubleday.

United Nations (UN). 2006. *Convention on the Rights of PwDs.* Geneva: New York <https://www.un.org/development/desa/disabilities/convention-on-the-rights-of-persons-with-disabilities/convention-on-the-rights-of-persons-with-disabilities-2.html> [accessed 11 April 2021].

United Nations (UN). 2014. Committee on the Rights of PwDs. Communication No. 22/2014. CRPD/C/18/D/22/2014.

United Nations (UN). 2016a. '10th Anniversary of the Adoption of Convention on the Rights of PwDs (CRPD)'. Department of Economic and Social Affairs: New York <https://www.un.org/development/desa/disabilities/convention-on-the-rights-of-persons-with-disabilities/the-10th-anniversary-of-the-adoption-of-convention-on-the-rights-of-persons-with-disabilities-crpd-crpd-10.html> [last accessed 10 March 2022].

United Nations (UN). 2016b. 'Toolkit on Disability for Africa: Introducing the United Nations Convention on the Rights of PwDs'. Geneva: UN <https://www.un.org/development/desa/dspd/2016/11/toolkit-on-disability-for-africa-2/> [last accessed 10 March 2022].

United Nations (UN). 2018. *Report of the Independent Expert on the Enjoyment of Human Rights by Persons with Albinism on the Expert Workshop on Witchcraft and Human Rights.* Geneva. A/HRC/37/57/Add.2.

United Nations (UN). 2020a. 'Best Practices in the Protection of Human Rights of Persons with Albinism', Addendum to the Report of the Independent Expert on the Enjoyment of Human Rights by Persons with Albinism'. A/75/50343.

United Nations (UN). 2020b. *Protection of Persons with Albinism,* Thematic Report by the Independent Expert on the Enjoyment of Human Rights by Persons with Albinism to the 75th Session of the General Assembly. A/75/170.

2

Legislation as a Care Institution? The CRPD and Rights of Adults with Intellectual Disabilities in South Africa

CHARLOTTE CAPRI

Introduction

South Africa is often hailed for its progressive Constitution, which includes a Bill of Rights as its second chapter, and for the development of an advanced body of human rights jurisprudence by its Constitutional Court (Republic of South Africa [RSA], 1996). It was among the earliest States to sign the United Nations (UN) Convention on the Rights of Persons with Disabilities (CRPD) and its Optional Protocol, on 30 March 2007, followed by ratification.[1] Despite this encouraging start, South Africa's dualist legal system is yet to incorporate the Convention into domestic law. By implication, the capacity of adults with intellectual disabilities (ID) to make decisions with legal consequences (i.e. their legal capacity) is still regulated by common law.

From the age of sixty and sixty-five years for women and men respectively, South Africans are protected by the Older Persons Act (No. 13 of 2006) (Department of Justice [DoJ], 2006), while the Mental Health Care Act (No. 17 of 2002) (Department of Health [DoH], 2002) assumes responsibility for the care and property administration of adults with severe and profound ID admitted into institutional care facilities as 'state patients'. Yet laws that safeguard the interests of groups regarded as vulnerable, like children (the Children's Act (No. 38 of 2005) (DoJ, 2005) or older persons, lack safeguards for adults with ID. For South Africans who may be regarded as vulnerable, protection under the

[1] The CRPD was adopted by the UN General Assembly by Res A/RES/61/106. It opened for signature by States and regional integration organizations on 30 March 2007 (Article 42).

Children's Act expires on their eighteenth birthday; this leaves a major gap in the South African legislative and policy framework. Using life histories from two persons with intellectual disability (PwID), Mike and Cheryl, we will attempt to illustrate the implications of a lack of such statutory legislation.

Despite the protracted Esidimeni tragedy emerging in 2018,[2] a lack of political will to safeguard, monitor, or track adults in communities with any level of ID who require support still remains (Capri *et al.*, 2018a). This history of death, torture, and disappearance arose from a decision by the Gauteng Province Department of Health (the Department) to transfer mental healthcare users[3] from the Life Esidimeni care facility, which provided services under a longstanding contract with the Department. Following contract termination in September 2015, 1,711 service users were transferred to hospitals, non-governmental organizations (NGOs), or familial homes between October 2015 and the end of June 2016. This process lacked consultation with and the involvement of families, health professionals, and service users themselves. In fact, despite the Department's own clinicians cautioning against the transfers based on harm to service users, the Department persisted (Bornman, 2018; Capri *et al.*, 2018a; Lund, 2016; Rahlaga, 2018). Its disregard for these concerns culminated in the ill-conceived 'Gauteng Mental Health Marathon Project'; the result was the known deaths of 140 mental health care users. Although 1,418 people survived, they were exposed to trauma and morbidity, nonetheless. At the time of the eventual arbitration proceedings discussed below, the whereabouts of 44 service users remained unknown (Bornman, 2018; Capri *et al.*, 2018a; Lund, 2016; Rahlaga, 2018).

It must be noted that South Africa ratified the Convention and its Optional Protocol ten years prior to Esidimeni. Yet the State continues to operate with no obligation to implement any international laws, assimilate any part of the Convention into domestic law on behalf of PwID, or abide by the Committee on the

2 The 'Esidimeni tragedy' refers to the deaths of 143 persons with mental illness who had been transferred from homes run by an experienced government-contracted provider (Life Esidimeni) to a series of poorly equipped NGOs after the South African government cancelled the contact with Life Esidimeni (Durojaye and Agaba, 2018).

3 Definition according to Mental Health Care Act (No. 17 of 2002) (DoH, 2002).

Rights of Persons with Disabilities (CoRPD)'s recommendations on citizen appeal. By April 2019, shortly after the Life Esidimeni Arbitration Award of 19 March 2019, South Africa was one of four signatories of the African Union (AU) Protocol on the Rights of Persons with Disabilities. Ironically, it aims to promote, protect, and ensure the human rights of PwDs in a similar way to the Convention, and to ensure respect for their inherent dignity.

Aims and Objectives

This chapter's main objectives are threefold: to comment on care justice in South Africa by exploring the reality of the State's commitment to rights Conventions on international, continental, and domestic levels; to discuss the usefulness of potential legislation to consider and address the well-being and rights of PwIDs in South Africa; and to highlight the implications that a lack of such consideration continues to have.

It aims to meet these objectives by explaining the need for designated ID legislation and starts with the existing legal frameworks of the CRPD and the South African Constitution (Act 108 of 1996) in order to motivate the mobilization of legislative support for PwID. Descriptions from the life histories of Mike and Cheryl aim to illustrate the reality of the current position of PwIDs in South Africa regarding issues of unnecessarily complex access to healthcare, socio-economic justice, and the practice of consent.

Methodological justification for including Mike and Cheryl's lived experiences (in other words, capturing a history of socio-economic equity, accessing appropriate treatment and care, and practising consent) lies in our objective of contributing to building care legislation that, although influenced by power relations, will be shaped by the historical, political, and social inequalities that PwIDs in South Africa are subjected to (Ssali, Theobald, and Hawkins, 2015; Wright, 2019). In the telling of their life history, Mike and Cheryl were asked to use their own words and timelines and select events which they remembered well (Ssali, Theobald, and Hawkins, 2015; Wright, 2019).

In acknowledging the importance of an ethical State's relationship to PwIDs, suggestions are made regarding what caring for PwIDs could look like under such a State. In order to strengthen care justice arguments *not* supported by obligatory implementation in South Africa as elsewhere in the world, we will also turn to feminist care justice theory and ethics by drawing on Tronto's (2010) 'caring society' and Kittay's dependency care work (Kittay 2001, 2009, 2011; Kittay, Jennings, and Wasunna, 2005). We aim to identify flashpoints for debate, discuss their implications, consider interwoven philosophical issues, and make suggestions for future legislation and socio-political engagement with PwIDs.

Clarification of Terms

Intellectual Disability (ID)

Intellectual disability is

> [c]haracterised by significant limitations in intellectual functioning (reasoning, learning, problem solving) and adaptive behaviour, covering a range of everyday social and practical skills. Intellectual disability forms a subset of *developmental disability*, but the boundaries are often blurred as many individuals fall into both categories to differing degrees and for different reasons (Human Rights Watch, 2015: iii).

Just as there are different ways of thinking about intellectual impairment, there is no 'single kind' of intellectually impaired person (McDonagh, 2008; Nakken and Vlaskamp, 2007). Some individuals can resist subordination, practise self-determination, participate autonomously as researchers or voters, and achieve their potential with little assistance, while others require support in such endeavours. Among the lenses through which to conceptualize ID, the medical and social models are a good way of illustrating distance on what can be thought of as a continuum of understanding disability (Swartz *et al.*, 2012).

Medical definitions ascribe ID to deficits in intellectual and adaptive functioning which occur across various domains during the developmental period (American Association on Intellectual and Developmental Disabilities, 2017; American Psychiatric Association, 2017; Crnic *et al.*, 2017). No longer categorized solely by scores on intellectual assessments, individuals now shift along a continuum of domains that include conceptual, social, and practical functioning and that inform on mild, moderate, severe, or profound ID (APA, 2013). Where limitations are irreversible, adaptive skills can be developed, while supported decision-making and individualized care can help PwIDs negotiate limitations. Support requirements vary according to the severity of the ID and levels of support needs. Regardless of subjective experiences, the medical model regards disability as an inherent problem of the individual (Nash and Navias, 1992; McKenzie and Macleod, 2012a; Roy, Roy, and Roy, 2012).

The Social Model of Disability

The social model resists pathologizing impairment and separates bodily impairment from a socio-political unwillingness to accommodate an individual's needs (Goodley, 2001; McKenzie and Macleod, 2012a; Shakespeare, 2017; Swartz *et al.*, 2012): whereas individuals live with impairment, their political and social environments do the disabling. The social model argues that disability occurs not because of individual impairment, but rather as the result of interactions among physical environments and social relationships that further encumber impairment (Young and Berry, 2016). Discriminatory attitudes towards disablement and impaired citizens as key obstacles to socio-political inclusion sit alongside difficult-to-navigate political and social environments (Barnes, 2012; Goodley, Hughes, and Davis, 2012; Kelly, 2013; Shakespeare, 2006; Stein and Stein, 2007). The disenfranchisement of PwIDs perpetuates their vulnerability to exploitation, marginalization, and inequality in systems where the distribution of care and services hardly ever occurs in their favour and very seldom adequately (Adnams, 2010).

Ableism

People with ID are subjected to whatever form care may take without appropriate supportive decision-making or opportunity to assert access to recourse. Denying such support perpetuates ableism, which refers to dominant societal attitudes that devalue and limit the potential of persons with impairment and give rise to practices and beliefs that assign inferior value to individuals with intellectual impairments (Nonnemacher and Bambara, 2011; Stainton, 2005; Stein and Stein, 2007; Watson, Wilson, and Hagiliassis, 2013). Ableist societies negatively evaluate impaired individuals against able-bodied standards, resulting in socio-political environments that essentially exclude impaired individuals by means of attitudinal or systemic barriers (Smith, Foley, and Chaney, 2008; Stop Ableism, 2009; Wolbring, 2008).

Care

Care is conceptualized as more than just a task – it also refers to our capacity for reflection on the nature of our participation in its practices. We care by addressing barriers that 'undermine or interfere with the freedom to exercise whatever capacities one has or can develop' (Kittay, Jennings, and Wasunna, 2005: 458). Care can be good or bad, but all care is person-making (Tronto, 2010). Morris (2001) refers to Kitwood and Bredin (1992: 44) to explain that '"[b]ad" care fails to take personhood seriously, and allows the individual to fall apart ... "[g]ood" care honours personhood and provides increasing interpersonal compensation and reassurance as individual powers fail'. But evaluations of care have rarely been sourced from PwID, and viewing them as incompetent to pass judgement perpetuates disabling and discriminatory treatment (Kittay, 2009, 2011; Tronto, 2010).

Existing Legal Framework

An adult at risk is any person aged eighteen years or over who is vulnerable to abuse or neglect because of their care and/ or support needs. Beyond the Mental Healthcare Act (DoH, 2002) or Older Persons Act (DoJ, 2006), the State has no legal obligation to intervene on behalf of adults with ID at risk of abuse and death (Makgoba, 2017). State care for adults with severe and profound ID is supported by the Mental Health Care Act (DoH, 2002) and General Regulation Amendment (DoH, 2016) but omits governance for adults with ID of any severity living in community settings.

The United Nations Convention on the Rights of Persons with Disabilities (CRPD)

Adopting the Convention in 2006 can be seen as a watershed moment in the development and recognition of disability rights. As the first international human rights treaty to expressly and exclusively deal with the rights of PwDs and described as having the 'potential to become a transformative international legal instrument' (Lewis, 2010: 98), the Convention is noteworthy for two reasons: it sets out the interpretation of existing human rights in respect of disability, and it clarifies the State obligations arising from recognizing these rights.

A major potential value of the Convention is that it is legally binding on ratifying States (referred to as States Parties). In terms of international law, this means that States Parties, such as South Africa, have a general, overarching obligation to give effect to Convention provisions. Article 4(1) explains that States are required to undertake commitments to ensure realization of all rights for all PwDs. This includes the adoption of appropriate legislative and other measures for implementing recognized rights in this document (Article 4[1][a]); modifying or abolishing existing laws and practices that constitute discrimination against PwDs (Article 4[1][b]); refraining from any act inconsistent with the Convention; and ensuring that public authorities and institutions act in conformity with the present Convention (Article 4[1][d]). A State Party also considers whether any legislative or other measures should be adopted in order to implement the Convention.

These 'operational' provisions are similar to comparable human rights instruments and, at a minimum, require a review of States Parties' existing laws and policies to investigate whether these discriminate against PwDs. In this regard, it is necessary to consider the concept of indirect discrimination, where a rule or legislative provision appears neutral but, in practice, has a disproportionately negative effect on a particular group of people.

Apart from Article 4, most provisions in the Convention that set out different rights also stipulate additional duties specific to the right in question. For example, Article 13, which deals with access to justice, requires States Parties to ensure effective access for PwDs in order to facilitate their participation in all legal proceedings (Article 13[1]).

It is generally accepted that human rights impose three types or levels of obligations on States, i.e. to respect, protect, and fulfil the right concerned (Committee on Economic, Social and Cultural Rights [CESCR], 2000). The duty to respect requires States to refrain from interfering directly or indirectly with the enjoyment of the right, whereas the obligation to protect requires it to take measures preventing third parties from interfering with the guaranteed right. The obligation to fulfil requires States to adopt legislative, budgetary, promotional, and other measures to ensure full realization of the right.

Article 12, which deals with equal recognition before the law, clarifies that PwDs have a right to legal capacity that is equal to that enjoyed by persons without disabilities, as well as the right to exercise this capacity on an equal basis with others. In terms of respecting, protecting, and fulfilling the right, equitable support is then provided to prevent abuse, in accordance with international human rights law. This could take the form of assistance that respects the will and particular preferences of the PwIDs (Capri and Swartz, 2018).

Despite successful lobbying in the past and, for example, the government being pressurized to provide access to educational environments for learners with any level of ID, the South African State struggles to maintain an interest in PwIDs and the issues they face once acute scrutiny passes (see the 11 November 2010 ruling in *Western Cape Forum for Intellectual Disability v. Government of the Republic of South Africa and Government of the Province of Western Cape*, ESCR-NET, 2010). Should a State Party like South Africa continue to fail to comply with its signatory duties, the application of shame through media exposure could be mobilized (Baehr, 1996). Governments and politicians, in particular, might be more likely to take persuasive human rights action if threatened by media attention. Still, even in the electronic and social media era, such publicity and public pressure remain a last resort when trying to change government attitudes and behaviour. Although it is more effective in countries that pay attention to public opinion, few governments can afford to ignore image management. Such exposure may also lead to external pressure by other governments or intergovernmental organizations.

Mobilizing Legislative Action for PwIDs: Naming and Shaming as Recourse

The Esidimeni transfer project culminated in arbitration proceedings[4] between the families of deceased and surviving mental healthcare users, the government of South Africa (represented by the national minister of health), the premier of Gauteng Province, and a member of the executive council for health. The government had conceded liability by this time, so the only aspect to be decided by the arbitrator was the amount to be awarded. Given testimony from sixty witnesses, retired Deputy Chief Justice (DCJ) Moseneke ordered the government to pay not only an amount of R180,000 to each claimant as compensation for shock and psychological trauma, but an additional R1,000,000 per claimant as constitutional

[4] Whereas courts are involved in the case of litigation (lawsuits), a settlement between the parties is done outside of court, in arbitration.

damages for the 'unjustifiable and reckless' violations of several provisions in the Constitution (see below), as well as breaches of the Mental Health Care Act of 2002 and National Health Act of 2003.

Of importance here is DCJ Moseneke's careful analysis of the regulatory framework applicable to the care of mental healthcare users: notably, as viewed in light of international human rights obligations, government duties towards mental healthcare users originate from the Constitution, domestic legislation, and policy. Reference is made to the Universal Declaration of Human Rights (UDHR), the African Charter on Human and Peoples' Rights, and several CRPD provisions as discussed earlier. In turn, the Constitution stipulates that its provisions bind all organs of State – that is, every State official entrusted with public power (Section 8[1]) (RSA, 1996). All public office-bearers and State officials who made decisions on the transfer project were thus required to effect constitutional imperatives (para. 155) (RSA, 1996). This extends to the NGOs who acquired constitutional obligations when they assumed the duties of an organ of the State.

These State organs and NGOs were enjoined to respect, protect, and promote mental healthcare users' constitutional rights, which include the right to life, human dignity, freedom and security of the person, and especially the right not to be tortured in any way (para. 156) (RSA, 1996). While one may take issue with the arbitrator's observation that this regulatory regime is in line with 'mental health care norms of a very high order' and international human rights, his conclusion is unassailable (Moseneke, 2018: 73):

> But what stands out is the breadth and depth and frequency of the arrogant and deeply disgraceful disregard of constitutional obligations, other law, mental health care norms and ethics by an organ of state, its leaders and employees.

The question brought to mind is whether, even if in place at the time, legislation would have prevented these egregious rights violations by the State against persons with ID.

The South African Constitution

Rights realizations for PwIDs require eliminating stereotypes and presumptions, encouraging inclusive practices, creating opportunities for occupational skills development (job coaching and supportive employers), and pathways out of poverty. Lobbying efforts might increase political will for legislative support and quality primary ID healthcare, and could reduce life-threatening discrimination against PwIDs (Makgoba, 2017). Although the Convention's Article 8 addresses prejudice and stereotyping and Articles 29 and 30 pertain to political and social participation, safe inclusion of PwIDs in South African communities is yet to align with these principles (McKenzie, McConkey, and Adnams, 2013b; UN, 2006).

Domestically, one can look to protect, respect, and promote the Bill of Rights of the South African Constitution (Chapter 2 of Act No. 108) (RSA, 1996), but without guarantee. There are, in lieu of a specific article dedicated to the rights of PwIDs, a number of directly relevant provisions in the Bill of Rights. These include prohibiting unfair discrimination based on disability (Section 9[3]), provisions relating to human dignity (Section 10), the right to the freedom and security of the person (Section 12), access to adequate housing (Section 26) and healthcare services (Section 27[1]), and the right to basic education (Section 29[1][a]) (RSA, 1996). Chapter 2, Section 7(2) of the Constitution enjoins the State to respect, protect, promote and fulfil the rights in the Bill of Rights; this wording significantly recalls the three levels of duties noted above in the Existing Legal Framework section (respecting, protecting, and fulfilling human rights). Law or conduct inconsistent with the supreme law is thus invalid, and obligations imposed in terms of the Constitution must be fulfilled (RSA, 1996).

If citizenship under the Constitution provides legal status and political participation without restraint while honouring various rights and duties, then viewing people with intellectual impairment as a politically 'unfit' homogeneous group disables the political rights of individuals with competence and capacity to make political decisions (Dowse, 2009; McDonagh, 2008; McKenzie and Adnams, 2014; Smith, Foley, and Chaney, 2008; Stein and Stein, 2007; Yeung, Passmore, and Packer, 2008). South Africa's political rights (Section 19[3][a]: RSA, 1996) indiscriminately entitle prison inmates to vote in elections, whereas citizens with ID must do battle for the very same right (Combrinck, 2014; Hartley, 2013; Kopel, 2017). The notion of being of 'unsound mind' is also used in South Africa but is not clearly enough defined and can endanger freedom of the person (Szwed, 2020). This aphorism continues to disenfranchise

PwIDs, regardless of contemporary support for successful suffrage elsewhere in the world (UN, 2006: Article 29[a]; Hood, 2014; Kjellberg and Hemmingsson, 2013).

Ironically, the medico-psychological model's reinforcement of 'different' or 'special treatment' and 'extra protections', as exemplified in separate-from-mainstream special health facilities like Alexandra Hospital[5] and schools for learners with special education needs, might actually risk the independence of PwIDs – as citizens with political choices – to assert participatory rights (McKenzie and Macleod, 2012b). However, equitable participation (e.g. voting), appropriate services (support while voting), and protections (against voter intimidation) can dispel the assumption that needs for equitable supports are irreconcilable when realizing the political rights of PwIDs (McKenzie and Macleod, 2012b; Pieterse, 2006).

Current Position: PwIDs in South Africa

Globally, approximately 200 million people live with ID, making it the world's most prevalent disability (World Health Organization [WHO] and World Bank [WB], 2011). Compared to the general population and other disability groups, PwIDs are: more at risk for poverty due to unemployment, lack of health, and independent community-living services; excluded from political and other forms of social participation; more at risk of violence, exploitation, and abuse; and lacking in access to justice both as witnesses and when accused (Merrells, Buchanan, and Waters, 2017; WHO, 2011; Wilson *et al.*, 2017). Among the many challenges facing PwIDs in Africa, high prevalence, discrimination, and access to justice and education are key considerations – without exception, these challenges are 'coupled with poor resource allocation' (Njenga, 2009: 457). Yet recognition of and provision for the needs of PwIDs in Africa carries low priority, despite the finding that the prevalence rate of ID in Africa is greater than in high-income countries (Molteno, Adnams, and Njenga, 2011; De Vries *et al.*, 2013).

5 Located in Cape Town, Alexandra Hospital is a specialized facility offering treatment and rehabilitation services for 'complex mental health' cases and PwIDs (https://www.westerncape.gov.za/facility/alexandra-hospital [accessed 14 March 2022]).

Since it is an important area of public health need, De Vries *et al.* (2013) also considers the resources and priorities associated with ID in African countries, given the importance of potential causes (like tuberculous meningitis, HIV/AIDS, and other opportunistic infections) that might differ from those in higher-income settings. For example, prenatal alcohol exposure can result in a range of lifelong impairments known as foetal alcohol spectrum disorders (FASD). South Africa has among the highest reported rates of FASD in the world (Katwan, Adnams, and London, 2011; May and Gossage, 2001; Urban *et al.*, 2008), and ID and neuroregression are documented as presenting features of HIV encephalopathy in up to 80% of cases of children with cognitive delays (Potterton *et al.*, 2010; Samia *et al.*, 2013).

Despite a higher ID prevalence in South Africa than in high-income countries, reliable ID data are rare (Du Plessis, 2013; Fujiura, Rutkowski-Kmitta, and Owen, 2010; Maulik *et al.*, 2011; McKenzie, 2016; Tomlinson *et al.*, 2014; WHO and WB, 2011). Accurate prevalence data were last gathered in the 1990s among children aged two to nine (Christianson *et al.*, 2002; Kromberg *et al.*, 1997, 2008). Claiming 'limited questions on disability in Census 2011' (Statistics South Africa [SSA], 2014: 24), South African ID prevalence data from the 2011 national censuses fared no better than in 2001 and, admittedly, '[i]ntellectual disability was not measured directly' (SSA, 2014: 23). But if 3.2% of persons aged five years and older were reported nationally as having mild and 1%, severe difficulties 'in remembering or concentrating' (SSA, 2014: 34), we cautiously estimate a 4.2% prevalence of this difficulty in persons aged five years and older.[6]

Since PwIDs face limitations to self-advocacy and prioritization of their interests, oversights by the South African Statistician-General and legislature are not inconsequential. Such omissions trivialize core issues of the societal exclusion of PwIDs that touch on pervasive ableism and inequality and the distribution of resources, protections, rights claims, justice, and citizenship. Excluding PwIDs from contributing to policies and laws that directly impact their lives is viewed as morally abusive (Kittay, 2009: 620). Such disenfranchisement perpetuates the marginalization of PwIDs in disempowering systems (Capri *et*

[6] The estimated South African population is 55,908,865 (WB, 2017), implying that more than 2,000,000 individuals may be living with difficulties in remembering or concentrating.

al., 2018b). In the absence of recourse, PwIDs are vulnerable to whatever form support may take – even if abusive, neglectful, or deadly (Makgoba, 2017).

Since they are faced with service barriers and low prioritization of care politically, PwIDs struggle more to exercise constitutional rights than the general population (Capri *et al.*, 2018b; DoH, n.d.; Donohue, Bornman, and Granlund, 2014; Huus *et al.*, 2015). By interpreting the UN Convention on the Rights of the Child (UNCRC) (UNICEF, 1989), protecting vulnerable children is legislated in South Africa's Children's Act (No. 38 of 2005) (DoJ, 2005). This legally requires the departments of social development and health to intervene on behalf of children at risk. But what of adults with ID at risk of neglect, abuse, and death?

Access to Health, Social and Criminal Justice, and the Practice of Consent

Health and well-being

Prejudice increases violence against PwIDs, while misconceptions may both contribute to and result from a lack of public campaigns on the health and safety of PwIDs, who face compound difficulties in accessing justice, health, education, employment, and welfare services (Adnams, 2010; McKenzie, McConkey, and Adnams, 2013a; Molteno, Adnams, and Njenga, 2011). In South Africa, children with ID are five times less likely to receive rehabilitation services than children with physical disabilities ($p < 0.0001$) (Saloojee *et al.*, 2007). Basic education and skills development programmes for PwIDs are rare, appropriate work placements are hard to find without help, and isolation and victimization in communities continues (Capri *et al.*, 2018b). Most adults with ID who live in community settings stay with family and have limited options when caregivers burn out or die. Few relatives willingly take on the support needs of PwIDs, so neighbours step in sometimes, while community care facilities are in short supply and have years-long waiting lists (Capri *et al.*, 2018b; Geiger, 2012). The need for participatory community-based services, developed and monitored in line with purposeful care and safe community inclusion, is urgent.

Rights to health are hampered by shortages of professionals able to competently treat PwIDs with physical and mental health problems, unavailability of typically used medications, obstructive referral pathways, users having to travel to multiple medical facilities for various interventions (but without supportive public transport), and poverty (Huus *et al.*, 2015). Given that they have the right to inclusion in South Africa, PwIDs should have their health needs met at a primary healthcare level, but they are often redirected to specialist settings for services that are available at their local clinics. A lack of ID awareness at a primary care level also results in PwIDs getting lost to referral services when they should have been receiving specialist intervention (Capri *et al.*, 2018b).

Adults with ID who also have behavioural and physical and/ or mental health difficulties face multiple barriers to accessing necessary services (De Vries *et al.*, 2013; McKenzie, McConkey, and Adnams, 2013b). Primary healthcare nurses are often the first professional contacts for those caring for PwIDs, but PwIDs are often ill-treated by health workers that could be potential sources of support (Bornman and Alant, 2002; Newton and McGillivray, 2017). While primary healthcare professionals could be up-skilled with knowledge of ID care (Bornman and Alant 2002), community-based services could implement task-shifting of appropriate assessment, intervention, and referral services (Geiger, 2012; Petersen, 2004; Shabalala and Jasson, 2011). In these ways, universal services can foster integration of PwIDs into the national health system (Molteno, Adnams, and Njenga, 2011; Petersen, 2004; Pillay and Siyothula, 2011).

Candidate practitioners from various disciplines will be better able to meet the care requirements of all patients if trained to practise multiple and diverse means of assessment and treatment, including the care needs of PwIDs (Geiger, 2012; Roberts *et al.*, 2016). Instructors with ID can broaden practitioner understanding, and future service designs can integrate the experience and knowledge of PwIDs and their caregivers (Grut *et al.*, 2012). Continuous professional development and journal clubs can keep practitioners current on best practice (Donohue and Bornman, 2015).

Most PwIDs in South Africa likely suffer poor nutrition and live in socio-economically distressed areas that further predispose them to negative outcomes (Pillay and Siyothula, 2011; Slone *et al.*, 1998, 1999). Most families caring for dependent PwIDs rely on monthly social grants of R1600 (± USD105.60) (South African Social Security Agency, 2017), and 25% frequently go without food before the next grant payment cycle (Pillay and Siyothula, 2011). Poverty and unmet service needs create a dire situation for PwIDs.

In South Africa, familial caregivers to PwIDs are predominantly women, and experiences of minimal support and isolation are similar across race and class, albeit questionably so because of whites and the middle/upper classes generally having better access to housing and resources (McKenzie, 2016; McKenzie and McConkey, 2016). Care burdens restrict personal growth and opportunities to pursue employment, contribute to stress and burn-out, and pose risks to the care of PwIDs who have no alternative care options (Coetzee, 2015; McKenzie and McConkey, 2016). Yet there remains little evidence of integration among the South African government's health, education, and social development departments in servicing these needs; and the opportunity costs of informal ID care remain unrecognized (Adnams, 2010; De Vries *et al.*, 2013; McKenzie *et al.*, 2013b; Saloojee *et al.*, 2007; Tomlinson *et al.*, 2014).

Compared to the general population or other disability groups, PwIDs are more often unemployed or underemployed due to low expectations of competence ('they' can't do much) and high expectations of problems ('they' are difficult to deal with) (Capri *et al.*, 2018b; Carvalho-Freitas and Stathi, 2017; Merrells, Buchanan, and Rogers, 2017; WHO, 2011; Wilson *et al.*, 2017). One specific example is Mike,[7] an adult in his late thirties who lives with mild intellectual disabilities (mild ID). Having 'failed' a number of occupational and community-living residential placements, Mike is perpetually at risk of being fired from a fourth job or expelled from a third group home. Others fail to recognise that he has little understanding of the value of money or budgeting and struggles with time and dates. He is unable to pace out a period of two weeks, measure time (e.g. how long half an hour is), or track when three months ago was. It is not possible for him to place calendar dates (e.g. product expiry dates). Mike has successfully applied for shelf-packing jobs in grocery stores, and things usually start off well, but without appropriate employer coaching and job support, he inevitably receives numerous final warnings, resigns, or gets fired from a job after a short period, which reinforces his expectation that there will be problems.

Sadly, in part due to his misleadingly good expressive verbal skills, the blame is shifted onto Mike rather than on

[7] 'Mike Bauer' and 'Cheryl September' are both pseudonyms. Mike's and Cheryl's true identities have been protected by removing information that could render them identifiable or recognisable.

an unwillingness to understand and respond to his particular neurobiological profile and behavioural support needs. His expressive abilities do not always count in his favour, because this makes it easy to overestimate his other abilities, which are actually more compromised than they seem. This leads to expectations from others that are too high for him to meet. As his anxiety escalates, he becomes very reassurance-seeking (clingy). While he is actually desperate for help to cope in an overwhelming situation, his distress at rejection and abandonment increases as people are put off by his clinginess.

Soon Mike will become even more intrusive, because he struggles to read social cues and non-verbal communication. The unrealistic expectations held of him will end in another dismissal from work or expulsion from a home. As a result, Mike is again misunderstood as being argumentative, insecure (he always wants to be the centre of attention), inattentive, lazy, and manipulative; when in fact he really struggles with maintaining his own and others' boundaries, and with maintaining focus and concentration for long periods of time. Because he can't use words to adequately express his disappointment and grief, his lashing out will be labelled as violence directed towards others, resulting in security guards or the police attending with force to a person who should rather have been understood as being in severe distress. Mike's reputation is now one of being difficult, dependent, unlikeable, and aggressive. He is recognized as a 'problematic case' that cannot hold down a job and gets evicted from group homes. The few people who are aware of his difficulties are giving up, with social and economic exclusion his inevitable future.

Access to justice: Effective participation in legal proceedings

Individuals with ID are particularly easy targets for sexual offenders, with close relatives implicated in most cases of sexual assault against children with ID (Calitz *et al.*, 2014; Meel, 2009; Phasha, 2009, 2013). Fallacies maintaining that PwIDs feel no pain, have high sex drives, and have unusual power, or that sex with PwIDs can cure the perpetrator of disease or is an act of pity, perpetuate this abuse (Phasha and Myaka, 2014). PwIDs continue to face multiple difficulties with the justice system despite women with ID being at increased risk of sexual abuse and the widespread sexual abuse of teenagers with ID (Bornman and Rathbone, 2016; Calitz *et al.*, 2014; Meel, 2009; Phasha, 2009, 2013). Sexual assault survivors with ID are particularly vulnerable to its psychological effects, and present with higher symptom intensity and rates of post-traumatic stress disorder than ID individuals with non-sexual traumatic histories (Shabalala and Jasson, 2011). This foregrounds the necessity of communicative support for PwIDs by investigators and court officers, especially in cases where a person's ability to tell their story is compromised.

Persons with mild and moderate ID can be supported to learn about, develop, and maintain consensual and meaningful sexual relationships (Bornman and Rathbone, 2016; Kramers-Olen, 2016; Phasha and Myaka, 2014; Rohleder and Swart, 2009). Individuals with severe and profound ID, however, will find it harder to negotiate consent around sexual practices. Without promoting safe access to State-supported sexual health education programmes, PwIDs will struggle to protect themselves against unwanted sex and its possible consequences (Bornman and Rathbone, 2016; Meel, 2009; Rohleder and Swartz, 2009). Undoing harmful misconstructions about ID and sexuality might initiate beliefs, policies, and public services that are supportive of PwIDs entering into healthy significant human relationships. Formal interventions should be nationally implemented in various communities to reduce the prevalence of sexual abuse of PwIDs (Phasha and Myaka, 2014).

We appreciate that sexual assault cases involving complainants with ID challenge the South African investigative and judicial systems (Calitz, 2011; Pillay and Kritzinger, 2008), but we question whether sexual assault survivors who have ID, after suffering trauma and perhaps undergoing a medico-legal examination, must undergo further evaluations to be deemed fit to testify to their account of events (Pillay, 2008). Decisions about an ID survivor's ability to testify should consider issues of capacity and self-determination (Phaswana, Van der Westhuizen, and Krüger, 2013). While competence relates to doing something successfully or efficiently, capacity speaks to a person's ability to enter into legally binding relations, to know what they are doing or what is being done to them, or to know the principles and impact of what they are agreeing to when entering into agreements with others. In a court of law, capacity refers to both legal independence and participation during legal proceedings.

Appropriate legal support for ID rape or abuse survivors can aid justice and equality (Sections 9.1 and 9.2) (RSA, 1996). Less reductionist definitions of legal capacity requirements can emphasize adaptive abilities and challenge a medical underscoring of intellectual impairment. Because abilities to observe, recall events, and communicate can be established during testimony, defendants might be able to give evidence despite conventional 'test' findings of intellectual deficit (Pillay, 2008, 2012a, 2012b; Pillay and Kritzinger, 2008). Having ratified the Convention (UN, 2006), should the State not provide any means necessary to equitably meet the needs of PwIDs in the criminal justice system under Article 12(3) (UN 2006)?

Having one's experiences and accounts of events received in a court of law is important for building competence (Bornman *et al.*, 2011; McKenzie, 2013; Nash and Navias, 1992). This is shown clearly in the case of Cheryl September, a woman in her early forties who lives with moderate ID and a severe psychiatric disorder which causes her to become psychotic. As her history illustrates (discussed below), focusing on biomedical limitations can overshadow individual competencies, lower expectations for new learning, minimize subjective experiences, and reinforce unequal power relations (Donohue and Bornman, 2014; Geiger, 2012; McKenzie and Macleod, 2012a; Young and Berry, 2016). Denying competence and legal capacity are fundamental rights violations that reinforce social prejudice against PwIDs and perpetuate discrimination and exclusion (Pillay, 2012a; UN, 2006). Given contemporary interpretations of capacity and equality under the law (UN, 2006: Article 12), the onus of proving that PwIDs are (un)able to participate in legal proceedings should be on the court – not on the PwIDs.

Cheryl's story highlights a number of significant events, social antipathies, and failures by government institutions and health professionals that continue to do harm to a woman with ID and a history of multiple traumas. Abandoned on a rubbish dump as a new-born baby, her childhood entailed neglect, abuse, and exposure to violence and drugs. She was sexually assaulted by men in her foster family; her foster mother was aware of this but was afraid of losing custody and therefore losing Cheryl's social welfare grant.

Having murdered the man who murdered her toddler, Cheryl was sentenced to prison after a lengthy court process. There is no court record of psychological or psychiatric assessment, no indication that her ID was considered, and no statement of her account of the violence she endured. Nobody explained to her what to expect during the legal process or knew that she was pregnant for a second time. With ID and an undiagnosed mental illness, Cheryl was an easy target for other inmates, and she was victimized and gang-raped in prison. This resulted in a miscarriage. Neither the department of correctional services nor the department of social development knew what to do with Cheryl other than place her in a group home unequipped to deal with clients with ID, mental illness, and a criminal history. After a second short hospital admission to acute psychiatric services, the manager of Cheryl's group home at the time reported that Cheryl had committed a second murder.

This time, the court undertook assessments and found that Cheryl lives with moderate ID. It considered her competent to stand trial but did not consider her co-morbid mental illness or her incapacity to fully appreciate the implications of her actions. As a poor woman of colour living with ID and mental illness, Cheryl's chances of receiving appropriate judicial, social development, and mental health support and a fair trial were jeopardized from the outset. She is not able to think things through from different angles without support, she struggles to regulate and control her reactions without help, and she lives with post-traumatic stress, which causes her to 'zone out' from time to time. In addition, her ability to express herself is poor: it is difficult to understand what she is saying, she uses grammar incorrectly, and she mispronounces words. There was no recommendation on record to help her access a facilitator, court intermediary, or any other communication support during her murder trial.

This begs the question, though we cannot know the answer: had the State not failed its earlier obligations towards her, would she have committed this second murder and been made to carry the responsibility for its trial alone? Under South African law, any accused person, no matter the crime, must be afforded a fair trial, have their charges explained to them until they understand fully, be given the chance to give their version of events, stand trial without too much time going by, and be allowed to answer questions from investigators and prosecutors. Because Cheryl did not receive any support, she was not made aware of her rights and was unable to understand what was happening or what she could do about it. In the end, due to no fault of her own, Cheryl was not considered a credible witness, and the case was dismissed due to a lack of evidence. Cheryl knew what had happened to her, remembers it, thinks about it, and tries to make sense of it. Denying her an opportunity to testify to any of this is an injustice.

We have to wonder if this decision serves Cheryl or the public well in any way. She remains at high risk of reoffending but is not given the right help or access to services. With no recognition from politicians or even society that it is necessary to fix these service gaps or that they even exist, people like Cheryl will continue to spend their days in danger of getting hurt or hurting others, but with no chance of getting help or getting better.

Cheryl will be forty-three soon. Images of her brain show that she is declining quickly. She is obsessed with the past, overcome with grief and guilt, and slowing down in her thinking and understanding. She has not killed anybody in eight years, did her time in prison, and has the right to get help and live without fear in safety. But she is becoming increasingly unable to manage her anger and rage without help. Despite the departments of justice, social development, or corrections surely having a share in the responsibility for her care needs, mental health practitioners are left to decide Cheryl's fate, since under the Mental Health Care Act (DoH, 2002), they alone – not law and order – have been left with the responsibility to make sure that she, and the public, stay safe.

Justice for offenders like Cheryl must be considered. Offenders with ID may understand truth, lies, and moral wrongfulness but be unable to link these to real implications. When capacity for social insight and adaptive skills are considered, therefore, it must be understood that knowing right from wrong should be differentiated from appreciating consequences of wrongfulness. A finding of intellectual impairment need not disqualify one from testifying, because defendants with adaptive functioning that is comparatively better than their intellectual functioning can be triable (Calitz *et al.*, 2007; Pilla, 2012a, 2012b). The disenfranchizing South African legal idea of not being of sound mind must be continuously criticized, since, as we can see from Cheryl's life history, PwIDs are not automatically without capacity (Combrinck, 2014; Phaswana, Van der Westhuizen, and Krüger, 2013).

Promotion and Protection: The Need for ID Legislation

People with ID may have limitations in advocating for themselves and ensuring that their best interests are prioritized, but not affording PwIDs support or opportunities for them to contribute to policies that directly impact their lives can be viewed as morally abusive (Kittay, 2009). Of importance for this discussion are issues regarding the societal inclusion and exclusion of PwIDs that touch on core questions of rights claims, justice, citizenship, equality, resources, and protections. Individuals may be intellectually or physically impaired, but it is their political and social environments that do the disabling (Shakespeare, 2017). An intellectually impaired person is *made* disabled when society restricts his or her status as a citizen, access to resources, or right to a humane life. A lack of legislation to address this can be viewed as ableist.

Legislation that promotes and protects the rights of PwIDs should incorporate issues of legal capacity and supported decision-making, a duty to intervene when protection is needed, and service provision standards inclusive of residential facilities. Purposeful legislation for adults who require support is yet to be taken up in South Africa, but recent examples we can turn to share common goals of preventing harm, reducing risk of abuse or neglect for adults with care and support needs, and safeguarding adults in ways that support their control over personal life choices (Capri *et al.*, 2018b).[8] Aligned with Article 12 of the Convention, such legislation could include the equal rights of PwDs to own or inherit property, control their own financial affairs, and have access to financial credit, and protect against their being arbitrarily deprived of property.

Still regulated by common law, the legal capacity of adults with ID in South Africa begs important and complicated questions which must be managed by the judicial and health systems. Determinants of capacity (making decisions with legal consequences) cannot solely rely on intellectual-functioning assessment scores. They must also involve one's understanding of the environment, speech and language proficiency, quality of education, reasoning ability, and the way in which a person makes decisions with legal consequences (Calitz *et al.*, 2007). A finding of ID does not necessarily exclude individual accountability, and

[8] See the United Kingdom Care Act (DoH UK, 2014); Safeguarding Policy of the Office of the Public Guardian (Office of the Public Guardian England and Wales, 2015); Vulnerable Adults Act Draft Bill (Government of Singapore 2016); Protection of Vulnerable Adults from Financial Exploitation Act (Alabama Securities Commission, 2016); and the Adult Protective Services Act (State of Illinois Department on Aging, 2013).

a person with ID can be held answerable to legal consequences (Calitz *et al.*, 2007). Accordingly, individualized management plans to assist adults living with support needs are not limited to health, caregiving, and community environments but are also the purview of judicial systems.

Under a future act yet to come into being (let's call it a 'Promotion and Protection of Rights for Adults Requiring Support Act', for the sake of argument), supported decision-making will hold the core principle that PwIDs manage personal choices with support from non-ID assistants of their choice (Capri and Swartz, 2018). The egalitarian ethos behind this recognizes that a PwID holds true ID expertise that cannot be understood by their non-ID assistants, respects the specific needs of PwIDs, who set the kinds and levels of necessary assistance, and provides equitable support, even if core requirements are exceeded. Accepting assistance, or not, is the individual's choice and the point of voluntary-assisted decision-making (Capri and Swartz, 2018).

Intersecting advocacy and policy design, voluntary-assisted decision-making might be useful for informing legislation, foregrounding self-identified life requirements, designing service standards and care practices, lobbying for rights implementation, developing political behaviour, realizing socio-economic participation, and facilitating engagement among those wishing to change restrictive socio-political conditions. By means of voluntary-assisted advocacy, PwIDs can represent issues in committees or boardrooms and consult on future standards for healthcare. People with ID and assistant advocates could comment on draft bills, work on legislation, write to newspaper editors, lobby for socio-political inclusion, participate in justice proceedings (e.g. the Esidimeni hearings – see p. XX), or insist that the National Census accurately includes South Africans with ID (Capri and Swartz, 2018).

Analogous to the Older Persons Act (No. 13 of 2006) (DoJ 2006), a law that promotes and protects the rights of adults who require support will frame a legislative environment for adult PwIDs that includes:

1. Development and compliance with national norms and standards;
2. Principles guiding service provision;
3. Registered support services and care programmes in community-based settings;

4. Regulations pertaining to home-based care;
5. Monitoring and evaluation of community-based care and support services.

A Promotion and Protection of Rights for Adults Requiring Support Act will thus legislate for services and PwID rights in residential facilities, prohibit unregistered facilities, and establish residents' committees. Notification of neglect of PwIDs will be legislated, abuse of PwIDs will be prohibited, procedures for bringing alleged abusers into enquiry or before a magistrate will be regulated, and special measures will combat the abuse of PwIDs (e.g. a register of abuse of PwIDs). In the absence of such legislation, the South African Esidimeni tragedy illustrates an unprecedented level of systems failure towards PwIDs.

Ethics of Care and Care Justice: Independence between an Ethical State and PwIDs Is an Illusion

To transform disabling structures and attitudes towards impaired individuals (Stein and Stein, 2007), we can no longer tolerate ableism, which must be approached with as much criticality as afforded to racism and sexism. As citizens, PwIDs should be able to live as full members of society, with equal duties, rights, and legal status; and enjoy the freedoms and obligations of belonging to a particular national space and place. Sadly, intellectually impaired individuals are often erroneously recognized as members of a homogeneous group, unfit for economic viability for suiting neither the liberal model of being independent and autonomous nor a materialist model of making financially measurable contributions (Carey, 2003; Dowse, 2009; McDonagh, 2008; Stein and Stein, 2007).

To resolve ableist practices, we must critically engage with the oppressive socio-political structures we comply with, the ableist policies and practices we collude with, the disabling assumptions and attitudes we hold, and the circumscribed spaces made available for the expression of intellectually impaired personhoods. An exclusive appeal to a traditional human rights model against ableism risks focusing on entitled protections ('having the right') rather than realizing these entitlements ('getting the right'). Despite having rights in law, South African intellectually impaired individuals' levels of socio-political participation remain limited due to implementation shortcomings, little political will, and a lack of accountability (Cary 2003; Stein and Stein 2007).

An Ethical State?

As an institution obliged to follow international human rights law and the Constitution, the legislation of the State must be underpinned by ethical action. These include policy implementation (involving the Executive), budget allocation (Treasury), and monitoring. If legal arguments for forcing the South African government to legislate in favour of adults with support needs remain unheard, we must alert the State to its complicity in the exploitation and disempowerment of PwIDs during the development and implementation (or lack) of lifesaving legislation.

What, then, of care justice? What if the State aligns CRPD adherence with ethics of care by committing to lawfully protecting PwIDs under a South African Promotion and Protection of Rights for Adults Requiring Support Act? Issues of autonomy amid discriminatory landscapes can be approached without losing sight of dignity and inclusion when considering adults who require legislative support in order to enjoy their rights.

As a normative project, ethics of care holds care as the most common human experience, describes good and bad care, holds us accountable, checks our behaviour towards others, and helps us think about our effect on others. Since '[w]e human beings are the sorts of beings we are because we are cared for by other human beings' (Kittay, 2009: 625), the consequences of our thoughts and actions towards individuals who depend on our decisions are inseparable from political aspects of ID care.

This approach informs the interdependent nature of the relationship between the State, legislators, and PwIDs as care partners. In fact, interdependence is such a central feature of human life that independence between States and PwIDs is impossible. States thus have a perpetual duty to the flourishing of PwIDs, no matter how much assistance this requires. Care, in the form of legal protections and safeguarding, is provided when and where necessary, and any barrier to such care is eliminated in an ethical State.

Kittay's myth of independence helps us realize that being human is better defined by shared characteristics of able minds and body impermanence, and, as such, never being independent.

Still occupying a space on the fairly healthy end of Swartz *et al.*'s (2012) impairment continuum, legislators may struggle to imagine themselves in an inevitably disabled body. We encourage them, as agents of the State, to recognize their own frailty so they, too, can face their future impairment with dignity, secure in justice and protected from abuse.

What Would Just Care Look Like under an Ethical State?

Within an ethics of care model, we are required to conduct ourselves constitutionally, recognize a common humanity, and consider the kinds of personhoods our lack of legislative care produces. 'Good' legislation for adults requiring rights support will respond to a common humanity, consider the kinds of persons it produces, and remove barriers to exercising capacity. In following Morris (2001), an ethical State will take the personhood of PwIDs seriously and provide reassurance, interpersonal support, and protection as individual powers fail. It will not erode independence, allow individuals to fall victim to ableism, or dominate the lives of those in need of safeguarding. 'Good' legislation for adults requiring rights support encourages dignity, promotes well-being, and fosters autonomy.

Legislating for South Africans with ID is considered politically in terms of purpose, power relations, and particularity (Tronto, 2010). While purpose addresses the function and end result of deliberate legislation, such a law will also be a site for the enactment of power relations. Inherent power relations must be interrogated so that asymmetry – fertile ground for discrimination and oppression – is placed under constant critique. Given the inescapable interdependence of the State and PwIDs, we further argue that 'good' legislation will be the product of, and produce, egalitarian relations between legislators and PwIDs.

A Promotion and Protection of Rights for Adults Requiring Support Act will face constant exposure to the ways in which PwIDs are thought about and responded to and, as with the CRPD, also needs to consider challenges to implementation. The Act will be a care performance by an ethical State – thought about, planned, and formulated into being. In learning from Goffman's (1961/1991) seminal work, ethical care, in the form of legislating for adults in need of rights support, does not infantilize, depersonalize, or contribute to the physical and psychological deterioration of its participants.

As a virtuous performance of a caring attitude, Kittay's work (2001, 2011) would encourage a worldview of care among legislators that manifests in designated law for PwIDs. Such a product of care work sustains others in need. Currently, the State's care is noticeable in its absence of inclusive services for PwIDs and lack of legislation, but changes to this system will be most appreciated by those least able to reciprocate. Designated legislation, as a statutory statement of caring, will demonstrate beneficent investments in the well-being of PwIDs without expectations of economically viable returns. Without beneficence and political will, both essential to understanding what someone with ID needs, the level of responsiveness required from the State to make a good law will not be achieved. Bringing an Act into being without interrogating the aforementioned emotional work will not produce laws that care well, as Tronto's (2010) end to which it is enacted (caring about South Africans with ID in the form of deliberate legislation) lacks well-being and is thus pointless.

Designing and producing designated legislation without harming the agency and dignity of PwIDs necessitates skill, and the care process requires a particular kind of reciprocity: the execution of the care task (the Act) must be evaluated and legitimized by PwIDs if an ethical State's care process is to be complete. In the absence of such validation, even promulgated care legislation is incomplete and cannot be claimed by a 'caring' State. However, producing legislation in the caring way described above might, in turn, create caring legislators for an ethical State.

How Do We Start?

Everyone, including PwIDs, gains knowledge about themselves through the ways in which legislators think about them. People treated in debasing ways know themselves as unequal. When we move our care ethic only into spaces created for equality, enabling care legislation can become incompatible with disabling assumptions about others. How do we expand the scope of ID care beyond intimate spaces into national and international socio-political ones, where caring about care also unfolds? Quite simply, by means of consultation and gathering information from experts, draft legislation must rely on the expertise of PwIDs, families, caregivers, and the individuals and organizations that support their needs. If ruling relations and practices, socio-political attitudes, and fiscal decisions sustain a person whose rights are respected and enacted, whose powerlessness is reduced, and whose autonomy of personal choice is routinely considered, we might begin to shape societies that practice ethical caring.

Conclusion

Can legislation become a care institution? As a signatory of the CRPD, the South African State is in effect signalling respect for different support needs and the variant ways of promoting, not disabling, human flourishing. Abuse, exploitation, and neglect is devastating for anyone. Protecting PwIDs as a particular group will have to be balanced with planning for heterogeneous, evolving support needs. Because care is relational, it influences the kinds of persons made during its planning and practice (Tronto, 2010). But care is never a simple good–bad binary, and we can at a minimum reject gradation among humans, foreground inclusion, emphasize mutually satisfying participation, and interrogate our hand in making enabled or PwDs (Smith-Chandler and Swart, 2014; Stein and Stein, 2007). The government vows that 'Esidimeni' will not be repeated (Phakgadi, 2018) but has no input from PwIDs on avoiding such futures.

Our ambitious idea of a Promotion and Protection of Rights for Adults Requiring Support Act raises questions about feasibility, implementation, and monitoring. Perhaps the South African State can start shifting towards a conscious ethics of care practice, reflected in the ways in which words are selected, decisions, made and the societal position of PwIDs investigated; in the State's duties and interactions towards humans cast into intellectually impaired lives; in its conduct as a care participant; and in the care institutions legislators create for their own inevitable impairments to be lived with one day.

Bibliography

Adnams, C.M. 2010. 'Perspectives of Intellectual Disability in South Africa: Epidemiology, Policy, Services for Children and Adults', *Current Opinion in Psychiatry* 23(5): 436–40.

Alabama Securities Commission. 2016. *Protection of Vulnerable Adults from Financial Exploitation Act 2016* <http://asc.alabama.gov/News/2016%20News/4-18-16%20Protection%20of%20Vulnerable%20Adults%20Act%202016.pdf> [accessed 10 March 2022].

American Association on Intellectual and Developmental Disabilities (AAIDD). 2017. 'Defining Criteria for Intellectual Disability' <http://aaidd.org/intellectual-disability/definition#.WZ78DSgjHIU> [accessed 3 August 2017].

American Psychiatric Association (APA). 2017. 'What Is Intellectual Disability?' <https://www.psychiatry.org/patients-families/intellectual-disability/what-is-intellectual-disability> [accessed 3 August 2017].

Baehr, P.R. 1996. *Mobilization of the Conscience of Mankind: Conditions of Effectiveness of Human Rights NGOs.* UNU Public Forum on Human Rights and NGOs, 18 September 1996, Tokyo, Japan <http://www.gdrc.org/ngo/lecture14.html> [accessed 10 March 2022].

Barnes, C. 2012. 'Disability, Work and Welfare', *Sociology Compass* 6(6): 472–84.

Bornman, J., and Alant, E. 2002. 'Community Nurses' Perceptions of and Exposure to Children with Severe Disabilities and their Primary Caregivers', *Health SA Gesondheid* 7(3): 32–55.

Bornman, J., and Rathbone, L. 2016. 'A Sexuality and Relationship Training Program for Women with Intellectual Disabilities: A Social Story Approach', *Sexuality and Disability* 34(3): 269–88.

Bornman, J. 2018. 'Life Esidimeni Victims Must Not Qualify for Constitutional Damages – State', *News24*, 9 February 2018 <http://www.news24.com/SouthAfrica/News/life-esidimeni-victims-must-not-qualify-for-constitutional-damages-state-20180209> [accessed 10 October 2021].

Bornman, J., Nelson Bryen, D., Kershaw, P., and Ledwaba, G. 2011. 'Reducing the Risk of Being a Victim of Crime in South Africa: You Can Tell and Be Heard!' *Augmentative and Alternative Communication* 27(2): 117–30.

Calitz, F.J.W. 2011. 'Psycho-legal Challenges Facing the Mentally Retarded Rape Victim', *South African Journal of Psychiatry* 17(3): 66–72.

Calitz, F.J.W., van Rensburg, P.H.J.J., de Jager, P.P., Olander, M.L., Thomas, L., Venter, R. *et al.* 2007. 'Psychiatric Evaluation of Intellectually Disabled Offenders Referred to the Free State Psychiatric Complex, 1993–2003', *South African Journal of Psychiatry* 13(4): 147–52.

Calitz, F.J.W., de Ridder, L., Gericke, N., Pretorius, A., Smit, J., and Joubert, G. 2014. 'Profile of Rape Victims Referred by the Court to the Free State Psychiatric Complex, 2003–2009', *South African Journal of Psychiatry* 20(1): 1–6.

Capri, C., Watermeyer, B., McKenzie, J., and Coetzee, O. 2018a. 'Intellectual Disability in the Esidimeni Tragedy: Silent Deaths', *SAMJ: South African Medical Journal* 108(3): 153–54.

Capri, C., Abrahams, L., McKenzie, J., Coetzee, O., Mkabile, S., Saptouw, M., Hooper, A., Smith, P., Adnams, C., and Swartz, L. 2018b. 'Intellectual Disability Rights and Inclusive Citizenship in South Africa: What Can a Scoping Review Tell Us?' *African Journal of Disability* 25(7): a396.

Capri, C., and Swartz, L. 2018. 'The Right to be Freepeople: Relational Voluntary-Assisted-Advocacy as a Psychological and Ethical Resource for Decolonizing Intellectual Disability', *Journal of Social and Political Psychology* 6(2): 556–74.

Carey, A.C. 2003. 'Beyond the Medical Model: A Reconsideration of "Feeblemindedness", Citizenship, and Eugenic Restrictions', *Disability and Society* 18(4): 411–30.

Carvalho-Freitas, M.N.D., and Stathi, S. 2017. 'Reducing Workplace Bias toward People with Disabilities with the Use of Imagined Contact', *Journal of Applied Social Psychology* 47: 256–66.

Christianson, A.L., Zwane, M.E., Manga, P., Rosen, E., Venter, A., and Downs, D. 2002. 'Children with Intellectual Disability in Rural South Africa: Prevalence and Associated Disability', *Journal of Intellectual Disability Research* 46: 179–86.

Coetzee, O. 2015. 'Caregiving Experiences of South African Mothers of Adults with Intellectual Disability Who Display Aggression: Clinical Case Studies'. Unpublished doctoral dissertation, University of Cape Town, Cape Town.

Combrinck, H. 2014. 'Everybody Counts: The Right to Vote of Persons with Psychosocial Disabilities in South Africa', *African Disability Rights Yearbook* 2: 75–100.

Committee on Economic, Social and Cultural Rights (CESCR). 2000. 'Fact Sheet No. 16 (Rev.1), United Nations' <https://www.ohchr.org/Documents/Publications/FactSheet16rev.1en.pdf> [accessed 10 March 2022].

Crnic, K.A., Neece, C.L., McIntyre, L.L., Blacher, J., and Baker, B.L., 2017. 'Intellectual Disability and Developmental Risk: Promoting Intervention to Improve Child and Family Well-being', *Child Development* 88(2): 436–45 <https://doi.org/10.1111/cdev.12740>.

De Vries, P.J., Venter, A., Jacklin, L., and Oliver, C. 2013. 'Behavioural Phenotypes and Neurodevelopmental Disorders in Africa', *Journal of Intellectual Disability Research* 57(9): 793–95.

Department of Health (DoH) (UK). 2014. United Kingdom Care Act 2014 <http://www.legislation.gov.uk/ukpga/2014/23/pdfs/ukpga_20140023_en.pdf> [accessed 10 March 2022].

Department of Health (DoH). n.d. *Policy Guidelines: Child and Adolescent Mental Health* <https://www.health-e.org.za/wp-content/uploads/2013/11/child_mental_health.pdf> [accessed 10 March 2022].

Department of Health (DoH). 2002. *Mental Health Care Act, 2002.* Cape Town: Government Gazette.

Department of Justice (DoJ). 2005. *Children's Act No. 38 of 2005* <http://www.justice.gov.za/legislation/acts/2005-038%20childrensact.pdf> [accessed 10 March 2022].

Department of Justice (DoJ). 2006. *Older Persons Act No. 13 of 2006* <http://www.justice.gov.za/legislation/acts/2006-013_olderpersons.pdf> [accessed 10 March 2022].

Donohue, D.K., and Bornman, J. 2014. 'The Challenges of Realizing Inclusive Education in South Africa', *South African Journal of Education* 34(2): 1–14.

Donohue, D.K., and Bornman, J. 2015. 'South African Teachers' Attitudes toward the Inclusion of Learners with Different Abilities in Mainstream Classrooms', *International Journal of Disability, Development and Education* 62(1): 42–59.

Donohue, D.K., Bornman, J., and Granlund, M. 2014. 'Examining the Rights of Children with Intellectual Disability in South Africa: Children's Perspectives', *Journal of Intellectual and Developmental Disability* 39(1): 55–64.

Dowse, L. 2009. '"Some People Are Never Going to Be Able to Do That": Challenges for People with Intellectual Disability in the 21st Century', *Disability and Society* 24(5): 571–84.

Du Plessis, M. 2013. 'The Social Model of Disability, Rights Discourse and the Impact of South Africa's Education White Paper 6 on Access to the Basic Education System for Persons with Severe or Profound Intellectual Impairments', *Law, Democracy and Development* 17: 202–25.

ESCR-NET. 2010. *Western Cape Forum for Intellectual Disability v. Government of the Republic of South Africa and Government of the Province of Western Cape, Case no: 18678/2007* <https://www.escr-net.org/caselaw/2011/western-cape-forum-intellectual-disability-v-government-republic-south-africa> [accessed 25 April 2021].

Fujiura, G.T., Rutkowski-Kmitta, V., and Owen, R. 2010. 'Make Measurable What Is Not So: National Monitoring of the Status of Persons with Intellectual Disability', *Journal of Intellectual and Developmental Disability* 35(4): 244–58.

Geiger, M. 2012. 'Communication Training for Centre-Based Carers of Children with Severe or Profound Disabilities in the Western Cape, South Africa', *African Journal of Disability* 1(1): 1–7.

Goffman, E. 1961/1991. *Asylums: Essays on the Social Situation of Mental Patients and Other Inmates.* London: Penguin.

Goodley, D., 2001. '"Learning Difficulties," the Social Model of Disability and Impairment: Challenging Epistemologies', *Disability and Society* 16(2): 207–31.

Goodley, D., Hughes, B., and Davis, L. Eds. 2012. *Disability and Social Theory: New Developments and Directions.* Houndmills: Palgrave Macmillan.

Government of Singapore. 2016. *Vulnerable Adults Act Draft Bill* <https://www.reach.gov.sg/-/media/reach/old-reach/2016/pc/msf/vaa-draft-bill-2016.ashx> [accessed 1 November 2016].

Grut, L., Braathen, S.H., Mji, G., and Ingstad, B. 2012. 'Accessing Community Health Services: Challenges Faced by Poor People with Disabilities in a Rural Community in South Africa', *African Journal of Disability* 1(1): e1–e7.

Hartley, W. 2013. 'IEC Rejects Suggestions that Mentally Impaired Be Allowed to Vote', *Business Day*, 16 September <https://www.businesslive.co.za/bd/national/2013-09-16-iec-rejects-suggestions-that-mentally-impaired-be-allowed-to-vote/> [accessed 11 March 2022].

Hood, I. 2014. 'How Will Scots with Learning Disabilities Be Voting in the Referendum?' *Guardian* <https://www.theguardian.com/society/2014/sep/16/scots-learning-disabilities-independence-referendum> [accessed 10 March 2022].

Human Rights Watch. 2015. 'Complicit in Exclusion: South Africa's Failure to Guarantee an Inclusive Education for Children with Disabilities' <https://www.refworld.org/docid/55d594994.html> [accessed 15 October 2021].

Huus, K., Granlund, M., Bornman, J., and Lygnegård, F. 2015. 'Human Rights of Children with Intellectual Disabilities: Comparing Self-ratings and Proxy Ratings', *Child: Care, Health and Development* 41(6): 1010–17.

Katwan, E., Adnams, C., and London, L. 2011. 'Childhood Behavioural and Developmental Disorders – Association with Maternal Alcohol Consumption in Cape Town, South Africa', *South African Medical Journal* 101(10): 724–27.

Kelly, C. 2013. 'Building Bridges with Accessible Care: Disability Studies, Feminist Care Scholarship, and Beyond', *Hypatia* 28(4): 784–800.

Kittay, E.F. 2001. 'When Caring Is Just and Justice Is Caring: Justice and Mental Retardation', *Public Culture* 13(3): 557–79.

Kittay, E.F. 2009. 'The Personal Is Philosophical Is Political: A Philosopher and Mother of a Cognitively Disabled Person Sends Notes From the Battlefield', *Metaphilosophy* 40(3–4): 606–27.

Kittay, E.F. 2011. 'The Ethics of Care, Dependence, and Disability', *Ratio Juris* 24(1): 49–58.

Kittay, E.F., Jennings, B., and Wasunna, A.A. 2005. 'Dependency, Difference and the Global Ethic of Longterm Care', *Journal of Political Philosophy* 13(4): 443–69.

Kitwood, T., and Bredin, K. 1992. 'A New Approach to the Evaluation of Dementia Care', *Journal of Advances in Health and Nursing Care* 1(5): 41–60.

Kjellberg, A., and Hemmingsson, H. 2013. 'Citizenship and Voting: Experiences of Persons with Intellectual Disabilities in Sweden', *Journal of Policy and Practice in Intellectual Disabilities* 10(4): 326–33.

Kopel, C. 2017. 'Suffrage for People with Intellectual Disabilities and Mental Illness: Observations on a Civic Controversy', *Yale Journal of Health Policy, Law, and Ethics* 17: 209–50.

Kramers-Olen, A. 2016. 'Sexuality, Intellectual Disability, and Human Rights Legislation', *South African Journal of Psychology* 46(4): 504–16.

Kromberg, J., Zwane, E., Manga, P., Venter, A., Rosen, E., and Christianson, A. 2008. 'Intellectual Disability in the Context of a South African Population', *Journal of Policy and Practice in Intellectual Disabilities* 5(2): 89–95.

Kromberg, J.G.R., Christianson, A.L., Manga, P., Zwane, M.E., Rosen, E., Venter, A. *et al.* 1997. 'Intellectual Disability in Rural Black Children in the Bushbuckridge District of South Africa', *Southern African Journal of Child and Adolescent Mental Health* 9(1): 2–11.

Lewis, O. 2010. 'The Expressive, Education and Proactive Roles of Human Rights: An Analysis of the United Nations Convention on the Rights of PwDs'. In: B. McSherry and P. Weller. Eds. *Rethinking Rights-based Mental Health Laws* (pp. 97–128). Oxford: Hart Publishing Company.

Lund, C. 2016. 'Mental Health and Human Rights in South Africa: The Hidden Humanitarian Crisis', *South African Journal on Human Rights* 32(3): 403–5.

McDonagh, P. 2008. 'Innocence, Economics and Institutions: Changing the Idea of Idiocy in the 1840s', *Journal of Intellectual Disability Research* 52(8): 706.

McKenzie, J. 2013. 'Models of Intellectual Disability: Towards a Perspective of (Poss)ability', *Journal of Intellectual Disability Research* 57(4): 370–79.

McKenzie, J. 2016. 'An Exploration of an Ethics of Care in Relation to People with Intellectual Disability and Their Family Caregivers in the Cape Town Metropole in South Africa', *Alter* 10(1): 67–78.

McKenzie, J., and Adnams, C. 2014. 'South African Adults with Intellectual Disability Speak about Residential Options', *Journal of Applied Research in Intellectual Disabilities* 27(4): 347.

McKenzie, J., and McConkey, R. 2016. 'Caring for Adults with Intellectual Disability: The Perspectives of Family Carers in South Africa', *Journal of Applied Research in Intellectual Disabilities* 29(6): 531–41.

McKenzie, J., and Macleod, C.I. 2012a. 'The Deployment of the Medico-Psychological Gaze and Disability Expertise in Relation to Children with Intellectual Disability', *International Journal of Inclusive Education* 16(10): 1083–98.

McKenzie, J., and Macleod, C.I. 2012b. 'Rights Discourses in Relation to Education of People with Intellectual Disability: Towards an Ethics of Care that Enables Participation', *Disability and Society* 27(1): 15–29.

McKenzie, J., McConkey, R., and Adnams, C. 2013a. 'Health Conditions and Support Needs of Persons Living in Residential Facilities for Adults with Intellectual Disability in Western Cape Province', *South African Medical Journal* 103(7): 481–84.

McKenzie, J., McConkey, R., and Adnams, C. 2013b. 'Residential Facilities for Adults with Intellectual Disability in a Developing Country: A Case Study from South Africa', *Journal of Intellectual and Developmental Disability* 39(1): 45–54.

Makgoba, M.W. 2017. *The Report Into the Circumstances Surrounding the Deaths of Mentally Ill Patients: Gauteng Province – No Guns: 94+ Silent Deaths and Still Counting*, Health Ombudsman, Republic of South Africa <https://healthombud.org.za/publications/reports/report-into-the-circumstances-surrounding-the-deaths-of-mentally-ill-patients-gauteng-province/> [accessed 12 October 2021].

Maulik, P.K., Mascarenhas, M.N., Mathers, C.D., Dua, T., and Saxena, S. 2011. 'Prevalence of Intellectual Disability: A Meta-Analysis of Population-Based Studies', *Research in Developmental Disabilities* 32(2): 419–36.

May, P.A., and Gossage, J.P. 2001. 'Estimating the Prevalence of Fetal Alcohol Syndrome: A Summary', *Alcohol Research and Health* 25(3): 159–67.

Meel, B. 2009. 'Prevalence of HIV among Victims of Sexual Assault Who Were Mentally Impaired Children (5 to 18 years) in the Mthatha Area of South Africa', *African Journal of Primary Health Care and Family Medicine* 1(1): 3–5.

Merrells, J., Buchanan, A., and Waters, R. 2017. '"We Feel Left Out": Experiences of Social Inclusion from the Perspective of Young Adults with Intellectual Disability', *Journal of Intellectual and Developmental Disability*. Advance online copy <https://www.tandfonline.com/doi/abs/10.3109/13668250.2017.1310822> [accessed 27 May 2017].

Molteno, C., Adnams, C., and Njenga, F. 2011. 'Sub-specialties in Psychiatry in Africa-intellectual Disability: Editorial', *African Journal of Psychiatry* 14(1): 1–3.

Morris, J. 2001. 'Impairment and Disability: Constructing an Ethics of Care That Promotes Human Rights', *Hypatia* 16: 1–16.

Moseneke, DCJ 2018. 'Life Esidimeni Arbitration Award. 19 March 2018' <http://www.saflii.org/images/LifeEsidimeniArbitrationAward.pdf> [accessed 10 October 2021].

Nakken, H., and Vlaskamp, C. 2007. 'A Need for a Taxonomy for Profound Intellectual and Multiple Disabilities', *Journal of Policy and Practice in Intellectual Disabilities* 4(2): 83–87.

Nash, E.S., and Navias, M. 1992. 'The Therapeutic Sterilization of the Mentally Handicapped. Experience with the Abortion and Sterilization Act of 1975', *South African Medical Journal* 82(6): 437–40.

Newton, D.C., and McGillivray, J.A. 2017. 'Perspectives of Carers of People with Intellectual Disability Accessing General Practice: "I'd Travel to the Ends of the Earth for the Right Person"', *Journal of Intellectual and Developmental Disability*. Advance online copy, 14 June 2017 <https://www.tandfonline.com/doi/abs/10.3109/13668250.2017.1310821> [accessed 12 October 2021].

Njenga, F. 2009. 'Perspectives of Intellectual Disability in Africa: Epidemiology and Policy Services for Children and Adults', *Current Opinion in Psychiatry* 22(5): 457–61. doi:10.1097/YCO.0b013e32832e63a1.

Nonnemacher, S.L., and Bambara, L.M. 2011. '"I'm Supposed to Be In Charge": Self-Advocates' Perspectives on Their Self-Determination Support Needs', *Intellectual and Developmental Disabilities* 49(5): 327–40.

Office of the Public Guardian (England and Wales). 2015. *Safeguarding Policy: Protecting Vulnerable Adults* <https://www.gov.uk/government/publications/safeguarding-policy-protecting-vulnerable-adults> [accessed 5 October 2021].

Petersen, I. 2004. 'Primary Level Psychological Services in South Africa: Can a New Psychological Professional Fill the Gap?' *Health Policy and Planning* 19(1): 33–40.

Phakgadi, P. 2018. 'Makhura: Esidimeni tragedy will not happen again', *Eyewitness News*, February 17 <http://ewn.co.za/2018/02/17/makhura-esidimeni-tragedy-not-happen-again> [accessed 15 March 2022.]

Phasha, T.N. 2009. 'Responses to Situations of Sexual Abuse Involving Teenagers with Intellectual Disability', *Sexuality and Disability* 27(4): 187–203.

Phasha, T.N. 2013. 'Influences on Under Reporting of Sexual Abuse of Teenagers With Intellectual Disability: Results And Implications Of A South African Study', *Journal of Psychology in Africa* 23(4): 625–29.

Phasha, T., and Myaka, L. 2014. 'Sexuality and Sexual Abuse Involving Teenagers with Intellectual Disability: Community Conceptions In A Rural Village Of Kwazulu-Natal, South Africa', *Sexuality and Disability* 32(2): 153–65.

Phaswana, T.D., Van der Westhuizen, D., and Krüger, C. 2013. 'Clinical Factors Associated with Rape Victims' Ability to Testify in Court: A Records-Based Study of Final Psychiatric Recommendation To Court', *African Journal of Psychiatry* 16(5): 343–48.

Pieterse, M. 2006. 'Resuscitating Socio-economic Rights: Constitutional Entitlements to Health Care Services', *South African Journal on Human Rights* 22(3): 473–502.

Pillay, A.L. 2008. 'An Audit of Competency Assessments on Court-Referred Rape Survivors in South Africa', *Psychological Reports* 103(3): 764–70.

Pillay, A.L. 2012a. 'Intellectually Disabled Child and Adolescent Sexual Violence Survivors Face Greater Challenges in the Legal System', *Journal of Child and Adolescent Mental Health* 24(2): iii–vi.

Pillay, A.L. 2012b. 'The Rape Survivor with an Intellectual Disability vs. the Court', *South African Journal of Psychology* 42(3): 312–22.

Pillay, A.L., and Kritzinger, A.M. 2008. 'Psycho-legal Issues Surrounding the Rape of Children and Adolescents with Mental Retardation', *Journal of Child and Adolescent Mental Health* 20(2): 123–31.

Pillay, A.L., and Siyothula, E.B. 2011. 'Intellectual Disability Examinations and Social Context Variables among Patients of Low Socioeconomic Status', *Perceptual and Motor Skills* 113(2): 589–96.

Potterton, J., Stewart, A., Cooper, P., and Becker, P. 2010. 'The Effect of a Basic Home Stimulation Programme on the Development of Young Children Infected with HIV', *Developmental Medicine and Child Neurology* 52(6): 547–51.

Rahlaga, M. 2018. 'Creecy Discredits Health Dept's Claims in Esidimeni Hearings', *Eye Witness News*, 30 January 2018 <http://ewn.co.za/2018/01/30/creecy-discredits-health-department-s-claims-in-esidimeni-hearings> [accessed 6 October 2021].

Reeve, D. 2006. 'Towards a Psychology of Disability: The Emotional Effects of Living in a Disabling Society'. In: D. Goodley and R. Lawthom. Eds. *Disability and Psychology: Critical Introductions and Reflections* (pp. 94–107). New York: Palgrave.

Reeve, D. 2012. 'Psycho-emotional Disablism: The Missing Link?' In: N. Watson, A. Roulstone, and C. Thomas. Eds. *Routledge Handbook of Disability Studies* (pp. 78–92). London: Routledge.

Republic of South Africa (RSA). 1996. *Constitution of the Republic of South Africa Act 108 of 1996: Chapter 2 – The Bill of Rights* <https://www.gov.za/sites/www.gov.za/files/images/a108-96.pdf> [accessed 10 March 2022].

Republic of South Africa (RSA). 2002. *Mental Health Care Act 17 of 2002* <https://www.gov.za/sites/default/files/gcis_document/201409/a17-02.pdf> [accessed 25 September 2021].

Roberts, T., Chetty, M., Kimmie-Dhansay, F., Fieggen, K., and Stephen, L.X.G. 2016. 'Dental Needs of Intellectually Disabled Children Attending Six Special Educational Facilities in Cape Town', *South African Medical Journal* 106(6): 94–97.

Rohleder, P., and Swartz, L. 2009. 'Providing Sex Education to Persons with Learning Disabilities in the Era of HIV/AIDS', *Journal of Health Psychology* 14(4): 601–10.

Roy, A., Roy, A., and Roy, M., 2012, 'The Human Rights of Women with Intellectual Disability', *Journal of the Royal Society of Medicine* 105(9): 384–89.

Saloojee, G., Phohole, M., Saloojee, H., and IJsselmuiden, C. 2007. 'Unmet Health, Welfare and Educational Needs of Disabled Children in an Impoverished South African Peri-Urban Township', *Child: Care, Health and Development* 33(3): 230–35.

Samia, P., Petersen, R., Walker, K.G., Eley, B., and Wilmshurst, J.M. 2013. 'Prevalence of Seizures in Children Infected with Human Immunodeficiency Virus', *Journal of Child Neurology* 28(3): 297–302.

Shabalala, N., and Jasson, A. 2011. 'PTSD Symptoms in Intellectually Disabled Victims of Sexual Assault', *South African Journal of Psychology* 41(4): 424–36.

Shakespeare, T. 2006. 'The Social Model of Disability'. In: L.J. Davis. Ed. *The Disability Studies Reader* (2nd ed., pp. 197–204). New York: Routledge.

Shakespeare, T. 2017. 'Critiquing the Social Model'. In: E. Emens and M. Stein. Eds. *Disability and Equality Law* (pp. 67–94). London: Routledge.

Slone, M., Durrheim, K., Lachman, P., and Kaminer, D. 1998. 'Association between the Diagnosis of Mental Retardation and Socioeconomic Factors', *American Journal on Mental Retardation* 102(6): 535–46.

Slone, M., Durrheim, K., Kaminer, D., and Lachman, P. 1999. 'Issues in the Identification of Comorbidity of Mental Retardation and Psychopathology in a Multicultural Context', *Social Psychiatry and Psychiatric Epidemiology* 34(4): 190–94.

Smith, L., Foley, P.F., and Chaney, M.P. 2008. 'Addressing Classism, Ableism, and Heterosexism in Counselor Education', *Journal of Counseling & Development* 86(3): 303–9.

Smith-Chandler, N., and Swart, E. 2014. 'In Their Own Voices: Methodological Considerations in Narrative Disability Research', *Qualitative Health Research* 24(3): 420–30.

South African Social Security Agency. 2017. 'Social Grants' <https://www.sassa.gov.za/Pages/Care-Dependency-Grant.aspx> [accessed 26 September 2021].

Ssali, S., Theobald, S., and Hawkins, K. 2015. 'Life Histories: A Research Method to Capture People's Experiences of Health Systems in Post-Conflict Countries' <https://healthsystemsglobal.org/news/life-histories-a-research-method-to-capture-peoples-experiences-of-health-systems-in-post-conflict-countries/> [accessed 28 October 2021].

State of Illinois Department on Aging. 2013. 'Adult Protective Services Act 2013' <https://www2.illinois.gov/aging/Pages/default.aspx> [accessed 5 October 2021].

Statistics South Africa (SSA). 2014. *Census 2011: Profile of PwDs in South Africa* <https://www.statssa.gov.za/publications/Report-03-01-59/Report-03-01-592011.pdf> [accessed 10 October 2021].

Stein, M.A., and Stein, P.J. 2007. 'Beyond Disability Civil Rights', *Hastings Law Journal* 58: 1203–40.

Stop Ableism. 2009. 'What is Ableism?' <http://www.stopableism.org/p/what-is-ableism.html> [accessed 12 April 2021].

Swartz, L., van der Merwe, A., Buckland, A., and McDougall, K. 2012. 'Producing Boundary-breaking Texts on Disability Issues: The Personal Politics of Collaboration', *Disability and Rehabilitation* 34(11): 951–58.

Szwed, M. 2020. 'The Notion of "a person of unsound mind" under Article 5 § 1(e) of the European Convention on Human Rights', *Netherlands Quarterly of Human Rights* 38(4): 283–301 <https://doi.org/10.1177/0924051920968480>.

Tomlinson, M., Yasamy, M.T., Emerson, E., Officer, A., Richler, D., and Saxena, S. 2014. 'Setting Global Research Priorities for Developmental Disabilities, Including Intellectual Disabilities and Autism', *Journal of Intellectual Disability Research* 58(12): 1121–30.

Tronto, J.C. 2010. 'Creating Caring Institutions: Politics, Plurality, and Purpose', *Ethics and Social Welfare* 4(2): 158–71.

United Nations (UN). 2006. *United Nations Convention on the Rights of People with Disabilities (UNCRPD) A/RES/61/106* <https://www.un.org/development/desa/disabilities/convention-on-the-rights-of-persons-with-disabilities.html#Fulltext> [accessed 12 April 2021].

United Nations International Children's Emergency Fund (UNICEF). 1989. *Convention on the Rights of the Child* <https://www.unicef.org/sites/default/files/2019-04/UN-Convention-Rights-Child-text.pdf> [accessed 30 September 2019].

Urban, M., Chersich, M.F., Fourie, L., Chetty, C., Olivier, L., and Viljoen, D. 2008. 'Fetal Alcohol Syndrome among Grade 1 Schoolchildren in Northern Cape Province: Prevalence and Risk Factors', *South African Medical Journal* 98(11): 877–82.

Watson, J., Wilson, E., and Hagiliassis, N. 2013. 'Participation in Decision Making for People with Severe-Profound Intellectual Disabilities: What Can It Look Like?' *Journal of Policy and Practice in Intellectual Disabilities* 10(2): 182.

Wilson, N.J., Jaques, H., Johnson, A., and Brotherton, M.L. 2017. 'From Social Exclusion to Supported Inclusion: Adults with Intellectual Disability Discuss Their Lived Experiences of a Structured Social Group', *Journal of Applied Research in Intellectual Disabilities* 30(5): 847–58.

Wolbring, G. 2008. 'The Politics of Ableism', *Development* 51(2): 252–58.

World Health Organization (WHO) and World Bank (WB). 2011. *World Report on Disability* <http://www.who.int/disabilities/world_report/2011/report.pdf> [accessed 12 April 2021].

Wright, J.S. 2019. 'Re-introducing Life History Methodology: An Equitable Social Justice Approach to Research in Education', *Research Methods for Social Justice and Equity in Education* (pp. 177–89). London: Bloomsbury.

Yeung, P.H., Passmore, A.E., and Packer, T.L. 2008. 'Active Citizens or Passive Recipients: How Australian Young Adults with Cerebral Palsy Define Citizenship', *Journal of Intellectual and Developmental Disability* 33(1): 65–75.

Young, L.S. and Berry, J. 2016. 'Slipping and Holding Minds: A Psychosocial Analysis of Maternal Subjectivity in Relation to Childhood Disability', *African Journal of Disability* 5(1): 1–9.

3

Examining the Implementation of Inclusive Education in Zimbabwe

TSITSI CHATAIKA & LINCOLN HLATYWAYO

Introduction

Globally, PwDs are considered the world's largest minority, although they occupy other social categories as well, including: men, women, children; different races and cultures among all social classes; wealthy and poor; and highly educated and illiterate (Hagen, 2016). According to the WHO and World Bank (WB) (2011), many children with disabilities (CwDs) have been historically excluded from basic mainstream education and access it in separate specialized schools. CwDs are the most excluded in society, with an estimated 90% of CwDs from the Global South, Zimbabwe included, not attending school (United Nations Educational, Scientific and Cultural Organization [UNESCO], 2015). Many learners with disabilities (LwDs) also drop out of primary education due to barriers and do not progress to secondary and tertiary education. This makes PwDs, especially children and youth, vulnerable to exclusion and stigmatization later in life. The CRPD is a legal instrument that in its entirety seeks to achieve inclusion. While inclusive education (IE) is discussed in depth under Article 24 of the CRPD, there are also various indirect clauses and articles that implicitly relate to inclusion (UN, 2006).

This chapter examines the strides taken in the implementation of IE in Zimbabwe. Of particular interest are the evaluation reports for the Leonard Cheshire Disability Zimbabwe (LCDZ) Trust (Chakuchichi, Chataika, and Nyaruwata 2016; Chakuchichi and Chataika 2014; Chakuchichi, Nyaruwata, and Chataika 2012), a major stakeholder in the implementation of IE in the country in collaboration with the Ministry of Primary and Secondary Education (MoPSE). In this chapter, we also examine how Zimbabwe is faring in the implementation of direct and indirect provisions in the CRPD in relation to IE. We argue that an appropriate IE programme offers an opportunity to learn how to cater for all children regardless of their conditions and circumstances. Through reflection on these matters, we flag the achievements and challenges and discuss the way forward in order to realize Article 24 of the CRPD in Zimbabwe.

We understand IE as a process of restructuring the education system, cultures, policies, and practices to address and respond to the diverse needs of all learners (UNESCO, 2001). We are aware that IE focuses on ensuring that no child is left behind. As such, we understand that IE does not focus exclusively on LwDs. Rather, an appropriate IE programme offers learning opportunities for all and advocates for the removal of all forms of barriers to learning and participation (Muthukrishna, 2018; Global Campaign for Education, n.d.; Stubbs, 2002). Thus, every child has a right to education, including those who are usually excluded: students with different types of impairments, those coming from ultra-poor households, marginalized girls, and other vulnerable groups. However, this chapter focuses on the inclusion of LwDs, who – as we mentioned above – constitute the largest marginalized minority group in the world (WHO and WB, 2011).

Why Inclusive Education?

Good-quality education needs to be inclusive to ensure that all learners participate and achieve their potential in school in a manner that is responsive to individual learner differences. Therefore, IE can act as a catalyst for changing educational practice, leading to an improved standard of education (Ministry of Education Science and Technology [MoEST; Malawi], 2016). The combination of disability and poverty places many PwDs in the Global South at a greater disadvantage than those in the North (Chataika, 2019). Hence, when PwDs get the opportunity to receive a quality education, doors are opened and this enables them to secure other rights throughout their lifetime, fostering better access to jobs, healthcare, and other services. For education to play this role as 'an enabling right', it must be of a high quality, available equitably, and built to tackle discrimination, as well as allowing for each child to flourish according to their own talents and interests. In recent years, human rights frameworks have begun to inform a vision for delivering on the right to education for CwDs and articulating what this might look like in practice. The CRPD is a milestone in this regard, as it seeks to establish IE as the key mechanism to deliver the right to education for PwDs (WHO and WB, 2011). IE systems are grounded in a rights-based analysis which can empower learners, celebrate diversity, combat discrimination, and promote more inclusive societies. This can be a powerful tool in addressing inequalities. It can also tackle discrimination by challenging widely held attitudes and behaviours – helping us to celebrate and embrace the diversity in our societies. Furthermore, the creation of IE systems is fundamental to achieving better quality in education and realizing the human rights of all children. IE can raise the quality bar across education systems, by using strategies that cater to the naturally diverse learning styles of all students, while accommodating the specific learning needs of some students. It also serves to target and include other marginalized groups of children, helping to ensure inclusion for all. However, the current challenges faced by PwDs in realizing their right to education remain profound (Global Campaign for Education, n.d.).

The estimated one billion people with disabilities face a multitude of barriers to participating equally in society (WHO and WB, 2011). In particular, their right to education is often not realized, which in turn hinders their access to other rights and creates enormous obstacles to reaching their potential and effectively participating in their communities. The 2020 Global Education Monitoring (GEM) Report revealed that half of the world's out-of-school children are in sub-Saharan Africa, totalling ninety-seven million children and youth, with poverty been indicated as the main constraint to accessing education (UNESCO, 2020). Thus, without improvement, more than one in ten adults in the region will not have completed primary school by 2050. Despite the target to achieve universal upper secondary completion by 2030, there are at least sixteen sub-Saharan African countries, with hardly any poor rural young women completing secondary school (UNESCO, 2020).

Despite commitments to achieving IE by 2030, only 2% of countries in sub-Saharan Africa have an education law that is inclusive of all learners, no matter their background, identity, or ability (UNESCO, 2020). For example, Ghana's Inclusive Education Policy (Government of Ghana, 2015) incorporates

UNESCO's 1994 Salamanca Statement and its associated Framework for Action, the latter of which states that schools 'should accommodate all children regardless of their physical, intellectual, social, emotional, linguistic or other conditions' (UNESCO, 1994: 6). In its draft IE policy, Zimbabwe defines IE as 'an approach or process that seeks to ensure universal access to and participation in education for all learners through mainstreaming of responsive learner-centred support to overcome identified barriers to individual learners' full participation in formal, non-formal and lifelong educational settings and activities' (MoPSE, 2019: 2). This implies that all learners can attend and are welcomed by their neighbourhood schools in age-appropriate, mainstream classes and are supported to learn, contribute, and participate in all aspects of the life of the school. However, the next section focuses on indirect provisions that have a bearing on the provision of IE.

Inclusive Education in the Global South

While IE has generally been adopted in most countries, conceptualizations and implementation frameworks differ from country to country. Research studies also show that the Global South lags significantly behind in terms of implementing IE compared to the Global North (UNESCO, 2020). Regrettably, Grech (2014) suggests that for the most part, discourses on IE are still created in the Global North and transferred to the Global South, with little or no alertness to context or culture. In Global South countries, the traditional understanding of IE as the mere placement of LwDs in mainstream schools remains a commonly held view (UNESCO, 2020).

Kamenopoulou (2018) carried out a study in Colombia and established that IE was viewed as synonymous with disability, while special education teachers were equated with IE in practice. The study also found huge gaps in the preparation of teachers for enabling IE. The researcher concluded that IE is a Global North-created concept which can acquire different meanings in Global South contexts, and also argued that Colombia in particular needs time to make its understanding of IE a priority. From these findings, it can be concluded that stakeholders possess varied perspectives on IE in the Global South, which have implications on implementation processes.

Based on their personal experience and literature surveys, Lehtomäki *et al.* (2017) conclude that there is a need for the Global South to deliver intensive IE programmes. That is, there is a need to move beyond a simplistic understanding of what IE entails and who it is aimed at, and concentrate on long-term implementation plans to yield better results. The authors strongly recommended collaboration between stakeholders, including documentation of the voices of LwDs and other vulnerable groups, as well as their families, in order to create systemic and institutional transformation. The researchers emphasized the need for a paradigm shift towards viewing inclusion not just in the knowledge creation process, but also during the research communication process, while creating policy dialogues. Only then will contextually relevant information come to the fore to build strong education systems.

Antoninis *et al.* (2020) reported that most African countries get bad press publicity for their lack of progress in providing IE. Across the continent, just two in three children complete primary school on time, while the number of out-of-school children and youth is ninety-seven million and growing. Although many African countries are taking steps to make education more inclusive, they need to do more. This is even more important in recent times, as the 2020 GEM Report shows that the COVID-19 pandemic has worsened the situation (UNESCO, 2020). About 40% of the countries in sub-Saharan Africa have not been able to support disadvantaged learners, including those with disabilities, during school closures. Prior to the pandemic, African countries were taking different approaches to inclusion. Most of them educate CwDs in mainstream schools but have some separate arrangements for learners with severe impairments. Nearly a quarter, however, have laws calling for CwDs to be educated in separate settings. In these cases, most countries attempting to transition from segregated to inclusive systems face serious challenges. Among other things, they need to work out how to share specialist resources between schools so that all children can benefit. Fortunately, examples of how this can be done are found across the continent.

Angola and Nigeria, for example, are looking at transforming special schools into support bases for CwDs who are enrolled in mainstream schools. Angola set a target in 2017 of including 30,000 CwDs in mainstream schools by 2022. Kenya also recognizes special schools' pivotal role in the transition towards

IE. At present, almost 2,000 primary and secondary mainstream schools provide education for LwDs (UNESCO, 2020). Malawi is implementing a twin-track approach. Those with severe impairments are educated in special schools or resource centres, while those with mild impairments are mainstreamed. Thus, special schools at each education level are being transformed into resource centres. Instead of resource centres, Tanzania is mobilizing itinerant teachers offering specialist services. These teachers are trained and managed by Tanzania Society for the Blind and are each provided with a motorbike. They also perform vision screening, refer children to medical facilities, and organize community sensitization and counselling (UNESCO, 2020).

While the political will for change seems clear, there is often a gap between theory and practice. This is where the emphasis must lie from now until 2030. Throughout Africa, teachers mention that implementing IE is hard because they lack resources. For example, Malawi is increasingly encouraging LwDs to enrol in mainstream schools (UNESCO, 2020), but a lack of facilities forces many to transfer to special schools. McLinden *et al.* (2018) supported quality provisions for CwDs in resource-constrained early childhood development and education (ECDE) services in rural Malawi, by introducing the concept of emotional well-being and the involvement of CwDs. This intervention has had a positive impact on learning, behaviour, social cohesion, and friendships among children with and without disabilities, as well as individual well-being.

In Namibia, the shortage of resource schools in rural areas, a lack of accessible infrastructure, and unfavourable attitudes towards disability are just some of the barriers to implementing the government's IE policy. Similarly, in Tanzania, only half of children with albinism complete primary school. This is because they lack support and often end up being transferred to special schools. Ghana makes provisions for all learners in its education law. Its 2015 IE policy framework envisages transforming special schools into resource centres, while maintaining special units, schools, and other institutions for students with severe and profound impairments. Yet CwDs are still required to perform the same tasks within the same timeframe as their peers without disabilities, occupy desks placed far from the teachers, and are often physically punished by teachers for behavioural challenges, even in inclusive schools in the Ghanaian capital, Accra (UNESCO, 2020).

In South Africa, a 1996 law specifies that the right to education of children CwDs is to be fulfilled in mainstream public schools. However, South Africa reported to the Committee on the Rights of Persons with Disabilities (CoRPD) recently that it had created new segregated schools in basic education and lacked provisions for children with severe intellectual impairment (UNESCO, 2020). Walton *et al.* (2014) also looked at teacher training for IE in South Africa, arguing that the training of teachers in IE cannot be 'one size fits all', as several contextual issues have to be considered. One of their findings is that there is a need to consider the complexity of teachers' current work when they are trained in differentiated instruction. They argue that when providing training to teachers on IE, several issues should be taken into consideration. These include the institutional context and other constraints faced by teachers, such as lack of space, class sizes, assessment challenges, an enormous workload, and lack of support. This implies that several issues should be considered before successfully implementing IE.

A closer look at some of the main factors for consideration in IE shows that most of these are not experienced in the Global North due to the better levels of development attained to date (UNESCO, 2020). Thus, there is a clear divide between the North and the South in respect of implementing IE to ensure its success. Walton *et al.* (2014) also view inclusion as calculated steps that are to be taken to address exclusion and related barriers. Another finding from Walton *et al.* (2014)'s study is the tendency to exclude persons who experience exclusion from inclusion debates and platforms, which militates against the implementation of IE. Therefore, they recommended that such persons be included in these forums and that the histories and geographies of exclusion in certain contexts be acknowledged, while work goes on within and beyond the possibilities and constraints of the context.

Drawing from empirical investigations carried out in Kenya, Zimbabwe, and Sierra Leone, Kett, Deluca, and Carew (2019) highlighted the need for the Global South to seriously consider context in the delivery of IE. As if implying that IE in these countries is not working, they call for the need for more rigorous evidence to highlight that it is, and explore any available alternatives. The study also looked at the role of teachers in delivering inclusive primary education and emphasized the need to make learning fun for both learners and teachers. Kett, Deluca, and Carew (2019) also identified gaps in respect of accountability in IE programmes and recommended the three R's model – Rights, Resources, and Research – as a strong analytical tool to ensure accountability of IE programmes.

General Obligations of the CRPD on Inclusive Education Provision in Zimbabwe

General obligations are discussed in Article 4 of the CRPD. Primarily, States Parties are obliged to put in place constitutional, legislative, and policy framework, as well as administrative measures that ensure the realization and full enjoyment of rights by PwDs, as enshrined in the Convention (UN, 2006). Zimbabwe is making great strides in this regard. The country ratified the Convention on 23 September 2013, showing the importance it places on disability issues. However, the ratification came five years after the adoption of the Convention, and at the time of writing this book chapter, we are also still five years away from the CRPD being meaningfully operationalized in Zimbabwe. The adage 'justice delayed is justice denied' can be applied here. In other words, while the CRPD is an international law, it is regarded as a sub-law in the current Zimbabwean scenario, as people with disabilities cannot fully enjoy their rights without its domestication. Domestication entails the adaptation of local laws and policies in line with the provisions in the CRPD. Another interesting event to take place in Zimbabwe in 2013 was the adoption of the new Constitution Amendment. This was the first time in the history of the nation that the supreme law included very specific sections with regard to disability issues.

In terms of IE, Section 83 indicates that it is the responsibility of the state to provide special facilities for the education of LwDs and to provide state-funded education and training where they need it. This is a very encouraging development, as in general the provision of special facilities and funding are fundamental indicators of high-quality IE. While this section has been used in advocacy and lobbying by PwDs, disability organizations, and CSOs to fight for the educational rights of LwDs, very little success has been realized. This is because the constitutional provision has negative qualifications such as *'within the limits of the resources'*. Such statements have created disabling barriers within the disability rights frameworks. If they are not removed, many LwDs may never be enrolled in schools and may, therefore, continue leading the lives of sub-class citizens despite the ratification of the CRPD.

Although Zimbabwe currently does not have any specific policy or legislation in place relating to IE, it does have a range of policies that support and promote the inclusion of CwDs. There are also two recent pieces of disability-friendly laws that have been enacted: the Education Amendment Act 2020 and the Zimbabwe National Disability Policy 2021. The former indicates that every citizen and permanent resident of Zimbabwe has a right to a basic state-funded education, including adult basic education. The latter is clear on ensuring that PwDs are exempted from paying fees and levies at all public learning institutions. To this effect, the government of Zimbabwe announced on 21 April 2021, in its national newspaper, that all PwDs will have access to free education from primary school to university, which is a huge milestone in realizing Article 24 of the CRPD. Also, the National Disability Policy emphasizes that LwDs should be assessed upon enrolling in learning institutions and at regular intervals. In addition, reasonable accommodations should be made for each individual's requirements in relation to physical infrastructure, staffing, assistive technology (AT), teaching and learning methods, and information and materials. Thus, if the content of these laws is implemented, it will positively influence the provision of IE and other disability services in Zimbabwe.

In addition to the above laws, Circular number P36 of 1990 provides guidelines to placement procedures for special classes, resource units, and institutions; Secretary's Circular Number 2 of 2000 emphasizes the inclusion of learners with albinism with reference to meaningful inclusion in schooling and co-curricular activities; and the Director's Circular number 7 of 2005 offers guidelines for the inclusion of LwDs in all school competitions. The greatest challenge, however, is that Zimbabwe still needs to realign its Disabled Persons Act of 1992 with the CRPD, as some of its provisions militate against the Convention. It will be prudent for the lawmakers to ensure that the CRPD is used as the foundation from which the rights and services of PwDs are included when developing the new Persons with Disabilities Act. Also, the administration of IE in Zimbabwe has not changed for quite some time, and yet many stakeholders strongly believe that there is a need to restructure the department of learner welfare psychological services and special needs education (SNE), under whose ambit IE falls. Most decision-makers in this department are psychologists, but the majority do not have educational qualifications in general and special or IE in particular. This practice needs to be discontinued if IE goals are to be positively consolidated. Educationists should take the leading role in the organization of IE, with psychologists coming in to support the educational ecosystem and not vice versa.

Mnkandla and Mataruse (2002) observed that the most prevalent type of IE in Zimbabwe is unplanned or de facto inclusion. The situation still remains, despite the need for the country to fully implement the provisions in the CRPD. The vast majority of LwDs participating in unplanned inclusion are placed in schools by parents and guardians, often with the school taking no steps to document their specific impairments. They are in unplanned or de facto inclusion by default (i.e. due to an absence of options) rather than by design (Mnkandla and Mataruse, 2002). Unfortunately, learners with severe impairments are the least well served by unplanned or de facto inclusion as practised in Zimbabwean schools, because the majority of the schools lack the personnel and material resources to cater to a variety of significant learning needs. Also, with unplanned inclusion, LwDs are exposed to the full national curriculum in mainstream education settings. As a result, most learners with severe impairments in unplanned or de facto inclusion are likely to drop out of school by the third grade. Most schools claim to be practising IE by virtue of enrolling LwDs, which in most cases is merely integration, not education.

Moreover, one of the challenges in Zimbabwe is that there are no clear data and statistics on the number of LwDs, which should be available in line with Article 31 of the CRPD. This is because IE is understood differently by various stakeholders across the country. The major source of this lack of understanding is the failure by the government to fast track the domestication of the CRPD. Domestication will ensure that clear guiding principles and definitions of IE are provided. As a baseline, Table 3.1 provides the current educational provisions for CwDs in Zimbabwe.

Table 3.1 Educational provisions for CwDs in Zimbabwe.

Provision	Description
Inclusive schools	These are mainstream schools that welcome all learners, including those with disabilities. Learners with and without disabilities get instruction from the same classroom, accessing the same curriculum.
Special schools	LwDs receive instruction in their own schools. A twin-track curriculum is followed, whereby the mainstream curriculum is adapted to the learning levels and needs of those with disabilities and a school-based curriculum is offered alongside this.
Special classes	CwDs are placed in their own classrooms, which are in mainstream schools. The classes are manned by teachers trained to handle and manage LwDs. Some special classes have children with specific types of disabilities, such as hearing impairment only. However, due to a shortage of specialist teachers, a significant number of special classes have learners with all types of disabilities who are at various grade levels. This situation places teachers in very difficult circumstances, as they often do not possess all the competencies required to handle classes with such a wide range of needs.
Reverse inclusion schools	Zimbabwe now has three schools that are practising reverse inclusion. These are Danhiko, Emerald Hill School for the Deaf, and King George VI, former special schools that used to enrol LwDs only but now enrol learners without disabilities and employ inclusive pedagogies that cater for all.
Resource units	Resource units are repositories of expertise, adapted teaching-learning materials, and ATs that enhance the teaching and learning of those with disabilities within mainstream schools. LwDs receive instruction together with their non-disabled counterparts; however, they will be withdrawn from time to time to be taught by specialist teachers who manage the resource units. The resource room teacher provides services that reduce teaching and learning gaps between the mainstream teachers and CwDs.

(Sources: M.M. Mutepfa, E. Mpofu, and T. Chataika. 2007. 'Inclusive Education Practices in Zimbabwe: Curriculum, Family and Policy Issues', *Childhood Education (Special Issue: International Focus Issue)* 83(6): 342–6; MoPSE. 2020. *Practical Handbook for Primary and Secondary Schools*. Harare: MoPSE.)

The CRPD general obligations also mandate States Parties to provide accessible information to PwDs about AT, as well as other forms of assistance, support services, and facilities. Accessible information and provision of AT and facilities are the backbone of IE. Without these, the majority of LwDs can never be included. Section 83 of the Zimbabwean Constitution, Amendment number 20, indicates that the state shall take measures to provide special facilities for the education of LwDs as well as state-funded education and training. There have been positive indicators to support this provision. For example, in the 2016 national budget, about US$4 million was deliberately allocated for the purchase of AT for learners and other PwDs. In addition, import duty has been scrapped for all ATs that are used by PwDs. Through its partnerships with non-governmental organizations (NGOs) such as LCDZ, Christian Blind Mission, the United Nations Children's Fund (UNICEF), Save the Children, the JF Kapnek Trust, and many others, the government of Zimbabwe has managed to provide AT to many LwDs, particularly those at primary school level.

Despite achievements in AT, many Zimbabwean CwDs receive sub-standard education, as the majority of schools, especially those in rural areas, have not gained access to these technologies. Where ATs have been donated by NGOs, the government and educational institutions rarely put sustainability plans in place for if charity support is withdrawn. The Zimbabwe 2013 Living Conditions among Persons with Disability survey indicated that only 14.4% of PwDs were using AT (UNICEF, 2013). Of these, four out of ten indicated that the ATs provided to them were not in good working condition. In addition, about 67% reported sourcing their AT privately, while the government catered for 33%. Unfortunately, about 40% were not satisfied by their AT. From these statistics, it can be deduced that a significant number of CwDs are not attending school due to the non-availability of AT. Also, the cost of AT in Zimbabwe is beyond the reach of many. For example, a set of brand new digital hearing aids costs about US$4,000. This contravenes the CRPD, which clearly stipulates that AT for PwDs should be made available at reasonable costs (UN, 2006). It is also the duty of States Parties to ensure, undertake, or promote disability-related research, which enhances the development, availability, and use of new technologies.

There also seems to be a lack of political will on the government's part, as less than 5% of the US$4 million allocated for the purchase of AT in the 2016 national budget was released. This suggests that the government prioritizes other development initiatives at the expense of disability programmes, thereby violating the constitutional rights of PwDs. NGOs and UN agencies seem more committed than the government of Zimbabwe to adhere to the CRPD. UNICEF's Zimbabwe Country Office has made a commitment to complement government efforts towards the realization of the CRPD's provisions by promoting equality and opportunities for all CwDs. To its credit, the Country Office has formulated a Disability Strategy 2018–20 whose mandate is to achieve equality, dignity, and equal opportunities for CwDs in specific areas of its programming (UNICEF, 2018). This requires ensuring the best interests of the child, including independence, freedom of choice, and full and active participation in all areas of life and society.

Strides Taken in Implementing Article 24 of the CRPD in Zimbabwe

In Zimbabwe, like many other countries, the CRPD has influenced how IE is generally perceived and understood, particularly by development partners working in this area. This section looks at the achievements and gains made so far in respect of the implementation of the IE provisions as enshrined in the CRPD. Challenges associated with the implementation process are also interrogated.

Through a partnership between the MoPSE and LCDZ, a pilot project code-named '*The Cluster Model of Inclusive Education*' came into effect in January 2010. The three-year project was implemented at sixteen schools in three provinces: Harare, Mashonaland East, and Mashonaland West. The project registered significant gains in terms of enrolment. Reports indicate that over one thousand CwDs who had not been in schools due to lack of support and a disabling school environment eventually made it into school (Chakuchichi, Chataika, and Nyaruwata, 2016; Chakuchichi and Chataika, 2014). The project saw school infrastructures being adapted and learners provided with mobility as well as teaching and learning ATs according to their need. Teachers and communities were also trained on what IE entails. After the success of the pilot project, the model was extended for a further four years.

One of the authors of this chapter conducted an evaluation of the Cluster Model with particular reference to Mashonaland West Province. One of the authors of this chapter conducted an evaluation of the Cluster Model with particular reference to a project promoting IE in Mashonaland West Province undertaken by LCDZ. The evaluation indicated that promoting an inclusive primary education project was reported as relevant by 159 out of 175 teachers (90.86%) (Chakuchichi, Chataika, and Nyaruwata, 2016). The project intended to support the enrolment of 1,500 CwDs in 30 model schools and at the same time ensure the retention of 741 such children enrolled in model schools prior to its commencement. It was thus expected to provide access to primary education to a total of 2,241 CwDs in model schools. The project supported a total of 1,089 CwDs in model schools and a further 1,843 in cluster schools. Thus, 2,932 CwDs were supported in accessing mainstream primary school education. In addition, a total of 951 teachers were trained in how to teach CwDs within an inclusive setting through workshops. Parents and CwDs were also provided with training to enhance their skills in self-advocacy. Teachers rated the impact of the project highly. At least 93.14% of teachers viewed the LCDZ's '*Promoting Inclusive Primary Education*' project as having a positive impact on the CwDs, their parents, schools, communities, and the nation at large. Thus, the project has given rise to an increased understanding of the rights of CwDs in the model schools.

At the local community level, the participation of women was enhanced to such an extent that they have since taken leadership posts in school development committees. The participants of the study were quite confident that the project produced very good value for money. Through transport solutions and AT, it enabled most of the CwDs in the project areas to access education and be able to remain in school for more than 80% of the required time. The Cluster Model entails that one central school in a cluster with around ten other schools is adapted for disability inclusion. The adaptations include infrastructure, training of teachers and local leadership, and the provision of ATs to LwDs. The school becomes an inclusive one, and most LwDs in the cluster of the adapted school are expected to attend the school. The increase in CwDs accessing nearly all schools had a ripple effect that influenced school heads and teachers, who also participated in exchange visits. Such visits enabled neighbouring schools to adopt IE practices in their schools, so that the project's rollout ultimately had a multiplier effect.

The findings by Chakuchichi, Chataika, and Nyaruwata (2016) show that sustainability significantly correlated with the type of school, with model schools having stronger sustainability ratings than cluster schools. The participants reported that IE was an intervention that would cut the cycle of poverty at two levels: first, when CwDs go to school, they are likely to gain knowledge and acquire skills they can use for employment; second, when they go to school, their parents or caregivers have more time to do other economically productive activities. The results of the evaluation indicate that positive attitudes emerged from the participants at various levels. Children, who are the main beneficiaries, recognized education as their right and a right for CwDs. Parents reported noticing that inclusive primary education brought a significant reduction in stigma and prejudice. Children also viewed the model schools as having an enhanced image, and thus were proud of their school's ambience. The school heads were happy with the increased enrolments and high retention rates now being obtained at the schools as a total of 2,241 CwDs became permanently enrolled in the model schools.

It is pertinent to note that parents viewed the collaboration between LCDZ, teachers, parents, and community leaders as the impetus for the success of the project. The evaluation recommended that MoPSE adopt the model and roll it out to other provinces across the country. However, despite the success stories, the Ministry is still yet to take a clear-cut decision on what needs to be done, when, and by whom as far as IE is concerned, now that financial support from Save the Children has come to an end.

Following the withdrawal of LCDZ, most LwDs who initially enrolled on the programme with support are now at high risk of dropping out of school. In other words, the government has failed to come up with a funding mechanism for sustaining IE. The gains and strides made initially are being lost, and the future of most LwDs is in jeopardy. This is regrettable, considering the efforts and resources injected into the programme. The former director of LCDZ had this to say with regard to the seriousness with which his organization approached IE: 'We have engaged some local people in the communities to go around identifying CwDs in homes who are not yet going to school.'

In order to enhance access to an inclusive and high-quality education for all learners, including those with disabilities,

UNICEF, through MoPSE, provided improvement grants to 3,159 out of the 3,200 schools targeted (98%) across the country. The grants have contributed to the improvement of the schools' physical environment and the availability of teaching and learning materials. Income from the grants also enhanced the retention of poor children in school by subsidizing their overall costs of education. The number of CwDs enrolled in the general education system as a result of this project increased from 34,734 in 2015 to 49,692 in 2016 (UNICEF, 2018).

MoPSE, with UNICEF support and funding from the GPE, supported the training of over 80,000 primary school teachers in 2018 in a supplementary module to the in-service early reading initiative (ERI) and performance lag address programme (PLAP). The supplementary module supports teachers by providing them with knowledge and skills on how to accommodate the diverse educational needs of learners to enhance their numeracy and literacy. This was done in recognition that teachers needed the *know-how* of planning and delivering meaningful lessons for the benefit of learners who have diverse educational needs in their classes.

As indicated earlier, Zimbabwe is also implementing the reverse inclusion model at special schools such as Emerald Hill School for the Deaf and King George VI. The reverse inclusion model entails that special schools open their doors to learners without disabilities, and these children are enrolled in the same class. The greatest achievement associated with this model is the change of attitude by learners without disabilities towards their peers with disabilities. In line with the CRPD, this is a great step towards reduction of discrimination. The implementation of this model is being done without the support of the government. A five-year study of this model by Hlatywayo (2018) indicated that reverse inclusion has many benefits associated with it. However, educationists in authority seem to have little understanding of the model, which may be a stumbling block as it looks to upscale.

Having articulated the milestones covered by Zimbabwe, there remain several challenges facing IE, including a lack of adequate resources, inaccessibility of schools, ambiguity of laws and policies, lack of political will, cultural stereotypes and negative societal attitudes, high teacher–pupil ratios, curriculum inaccessibility, and research concerns (UNESCO, 2020; Sibanda, 2018). Still, there are opportunities provided by circumstances such as the huge interest of the government of Zimbabwe, which has invested significantly in general education since 1980. These investments have culminated in the construction of several mainstream schools, and the training of specialist and special education teachers can be exploited for full inclusion of LwDs (Sibanda, 2018). Such opportunities have increased the potential for the successful implementation of IE in Zimbabwe. Furthermore, the country has now developed a draft IE policy which, if adopted, could change the landscape of IE in Zimbabwe.

CRPD Indicators and Their Implementation Level in Zimbabwe

As a starting point for improvements, Table 3.2 illustrates IE indicators in line with the CRPD, with a scale showing how Zimbabwe is faring to date according to the evaluation by the authors, who are IE practitioners in Zimbabwe. The authors have also been involved in the evaluation of IE programmes in Zimbabwe and other African countries.

Table 3.2 CRPD indicators and their implementation level in Zimbabwe.

	Implementation level			
Indicators for Article 24 of the CRPD: Education	**1**	**2**	**3**	**4**
An education system that focuses on full development of human potential		■		
Development of an IE policy		■		
Development of the personalities, talents, and creativity, as well as the mental and physical abilities of PwDs to their fullest potential		■		
PwDs are not excluded from the general education system		■		
Access to inclusive, high-quality, and free primary education		■		
Provision of reasonable educational accommodations			■	
Availability of educational support systems, including individualized support		■		
Facilitating the learning of braille, augmentative and alternative modes, mobility and orientation skills		■		

Table 3.2 continued.

Indicators for Article 24 of the CRPD: Education	Implementation level 1	2	3	4
Facilitating the learning of sign language		■		
Delivery of instruction in the most appropriate modes			■	
Employment of teachers with appropriate qualifications such as in braille and sign language			■	
Training of teachers and other stakeholders in IE		■		
Access to tertiary and vocational education and training		■		

Key:
1 = not achieved; **2** = partially achieved; **3** = almost achieved; **4** = achieved.

(Source: D. Chakuchichi, T. Chataika, and L. Nyaruwata. 2016. 'Promoting Inclusive Education in Schools', Project Endline Evaluation Report. Harare: LCDZ, 19–20.)

This evaluation is premised on the following factors:

1. Lack of commitment on the part of the government to fund IE;
2. Lack of political will;
3. Unavailability of IE sustainability models;
4. Failure by government to domesticate CRPD;
5. Lack of consensus and agreement among stakeholders on available disability statistics;
6. Lack of documentation on available projects.

Conclusion

Zimbabwe has made great strides in developing constitutional, legislative, and policy frameworks in line with the CRPD. However, it is clear that the country lacks progress on implementation and sustaining its gains, which often quickly diminish. There has been no serious commitment on the part of government in terms of funding IE and other disability-related services, and this non-committal attitude has significantly militated against the provision of IE.

The Global Campaign for Education (n.d) has suggested key strategies that countries like Zimbabwe can adopt in order to ensure that IE becomes the national strategy for providing education to all, without leaving anyone behind. Table 3.3 outlines strategies that are specific to the Zimbabwean context.

Table 3.3 CRPD strategies and implementation plans in Zimbabwe.

Strategy	Implementation plan
Strategy 1: Create appropriate legislative frameworks and set out ambitious national plans for inclusion	• Abolish legislative or constitutional barriers to PwDs being included in mainstream education systems. • Develop ambitious yet realistic and time-bound IE plans within the overall education sector plan. • Involve PwDs and organizations in planning and monitoring education plans, at all levels.
Strategy 2: Provide the capacity, resources, and leadership to implement ambitious national plans on inclusion	• Allocate at least 20% of national budgets to education and ensure at least 50% is dedicated to basic education. • Ensure a time-bound and costed IE implementation plan with sufficient and specifically allocated resources. • Ensure MoPSE has the primary responsibility for the education of disabled children, with different levels of responsibilities clearly outlined across the whole education system, backed by high-level political leadership. • Invest in improving the knowledge and capacity of local and national government institutions so that they can deliver on IE (from decentralized local education authorities responsible for education planning, through to policymakers in the Education Ministry).
Strategy 3: Improve data on disability and education, and build accountability for action	• Improve data on disability and education and build accountability for action. • Ensure education data is disaggregated by disability and gender, and that it tracks both enrolment and retention (including in different schools, e.g. segregated or mainstream). • Ensure effective collection and analysis of data to improve planning and monitoring.
Strategy 4: Make schools and classrooms accessible and relevant for all	• Develop and enforce accessible building regulations for schools. • Provide accessible materials and AT to support learning. • Ensure that curricula are better able to adapt to a diversity of needs. • Develop national guidelines to support IE, such as guidelines on curriculum adaptation or screening, identifying, and addressing support needs.

Table 3.3 continued.

Strategy	Implementation plan
Strategy 5: Ensure enough appropriately trained teachers for all	• Reduce teacher–pupil ratios so that teachers can focus on individual learners' needs. • Ensure adequate pre-service and in-service training in IE. • Ensure that adequate support material and expertise in disability-specific skills are available. • Ensure that teachers that are being trained IE become resources to assist mainstream schools. • Promote the training and recruitment of teachers with disabilities.
Strategy 6: Challenge attitudes which reinforce and sustain discrimination	• Tackle the attitudes that keep CwDs out of schools by launching an awareness programme among parents, children, communities, and schools, and within the public and private sectors.
Strategy 7: Create an enabling environment to support IE, including through cross-sectoral policies and strategies that reduce exclusion	• Bring in additional policies and resources to support CwDs to go to school, i.e. social protection schemes, community-based rehabilitation programmes, early childhood development programmes.

(Source: Adapted from D. Gartner. 2009. *A Global Fund for Education: Achieving Education for All*. Washington, DC: Brookings Institution, 6.)

We recommend that the Zimbabwean government addresses these factors, without which compliance with the full provisions in the CRPD and SDG 4 will remain unattainable. Most importantly, Zimbabwe needs to introduce measures to devise longer-term IE plans. This will ensure that all PwDs, including those with physical, sensory, intellectual, psychosocial, and developmental impairments, will be included within the mainstream educational system in line with the CRPD's provisions – that is, from early childhood to vocational and university education. Such measures must also: ensure complete, free, local, equitable, and high-quality accessible primary and secondary education; ensure access to high-quality early childhood development, including pre-primary education; promote and use accessible communication methods, including ATs and languages, such as sign language; and provide equal access to affordable and high-quality technical, vocational, business, and tertiary education, including at university level (UN, 2006). In order to realize the above recommendations, it will be necessary to recruit teachers, instructors, and trainers with disabilities and to train all teachers in inclusive practices, including those relating to language and communication, through teacher education programmes that focus on the pedagogy and andragogy of education and inclusion. This will require training on the understanding and application of inclusive practices, as well as reasonable accommodations and individual support that facilitate access to knowledge, in line with the CRPD.

Critical to realizing SDG 4 and Article 24 of the CRPD is the inclusion and the participation of PwDs and their representative organizations in all phases of implementing IE, rather than merely opening up more classroom spaces for PwDs. This is because they are the true experts when it comes to their complete inclusion in society. Through consultations and by partnering with PwDs and their allies, the government will receive technical assistance, capacity-building, and access to data, which are essential to achieving inclusion and realizing the overarching principle of leaving no one behind. Bringing PwDs explicitly into mainstream development discourse will not only benefit them; it will also enable all Zimbabweans to realize that there is immense untapped potential to transform the country into a better place for all people.

In conclusion, we argue that, among other things, the inclusion of CwDs in mainstream schools will promote universal primary completion, can be cost-effective, and will contribute to the elimination of discrimination (McConkey, Mariga, and Myezwa, 2014; WHO and WB, 2011; Stubbs, 2002). These are important benefits, but the potential of IE, when properly and effectively utilized, goes even further, and can be fundamentally transformative for individuals, education systems, and society as a whole. IE creates inclusive communities, which are capable of embracing diversity and promoting inclusive development. It is our hope that Zimbabwe's draft IE policy will be adopted to ensure that all learners realize one of their fundamental rights: the right to inclusive and equitable education as enshrined in Article 24 of the CRPD.

Bibliography

Antoninis, M., April, D., Barakat, B., Bella, N., Cristina D'Addio, A., Eck, M., Endrizzi, F., Joshi, P., Kubacka, K., McWilliam, A., Murakami, Y., Smith, W., Stipanovic, L., Vidarte, R., and Zekrya, L. 2020. 'All Means All: An Introduction to the 2020 Global Education Monitoring Report on Inclusion', *PROSPECTS* 49: 103–9.

Chakuchichi, D., and Chataika, T. 2014. *Mid Term Review Report: 'Promoting Inclusive Education in Schools'*. Harare: Leonard Cheshire Disability Zimbabwe (LCDZ) Trust.

Chakuchichi, D. Chataika, T., and Nyaruwata, L. 2016. *'Promoting Inclusive Education in Schools' Project Endline Evaluation Report.* Harare: Leonard Cheshire Disability Zimbabwe (LCDZ) Trust.

Chakuchichi, D., Nyaruwata, L., and Chataika, T. 2012. *Leonard Cheshire Disability International Schools for All-Inclusive Education – Zimbabwe Evaluation Report.* Harare: Leonard Cheshire Disability Zimbabwe (LCDZ) Trust / Leonard Cheshire Disability International.

Chataika, T. 2019. 'Introduction: Critical Connections and Gaps in Disability and Development'. In: T. Chataika. Ed. *The Routledge Handbook of Disability in Southern Africa* (pp. 3–13). London: Routledge.

Gartner, D. 2009. *A Global Fund for Education: Achieving Education for All.* Brookings Institution.

Global Campaign for Education (GCE). n.d. *Inclusive Education for Children with Disabilities.* Global Campaign for Education.

Government of Ghana. 2015. *Inclusive Education Policy.* Ministry of Education (MoE), Accra: Ghana Education Service.

Government of Zimbabwe. 2013. *The Constitution of Zimbabwe Amendment Number 20.* Harare: Zimbabwe Government Printers.

Grech, S. 2011. 'Recolonizing Debates or Perpetuated Coloniality? Decentring the Spaces of Disability, Development, and Community in the Global South', *International Journal of Inclusive Education* 15(1): 87–100.

Grech, S. 2014. 'Disability, Poverty and Education: Perceived Barriers and (Dis)connections in Rural Guatemala', *Disability and the Global South* 1(1): 128–52.

Hagen, C. 2016. 'Barriers to Education for Youth with Disabilities in Malawi: A Qualitative Study of Policy and Practice in Urban and Rural Areas'. Unpublished Master's Thesis, Norwegian University of Life Sciences, Ås, Norway.

Hlatywayo, L. 2018. 'An Analysis of Reverse Inclusion as an Alternative Model in Deaf Education'. Unpublished PhD thesis, University of South Africa.

Kamenopoulou, L. 2018. 'Inclusive Education in the Global South? A Colombian Perspective: "When You Look Towards the Past, You See Children with Disabilities, and If You Look Towards the Future, What You See Is Diverse Learners"', *Disability and the Global South*, Open Access, 5(1): 1192–1214.

Kett, M., Deluca, M., and Carew, M. 2019. 'How Prepared Are Teachers to Deliver Inclusive Education: Evidence from Kenya, Zimbabwe and Sierra Leone'. In: N. Singal, P. Lynch, and S. Taneja Johansson. Eds. *Education and Disability in the Global South – New Perspectives from Africa and Asia* (pp. 203–24). London: Bloomsbury.

Lehtomäki, E., Janhonen-Abruquah, H., and Kahangwa, G.L. Eds. 2017. *Culturally Responsive Education: Reflections from the Global South and North*. London: Routledge.

McConkey, R., Mariga, L., and Myezwa, H. 2014. *Inclusive Education in Low-Income Countries: A Resource Book for Teacher Educators, Parent Trainers and Community Development Workers*. Cape Town: Atlas Alliance and Disability Innovations Africa.

McLinden, M., Lynch, P., Soni, A., Artiles, A., Kholowa, F., Kamchedzera, E., and Mankhwazi, M. 2018. 'Supporting Children with Disabilities in Low-and Middle-Income Countries: Promoting Inclusive Practice within Community-Based Childcare Centres in Malawi through a Bioecological Systems Perspective', *International Journal of Early Childhood*, 50(2): 159–74.

Ministry of Education, Science and Technology (MoEST) [Malawi]. 2016. *Inclusive Education Source Book: A Sourcebook for Pre-Service Teacher Educators and Practising Teachers*. Lilongwe: MoEST.

Ministry of Primary and Secondary Education (MoPSE). 2019. *Draft Inclusive Education Policy in Zimbabwe: Promoting Quality Education for All*. Harare: MoPSE.

Mnkandla, M., and Mataruse, K. 2002. 'The Impact of Inclusion Policy on School Psychology in Zimbabwe', *Educational and Child Psychology* 19: 12–23.

Muthukrishna, A. 2019. 'The Practice Architectures of Inclusive Education in Two African Contexts'. In N. Singal, P. Lynch, and S.T.

Johansson. Eds. *Education and Disability in the Global South – New Perspectives from Africa and Asia.* London: Bloomsbury.

Sibanda. 2018. 'A Review of the Implementation of Inclusive Education in Zimbabwe: Challenges and Opportunities,' *Scientific Journal of Pure and Applied Sciences* 7(9): 808–15.

Stubbs, S. 2002. *Inclusive Education Where There Are Few Resources.* Oslo: The Atlas Alliance.

UNESCO. 1994. *The Salamanca Statement and Framework for Action on Special Needs Education.* Adopted by the World Conference on Special Needs Education: Access and Quality. Salamanca, Spain: UNESCO.

United Nations Educational, Scientific and Cultural Organization (UNESCO). 2018. *Global Education Monitoring Report 2019.* Paris: UNESCO.

United Nations Educational, Scientific and Cultural Organization (UNESCO). 2020. 'Global Education Monitoring Report: Inclusion and Education – All Means All.' Paris: UNESCO.

United Nations Children's Fund (UNICEF). 2018. 'Summative Evaluation of UNICEF Support for Education in Zimbabwe EDF 2012–2015 and GPE 2014–2016.' Harare: UNICEF <https://mokoro.co.uk/wp-content/uploads/UNICEF_Zimbabwe_Education_Evaluation_Report__2018-002.pdf> [accessed 12 December 2019].

United Nations Children's Fund (UNICEF). 2013. 'The Zimbabwe 2013 Living Conditions Survey among Persons with Disability.' Harare: UNICEF <https://www.medbox.org/pdf/5e148832db60a2044c2d51ae> [accessed 15 November 2019].

United Nations (UN). 2008. Convention on the Rights of PwDs. GA Res, 61, 106. New York: UN.

United Nations (UN). 2016. 'Transforming Our World: The 2030 Agenda for Sustainable Development'. UN General Assembly Resolution. 25 September 2015, A/RES/70/1, at para. 1.

United Nations (UN). 2016. *High Level Political Forum Ensuring That No One Is Left Behind: Position Paper by PwDs* <https://www.internationaldisabilityalliance.org/resources/leave-no-one-behind-hlpf-2016-position-paper-persons-disabilities> [accessed 15 October 2019].

United Nations Educational, Scientific and Cultural Organization (UNESCO). 2015. *Education for All 2015 National Review Report: Zimbabwe.* (Harare: UNESCO).

Walton, E., Nel, N.M., Muller, H., and Lebeloane, L.D.M. 2014. '"You Can Train Us Until We Are Blue in Our Faces, We Are Still Going to Struggle": Teacher Professional Learning in a Full-Service School', *Education as Change* 18(2): 319–33.

World Health Organization (WHO) and World Bank (WB). 2011. *World Report on Disability.* New York: WHO.

4

Barriers to the Implementation of Education Article 24 of the CRPD in Kenya

BILLIAN OTUNDO

Introduction and Background

The Kenyan government's formal support for disability rights began with the Disability Act of 2003. This commitment continued with the signing of the United Nations (UN) Convention on the Rights of Persons with Disabilities (CRPD) in 2006 and the ratification of the Convention in 2018. Taken together, these actions created a public obligation for the government to respect, protect, and fulfil the provisions in the Convention, including inclusive education (IE). For example, Article 24 of the CRPD declares that 'States Parties shall ensure an inclusive education system at all levels and lifelong learning directed to enabling persons with disabilities [henceforth PwDs] to participate effectively in a free society' (UN, 2006). Article 33 speaks to enforcement, calling on signatories to implement and monitor the Convention's provisions (UN, 2008). The Kenyan government acknowledged this responsibility by incorporating the CRPD into Article 2(6) of the Kenyan Constitution of 2010, so that the Convention forms part of Kenyan law.

On paper, therefore, Kenya is firmly committed to IE. However, many learners with disabilities (LwDs) still do not have access to education, despite it being a fundamental right for all as enshrined not only in the CRPD and the Kenyan Disability Act but also in the Universal Declaration of Human Rights (UDHR) (Zandy, 2019). In this country, IE has been defined as a philosophy that focuses on the process of adjusting the home, school, and wider society to accommodate persons with special needs, including disabilities (Ngugi, 2000). However, a significant number of learners and trainees with disabilities are not in school, and those who are in school are enrolled in around 300 special schools and various special units throughout the country (Ministry of Education [MoE], 2005: 11).

Implementing Article 24 in Kenya is complicated by the complex web of interconnected challenges experienced by PwDs, including gender inequality, social and economic constraints, and barriers within mainstream education, all of which affect their ability to access IE. These challenges render a disproportionate number of children and adults with disabilities unable to access good-quality education and attain adequate levels of literacy. Very few young people living with disabilities remain in education beyond primary school level (Global Monitoring Report [GMR], 2012). This affects their chances of obtaining livelihoods. Most importantly, they face constraints in employment owing to their low level of education, little or no adaptation of their workplaces, and limited expectations among families and employers (Baboo, 2011). Kenya's National Survey on PwDs (Republic of Kenya [RoK], 2008) found that a quarter of PwDs work in family businesses, but a third do not work at all. Another study found that at the time of the survey in 2021, only 8% of PwDs aged fifteen to twenty-four worked for pay, and 14% had worked in the family business. In contrast, over 50% had not worked at all (GMR, 2012). According to the Kenya National Survey for Persons with Disabilities (KNSPWD), the largest proportion of PwDs who worked for pay was in Nairobi (32%) and the smallest was in the North Eastern province (3%) (RoK, 2008). Those working were more likely to be male (18%) than female (8%). Most importantly for our purposes, most PwDs with employment were likely to be better educated: 45% had a university education, 36% a middle-level education, and 22% a secondary or 'A' level, or post-primary vocational education (RoK, 2008). Even though the government of Kenya has declared the necessity to include LwDs in the mainstream school setting in line with the CRPD, the country has far to go before educational progress, access, and equality become a reality for these learners.

The quest for more inclusive educational practices underscores the need to fully comprehend the challenges and barriers to inclusion that LwDs face to successfully implement policies driven by international human rights values. This chapter explores the challenges and barriers in the implementation of the Education Article of the CRPD in Kenya. This will be accomplished in four sections: (a) an outline of the strides made by Kenya in addressing education for LwDs; (b) a brief on monitoring the implementation of the Convention in Kenya; (c) a description of the barriers and challenges faced at institutional and national levels; (d) a summary of the recommendations for improvement. The chapter will be guided by three research questions:

1. What efforts have been made to facilitate education for LwDs in Kenya?
2. How far has Kenya monitored and implemented Article 24 of the CRPD?
3. What barriers and challenges are evident in the implementation of Article 24 at institutional and national levels?

Efforts towards Education for LwDs in Kenya, 1940s–2000s

Education for LwDs in Kenya dates to the late 1940s, when Kenya's education sector and religious institutions made efforts for organized care and the provision of special needs education (SNE). The religious institutions included the Salvation Army Church and (much later) the Anglican, Catholic, Methodist, and Presbyterian churches. Until the 1970s, education for LwDs was offered solely in special schools (Mwangi and Aluko, 2014). In addition to the churches, after independence in 1963, the government of Kenya progressively engaged notable commissions, committees, and task forces to address the challenges facing the education sector. In 1964, the Kenya Education Commission (Ominde Report) was established to advocate for the integration of children with special needs into regular schools (RoK, 1964). In 1976, the National Committee on Educational Objectives and Policies (RoK, 1976) recommended the integration of LwDs into the mainstream education system by transferring them from special schools to regular schools. In 1986 the MoE established the Kenya Institute of Special Education (KISE) to build the capacity of SNE service providers through research, teacher training, and teacher in-servicing. In 1988 the government established the presidential working party on education and manpower training for the next decade and beyond (RoK, 1988), which mainly focused on: improving the quality and relevance of education; the intensive use of the media, and national programmes for sensitization on the needs of PwDs;

and the provision of education for learners with special needs in regular classrooms. In 1999 the commission of inquiry into the education system of Kenya (Koech Report, 1999) highlighted the need for early intervention for children with special needs and for improving the means of accessibility, equity, relevance, and quality, while foregrounding gender issues, PwDs, and disadvantaged groups.

In 2003 the MoE introduced free primary education (FPE), undertaking several measures to facilitate access to education for LwDs. In the same year, the Kenyan government provided several crucial additional interventions, including implementing the Persons with Disabilities Act (RoK, 2003); producing the report of the taskforce on SNE, led by SNE scholar Dr Edwards Kochung; increasing funding to SNE; and enhancing support for teacher training at KISE. Under the Persons with Disabilities Act, the National Council for Persons with Disabilities (NCPWD) was established and given responsibility for follow-up and enforcement of the law and formulating and developing measures and policies designed to achieve equal opportunities for PwDs (Sightsavers, 2018: 3; Kabare, 2018: 5). The implementation of FPE in 2003 led to an influx of new categories of students qualifying for IE initiatives, particularly in public schools. Many categories related to disability, including albinism, autism, cerebral palsy, deaf-blindness, Down syndrome, emotional and behavioural disorders, epilepsy, intellectual and developmental disabilities, learning disabilities (LDs), locomotor impairments, and speech/language disorders. Of these, the most common forms of disabilities in Kenya are associated with chronic respiratory diseases, cancer, diabetes, malnutrition, HIV/AIDS, other infectious diseases, and injuries such as those from road accidents, falls, land mines, and violence. Other categories which qualified for these initiatives were not connected specifically to a disability, although they could be related. These included gifted students, those with experiences of abuse, homelessness, heads of households, those from nomadic/pastoral communities, and internally displaced persons (RoK, 2008). Based on this classification, there have been increases in demands for education from teachers, parents, guardians, and caregivers of LwDs, which has overwhelmed the Ministry's resources.

Moving ahead to 2009, the MoE, along with stakeholders and other partners, developed the SNE policy framework to address profound issues concerning education for LwDs. The purpose of this policy is to guide the staff at the MoE and other stakeholders in IE at all levels of learning, as opposed to special schools and units attached to regular schools. The SNE policy of 2009 is a notable endeavour by the Kenyan government to domesticate the UN Educational, Scientific and Cultural Organization (UNESCO)'s Salamanca Statement of 1994, which urged all governments 'to give the highest policy and budgetary priority to improve education services so that all children could be included regardless of differences or difficulties' (UNESCO, 1994). The policy has also set several target areas, including: assessment and intervention; access to quality and relevant education; conducive environment, health and safety (an adaptation of facilities); specialized facilities and technology; curriculum development; capacity-building and development; participation and involvement; advocacy and awareness creation; partnerships and collaboration; gender mainstreaming; research and documentation; disaster preparedness; resource mobilization; guidance and counselling; and assessment and intervention. It is worth noting that the SNE policy of 2009 has been revised as the *Sector Policy for Learners and Trainees with Disabilities 2018* (RoK, 2018), to ensure that it is aligned with the CRPD on the principle IE (Sightsavers, 2018). In this current policy, the focus is on the adoption of IE approaches and strategies in the provision of education services to LwDs at all levels of education, from early childhood to university (Sightsavers, 2018).

Another crucial framework is the Constitution of Kenya 2010. In its Chapter 4 part 54, the Constitution stipulates that PwDs are entitled to 'access educational institutions and facilities for PwDs that are integrated into society to the extent compatible with the interests of the person', 'to use sign language, Braille, or other appropriate means of communication', and to 'access materials and devices to overcome constraints arising from the person's disability'. Worth mentioning is Kenya's National ICT Policy of 2016, which outlines the strategies for 'an accessible ICT environment in the country to enable PwDs to take full advantage of ICTs'. Other policy documents to this effect include the *Sessional Paper No. 1 of 2005 on A Policy Framework for Education, Training and Research* (RoK, 2005), and Kenya Vision 2030. Vision 2030 is a flagship project of the National Economic and Social Council (NESC) that unifies the country's macro-economic, social, and political objectives into a single, long-term national plan or 'vision'. The aim is to transform Kenya into a 'newly-industrializing, middle-income country' by 2030 through a series of successive five-year plans that began in 2007. This document commits to ensuring that issues directly affecting PwDs are adequately addressed in policies, legal frameworks, programmes, and projects. In 2016 the government, in partnership with Disabled People's Organizations (DPOs), devised the *National Plan of Action* on the implementation of the recommendations made by the NESC on the rights of persons living with disabilities in the Republic of Kenya. The functions of this plan include disability matters, and specifically the need to identify and concretize the objectives and milestones that Kenya must realize to ensure full implementation of the CRPD (RoK, 2016a). It is evident that since the 1940s, the general objective of the government of Kenya has been to provide equal access to education for all learners regardless of their physical or mental state.

Monitoring the Implementation of the CRPD in Kenya

In February 2011, the Kenya National Commission on Human Rights (KNCHR) was first designated as the monitoring agency for the implementation of the CRPD (Kabare, 2018: 18–19). Since then, concerted efforts have been made by the state, DPOs, and other members of civil society to drive forward the implementation of the CRPD in Kenya. In 2014, the monitoring mandate was vested in the National Gender and Equality Commission (NGEC), whose mandate is to promote gender equality and freedom from discrimination in compliance with Article 27 of the Constitution of Kenya 2010 (RoK, 2010). This mandate is achieved by monitoring, auditing, and facilitating the integration of principles of equality and inclusion in all national and county policies, laws, and administrative regulations in both public and private institutions. The NGEC particularly focuses on conducting audits on the status of special interest groups (SIGs), including minorities, marginalized groups, PwDs, women, youth, and children. The Commission is the organ of the State that ensures compliance with all treaties and Conventions ratified by Kenya relating to issues of equality and freedom from discrimination and relating to SIGs, including PwDs and children.

On 9 June 2017, the attorney general redesignated the KNCHR as the monitoring agency under the CRPD, and this is expected to work alongside the NGEC. However, the KNCHR Committee, which comprises eighteen independent experts, has recently indicated that it finds it difficult to receive and hear individual complaints because, despite the ratification of the CRPD, the government neither signed nor ratified its Optional Protocol, which would give the Committee competence to examine individual complaints concerning any alleged violation of the Convention by a State Party to the Protocol. Still, the Committee is obliged to report and make recommendations on the implementation of the Convention beginning in 2010 (two years after Kenya ratified the CRPD), and every four years thereafter. Under this guidance, Kenya initially owed its first state report in 2010 but did not submit it to the Committee on the Rights of Persons with Disabilities (CoRPD) until April 2012. Kenya's report on the CRPD was reviewed by the Committee during its fourteenth session in August 2015. Under its designation, the Commission has carried out monitoring of the implementation of the Convention in twelve counties (Bungoma, Busia, Kilifi, Makueni, Mombasa, Nyeri, Machakos, Kisii, Kiambu, Migori, and Uasin Gish) for the period 2011–13. The monitoring was conducted with the participation of PwDs and their representative organizations from the design of the monitoring frameworks through to collection of data and report writing, in line with Article 33(3) of the CRPD. Relevant to this chapter are the challenges experienced by the Commission in the implementation of Article 24 of the CRPD, including findings from other research and the baseline survey hereunder.

Barriers and Challenges to Implementation of Article 24 of the CRPD: Primary and Secondary Schooling

Schools are key players in the implementation of the practices of IE policies. Bell and Stevenson (2015) state that an institution's (school's) capacity to modify its strategies and systems to enhance accessibility for all learners is crucial to the implementation of IE. These strategies include authorization, financial investment, building an enabling environment, ethos, and the way the individuals, institutions, public sector, and community at large engage with one another to facilitate IE (Bell and Stevenson,

2015). There is more research on IE at the primary school level compared to early-childhood education and the secondary and post-secondary levels. As such, a detailed comparison of barriers across all levels is very difficult. While there is some literature on IE in primary schools in Kenya with several ongoing pilot projects, institutions of higher education remain neglected. With this limitation in mind, this section discusses barriers and challenges to IE at the primary level. The subsequent section presents Moi University as an illustrative case study of the barriers facing LwDs at the post-secondary level. Statistically, there are 15 secondary special schools and integrated programmes in Kenya and 1,882 primary and secondary schools that provide education for LwDs (KNCHR, 2016).

Access to IE in Kenya remains a huge challenge for LwDs, despite the ratification of the CRPD and enactment of legislation and policies that aim to increase accessibility. Recently, the UN promulgated twenty-two Standard Rules on the Equalization of Opportunities for Disabled Persons (1993). Related to IE, rule 6 states that countries 'should recognise the principle of equal primary, secondary and tertiary educational opportunities for children, youth and adults with disabilities. They should ensure that the education of PwDs is an integral part of the education system.' This rule not only affirms the equal rights of children, youth, and adults with disabilities to education but also states that education should be provided 'in integrated school settings' and 'in the general school setting'. The CRPD further affirms the right to education in an inclusive setting for all children. The key point here is to enable LwDs to enrol and remain in the school of their choice within their localities, as is supported fully by Kenya's Children Act 2001 (GoK, 2001). Despite Kenya's efforts to implement the Education Article of the CRPD, children with disabilities (CwDs) are still blocked from equity and inclusiveness in education. The discussion below provides a summary of the key difficulties, as raised by the KNHRC (2014) and other organizations.

Poor Attitudes, Marginalization, and Stigma

Persons living with disabilities in Kenya face stigma and discrimination that lead to enduring and humiliating stereotypes and prejudices, including being labelled as a curse, witchcraft, and a burden on society, undermining the human rights principles which are key to inclusion (Randiki, 2002;

Sightsavers, 2018: 4; KNCHR, 2016: 16, 21; Kabare, 2018: 10; Bunning *et al.*, 2017). In this country, LwDs face multiple forms of discrimination based on gender, form and severity of the disability, resource allocation, and regional disparities. This discrimination has led to poor attitudes towards IE by key stakeholders, misinterpretations of policies that support IE, and ineffective learning strategies. As a result, people with disabilities are disempowered and marginalized, violated, abused, and more often than not remain voiceless.

Approaches for supporting people living with disabilities should involve the training of not only specialized staff to deal with PwDs but also the community at large to alleviate societal barriers to progress. The Oriang Project, for instance, aimed to change the perceptions of teachers, parents, and the wider community by teaching them about the principle of inclusion that promotes the integration of CwDs in schools (GMR, 2012). Despite this, there is still a strong traditional mentality, particularly in rural areas, that PwDs should attend formal education in special schools, and even parents are not actively involved in the education of their children who are living with a disability (KISE, 2018). Additionally, the regular institutions have been accused of maltreatment of LwDs, and this explains why parents still opt for special schools despite the government's commitments to IE.

Poverty and Limited Access to Educational Spaces

According to the KNSPWD, 65% of PwDs in Kenya regard environmental factors such as temperature, terrain, accessibility of transport, and accessibility of health and educational facilities as major problems in their daily lives (RoK, 2008). Kenya's education system has been characterized by processes and facilities that are inadequate for responding to the challenges faced by LwDs. The 2010 GEM Report indicates that many schools, including those in Kenya, particularly in remote rural areas or in urban slums, are physically inaccessible to some LwDs. Furthermore, the majority of regular institutions have not made adjustments to make the facilities accessible to PwDs. This has forced LwDs in Tharaka Nithi County in Kenya, for instance, to either adjust to get access to education or drop out of school because of ineffective school strategies for overcoming physical barriers (Ireri *et al.*, 2020). Generally, institutions of learning, including those at the tertiary level lack ramps and accessible washrooms, as observed from the university case study sampled in this research.

Worth noting is the fact that parents of CwDs more often than not experience socio-economic hindrances which contribute to inaccessibility. Many special schools in Kenya are residential, which is appreciated by some parents (Sightsavers, 2018: 8). However, this means parents have to pay the boarding expenses for LwDs, which can be a challenge (Sightsavers, 2018: 8–9), because the majority of these parents live in poverty, so will often be forced to seek admission for their children in regular institutions. In turn, the lack of appropriate infrastructure in these mainstream schools means that LwDs are unlikely to complete their studies; indeed, their inability to access these institutions of learning has a negative impact on their rates of both enrolment (Wodon *et al.*, 2018) and completion when compared to peers without disabilities (Male and Wodon, 2017). Additionally, there is a lack of awareness within the school administrative structure, as most administrators and teachers, particularly in regular schools, are unaware of the provisions on the right to education for LwDs (Ohba and Malenya, 2020: 10).

Inadequate Funding, Assistive Devices, and Services

Despite the country's most conscious effort to address IE, it has provided neither adequate systems, facilities, and services that respond to the challenges faced by PwDs, nor adequate resources to audit the organizations and enforce the provision of the laws which promote access to IE (Sightsavers, 2018: 3), including access to related assistive devices required for a fully functional IE. Article 20 of the CRPD calls for effective measures to facilitate access to quality assistive devices and technologies for PwDs, delivered at affordable costs and in a manner and at a time of the choice. However, in Kenya, the majority of people that need these technologies do not have access to them, and many are not even aware of such technologies and their functionalities. Kenya's Persons with Disabilities Act (RoK, 2003) defines assistive devices and services to mean 'implements, tools and specialized services (including the services of qualified interpreters for the deaf and qualified teachers for the blind) provided to PwDs to assist them in education, employment or other activities'. The devices and services enhance the ability of PwDs to participate in day-to-day endeavours, including the activities in learning spaces required for formal education. The

KNSPWD has categorized these devices to include those related to information (hearing aids, magnifying glasses, braille) and communication (sign language interpreter, portable writer), as well as personal mobility (wheelchairs, crutches, walking sticks/frames) (Randiki, 2002; RoK, 2008; Sightsavers, 2018: 2; Kabare, 2018: 11). Other items relate to the home (flashing light on the doorbell, amplified telephone); personal care and protection (special fasteners, bath and shower seats, toilet-seat raisers); handling goods and products (gripping tongs, aids for opening containers); and computer-assisted technology (e.g. keyboards for the blind) (RoK, 2008).

In a study carried out between 2016 and 2017 in Nairobi's Kasarani sub-county and Marsabit's central division in fourteen schools, eight of which had special units, Ohba and Malenya (2020) documented that attempts 'towards inclusion were found in schools with specialized units' (p. 29). These efforts included LwDs participating in most school activities, attending regular classes, and the whole school learning basic sign language. Despite these measures, there was still evidence of practices that were not inclusive: LwDs used regular classroom desks that were unsuitable for wheelchair users and were segregated from other students and learned in separate units; school materials were often inaccessible; and some LwDs were made to transition to special secondary schools because the local schools were not ready to accommodate them (Ohba and Malenya, 2020: 12–13).

Recent developments with the COVID-19 pandemic have made the challenges faced by LwDs even harder. Kenya's MoE announced a progressive transition back to school during the pandemic, but the government seems to have neglected to factor in the needs of LwDs. For example, LwDs who are physically disabled cannot access amenities such as designated water points in the same way as students without disabilities. Also, some messages for containment measures have not been made available in braille for the visually impaired. Meanwhile, teachers have not been trained in how to handle LwDs during these unique times (Oyeng' and Kajilwa, 2020). Despite this, teachers have generally not been trained in IE, and much of the research indicates that the attitudes of teachers towards special needs children are key components for successful inclusion (Moodley, 2002; UNESCO, 2003; Van Reusen, Shoho, and Barker, 2001). In fact, when teachers are trained and have the skills and competence to handle children with special needs, they normally gain courage in their work and have a positive attitude towards LwDs (Carew *et al.*, 2019: 229; Moodley, 2002; Mutisya, 2010; UNESCO, 2003). Teachers with training in SNE have been found to favour mainstreaming more than those without (Mutisya, 2010; Njoroge, 1991). Although KISE has been training teachers specifically in IE, it has neglected the fact that in the regular schools the teacher–pupil ratio is quite high, rendering it doubtful whether LwDs get the needed attention (Mutisya, 2010).

Further to that, Ohba and Malenya (2020: 14) observe that education assessment and resource centres (EARCs) often advise placing LwDs at a great distance from their locality, owing to the local schools and environments lacking financial and human resources (Ohba and Malenya, 2020: 14). Moreover, these EARCs are underfunded and not easily accessible by all schools in the country, which undermines the identification and assessment process that is important for LwDs (Kiru, 2018: 185; Bii and Taylor, 2013: 29, 33). The *Policy Framework for Education and Training* (second draft) 2012 also flags the financing of special education as a major challenge, as well as the shortage of specialized teachers and inadequate facilities, among others (Rohwerder, 2020).

Gender and Regional Disparity

Despite Kenya's fundamental commitment to the principles of education-for-all and no-child-left-behind policies, gender, and regional disparities persist regarding admission, learning, progression, promotion, management, and monitoring and evaluation for LwDs. The 2019 census of Kenya showed that 1.9% of men are living with a disability compared to 2.5% of women and that there was a higher prevalence of disability in rural parts of the country (2.6%) than in urban areas (1.4%) (Owino, 2020: 6). Kenya has been slow to move towards gender equity in education, particularly for girls, who face a double disadvantage – gender and disability – and more so for those living in rural areas (RoK, 2009). The widest gender gaps for LwDs exist at the post-secondary education levels (RoK, 2009). Moyi (2017: 502) notes that CwDs, especially girls, are less likely to have ever been enrolled in school than children without disabilities. Notably, girls with disabilities are more prone to gender-based violence like sexual harassment and rape, among others (KNCHR, 2016: 39; RoK, 2009). This is due to the marginalization, stigma, and double discrimination that they face, including negative cultural practices and attitudes towards gender and disability biases (KNCHR, 2016: 39, 156). The SNE policy (RoK, 2009) noted that the dropout rate for girls with special needs and disabilities is higher compared to their male counterparts because of teachers who may not be sensitive to the needs of these learners, and more often than not they are left out of programmes such as sex education, life skills, and HIV and AIDS due to the belief that they do not engage in social activities and sex (RoK, 2009; RoK, 2018). Moreover, a traditional and conservative mentality on the role of women in society has reinforced 'the misconception about the ability of women and girls with disabilities to adequately perform their roles as other peers' (KNCHR, 2016: 39). This is not to mean that the male child with a disability enjoys access to IE: he is often exposed to child labour and other cultural practices that infringe on his right to education (RoK, 2018: 26).

Other regional disparities that pose a problem for access to IE for LwDs include the proneness of certain areas to natural calamities and arid and semi-arid areas. As an illustration, a 2012 countrywide survey found that access to, and participation in, schools by CwDs was relatively low across the country, and more so in the north-eastern region, which documented the lowest number of SNE units (Department of Education [DoE], 2012: 36). The MoE (RoK, 2018: 6) also noted that interventions such as mobile schools in arid areas are not adapted to serve learners and trainees with disabilities.

Inaccurate Data, Late Identification, and Low Enrolment

There is a general lack of reliable disability data in Kenya (Sightsavers, 2018: 4; Owino, 2020: 4), but more so for LwDs. The 2019 census data suggests that 2.2% of Kenyans aged five and above (0.9 million people) live with some form of disability (Owino, 2020: 6). A lack of disaggregated data, including on the extent of access to IE for LwDs, severely hinders efforts to improve their access to appropriate services, information, and resources (RoK, 2018). In Kenya, the county governments have been tasked with the provision of EARCs according to Article 46(1) of the Basic Education Act (RoK, 2013). The role of EARCs is to offer the early identification, assessment, intervention, and placement in educational services of children with special needs (Bii and Taylor, 2013: 13). This is significant, as identifying the special educational need of a child is critical to facilitating the provision of relevant support to enable the child to participate fully in quality learning in an inclusive setting. Moreover, early identification of a disability is likely to arrest its deterioration (RoK, 2018). This has been hindered due to a lack of strategies for early identification, poor access to healthcare, financial constraints, and social barriers such as stigma and discrimination (RoK, 2018). More emphasis has been placed on the traditional categories of disabilities – hearing impairment, visual impairment, intellectual disability (ID), and physical disability – to the exclusion of other disabilities like deafness, blindness, autism, and specific learning difficulties, among others, which has resulted in a lack of availability of accurate disaggregated data by disability, gender, region, and distribution in the institutions (RoK, 2018).

In 2013, Bii and Taylor found no accurate data on the dropout and transition rates of CwDs (Bii and Taylor, 2013). However, in 2020, it was documented that CwDs are less likely to complete school in comparison to children without disabilities, with 44% of the former completing primary school in comparison to 60% of the latter (Rohwerder, 2020). Further, the *SNE Policy Review Data Collection Report* (RoK, 2016b) showed that the high dropout rate of LwDs, including trainees with disabilities, was attributed to factors such as incontinence and poor management of menstrual health because of unaffordable sanitary towels. In such situations, the learners and trainees may find it challenging to cope in a classroom setting and opt to drop out of school altogether (RoK, 2018: 6). In another study, Wodon *et al.* (2017) noted that many CwDs have never enrolled in school and further observed that, among children aged twelve, the likelihood of having ever enrolled in school was ten percentage points lower for CwDs versus children without disabilities.

In 2015, the NGEC conducted an assessment to find out the extent to which CwDs were accessing FPE across the following counties in Kenya: Isiolo, Nyeri, Tharaka Nithi, Elgeyo Markwet, Taita Taveta, and Kisii. The assessment revealed that according to the chiefs, the majority of CwDs were not in school, and the county development officers had no records of CwDs (NGEC, 2016). Moreover, headteachers reported that they were aware of other CwDs in their catchment areas who had not been enrolled in any school, while parents also acknowledged the presence of children who stayed at home, especially those with severe disability (NGEC, 2016).

Unsuitable Curriculum and Rigid Assessment

In any education system, the curriculum is one of the crucial obstacles or tools to facilitate the development of inclusion (UNESCO, 2003), and in various settings, the curriculum is quite demanding, rigid, and difficult to adapt (Moodley, 2002). These barriers must be identified and addressed to accommodate LwDs. Ngugi (2000) recommended that curriculum diversification and adaptation of examinations are teaching and learning strategies that will promote inclusion in education. In spite of the competency-based curriculum (CBC) launched in Kenya in 2018, which is geared towards nurturing every learner's potential, including those with disabilities, by the provision of a differentiated curriculum stipulated in the sector policy, this curriculum still does not meet the needs of LwDs (Rohwerder, 2020). Further to that, schools still base their assessment on a mean score, which leads to low rates of transition across all levels of education for LwDs (Ohba and Malenya, 2020). This is particularly a challenge for children with intellectual disabilities. Regarding the CBC, Obha and Malenya (2020: 15) noted that many of the barriers to the participation of LwDs in learning were in the 'curriculum and school setup, which were actually the responsibility of the government' and that '[... i] nclusive education cannot be implemented without human and financial commitments'.

Laxity in Implementation of (Ambiguous) Policies

Education policies in Kenya before and after realignment into the country's Constitution seem not to have fully benefited LwDs, because many of them are still out of school (Kiru, 2018). Attempts have been made to revise Kenya's Education Act to guide IE, but the process has been very slow. Since 2009, the SNE policy has been in existence without implementing guidelines; this was noted as an impediment to implementation, with stakeholders expressing how challenging it has been for them to implement IE without concrete guidelines and guidance (RoK, 2018). Moreover, there were concerns that the policy is difficult and ambiguous for teachers to implement and that it fails to include salient definitions to facilitate a common way of addressing children said to be living with disabilities (Mwangi, 2013). As an example, Mwangi (2013: 305) noted that the definition of the term inclusion was in itself ambiguous, and that it created doubts over whether integration and inclusion are understood at the ministry level and whether it is clear where the responsibilities lie for the implementation of SNE. As a reaction to this and other drawbacks, the SNE policy of 2009 has been revised as the *Sector Policy for Learners and Trainees with Disabilities 2018* (RoK, 2018). However, Rohwerder (2020) notes that there is a reluctance to apply the guidance on the implementation of the policy and IE. Even though the government subscribes to the policy of IE and has recognized the challenges involved and even given a number of ways to address these challenges, it has also 'acknowledged that integration of all children with special needs in regular education and training programmes is professionally unachievable' (DoE, 2012: 96).

Barriers and Challenges to Implementation of Article 24 of the CRPD: Post-Secondary Schooling

To achieve implementation of IE at the post-secondary level, Kenya has on record twelve vocational rehabilitation centres (VRCs) dispersed throughout the country (KNCHR, 2016: 6). These VRCs have adopted a policy of taking on 60% of students with disabilities and 40% without (KNCHR, 2016: 36). Mainstream training institutes have largely benefited from the advice and skills training provided by these centres on how to communicate with visually impaired, deaf, and hard-of-hearing people (Baart and Maarse, 2017: 29). Notably, there are too few technical and vocational education and training institutes (TVETs) to cater for the needs of all the LwDs in Kenya alongside those without disabilities (Mueke, 2014: 25), and this is an even greater issue for universities. As mentioned earlier, there is a serious lack of research on IE in Kenyan post-secondary institutions. Opini (2009), for instance, found that poverty, sexual abuse, discrimination, indifferent reactions, limited learning resources, and physical access were some of the barriers to the participation of LwDs in university education in Kenya. To help bridge this gap in research, an excellent study of IE at Moi University was carried out by the author of this chapter, and can be used as a case study to highlight the main issues in making higher education accessible for PwDs.

Moi University was established by the government in 1984, and currently has the following campuses: Main Campus, Town Campus, Eldoret West Campus, Nairobi Campus, and Coast

(Mombasa) Campus. It has a total of 15 schools, 2 institutes, 9 directorates, and 3 centres of excellence. The student affairs division of the university has devised its 2015 Procedure for Student Support – Special Needs Services, which caters for LwDs. The purpose of this procedure is to ensure that LwDs access efficient support services that will produce an academically, physically, and socially conducive learning environment for all students. In the creation of this procedure reference materials have been adopted from documents on the rules and regulations governing the conduct and discipline of students, student constitutions and handbooks, the institution's strategic plan, statutes, and gender policy, and the Persons with Disabilities Act 2003. In Moi University, it is the principal responsibility of the dean of students to implement this procedure; its performance targets are shown in Table 4.1 below, alongside the corresponding monitoring and measurement activities.

Table 4.1 Performance target for IE at Moi University.

Performance Target	Monitoring and measurement
Identification and registration of special needs students	Available records in the unit
The orientation of special needs students	Reports at the end of every semester
Offering support services to special needs students	Deployment of students on the work-study programme to the unit at the beginning of every semester
Provision and repair of relevant equipment for special needs students	Memos and reports on the condition of the equipment

(Source: Adapted from Moi University 2015. *Moi University Procedures: The Procedure for Student Support – Special Needs Services [*7th edition]. Eldoret, Kenya: Moi University Press.)

Currently, the student population is slightly over 52,000. Of these, the university records state that 21 are visually impaired, 2 are hearing impaired, 19 are physically impaired, and there are 4 people with albinism. To cater to these learners, the institution indicated that the following resources were required for IE purposes: computer laboratory, laptops, wheelchairs, hearing aids, Perkins Braille machines, Braillo 200/600 embossers, and appropriate accommodation and transportation. The university has been successful in including LwDs in regular classes and some students with physical and visual impairment and albinism have graduated. The services of a Braille Officer to cater to the needs of learners with visual impairment in the regular lecture halls have also contributed to this success. However, a baseline survey revealed challenges that hindered the successful implementation of the procedure, as follows:

1. There were neither computer laboratories nor laptops assigned to LwDs and the hearing aids and wheelchairs were bought personally by the learners and not provided for by the institution.
2. The institution had no sign language interpreter.
3. There was only one Braille Officer to cater for 12 students, and his workload was to transcribe 10 unit exams, which required at least 360 hours. The Braille Officer was also tasked to handle the coordination of transport and accommodation for the students with disabilities. This situation was because of a lack of existing staff for the special needs section, and requests to this effect were futile, since the university management team was facing financial constraints.
4. Members of staff did not fully understand the issues of context and risks for the special needs unit.
5. The unit had stipulated only one quality objective, which was more of a requirement than an objective, and had no clear plan on how to achieve this.
6. LwDs had not been inducted with survival life skills within the institution during orientation.
7. There was no channel for consultative and counselling support for students with disabilities.
8. Although there was clear communication for coordination between the special needs unit and the transportation sector, the implementation of transportation for students with physical and visual disabilities within the university was problematic.
9. Moreover, there was no documentation regarding the enrolment of learners with other forms of disabilities like autism, Down syndrome, cerebral palsy, epilepsy, intellectual disabilities, emotional and behavioural disorders, LDs, and speech and language disorders, among others.

In Kenya, at the post-secondary level, as illustrated with a baseline survey of a major university in the country, the successful implementation of IE is still a major hurdle to overcome. Basing on the findings, there are recurring themes within the broad areas of access, retention, and transition that represent major barriers to the implementation of IE across the three levels of education. Though much of the research on this topic focuses on IE at primary and secondary levels, the findings from the case study have further supported the concerns regarding standards of implementation of IE in Kenya. Research at the pre-primary school level would also be of benefit to this field of inquiry, to improve understanding vis-à-vis practice, regarding the implementation, monitoring, and evaluation of IE across the country. This is crucial because ECDE is critical in preparing children to enter and succeed in their academic pursuits as well as in enhancing their physical, emotional, and social development (NGEC, 2016).

Conclusion

This chapter sought to respond to three research questions. With regard to the efforts made to facilitate education for LwDs, the government of Kenya took various measures between the early 1940s and 2000s. These measures included education for LwDs through religious institutions, especially in churches in the 1940s. Additionally, after independence in 1963, the government of Kenya progressively engaged notable commissions, committees, and task forces to improve education for these learners. In the 1970s education for LwDs was offered solely in special schools. In the 2000s the MoE introduced FPE, undertaking several measures to facilitate access to education for LwDs, including drafting several policies and passing acts to help this cause. Other crucial frameworks are the Constitution of Kenya 2010 and Kenya Vision 2030, which are committed to ensuring that issues directly affecting PwDs are adequately addressed in policies, legal frameworks, programmes, and projects. It is clear that since the early 1940s, the Kenyan government has been striving to provide equal access to education for all learners, including those with disabilities.

The second question explored the extent to which Kenya has monitored the strides towards implementation of the Education Article; it was found that between 2011 and 2017, several agencies, including the KNCHR, the NGEC, and DPOs, and other members of civil society drive the implementation. In spite of these, there is scanty information about monitoring and evaluation which culminated in the final research question of this chapter on the barriers and challenges that hinder the successful implementation of the Education Article of the CRPD in Kenya.

At both institutional and national levels, though intertwined, the barriers can be summarized in seven emergent themes: (a) poor attitudes, marginalization, and stigma; (b) poverty and limited access to educational spaces; (c) inadequate funding, assistive devices, and services; (d) gender and regional disparity; (e) inaccurate data, late identification, and low enrolment; (f) unsuitable curriculum and rigid assessment; (g) laxity in implementation of (ambiguous) policies. These challenges to IE in Kenya strongly suggest the need for a coordinated and multipronged action plan to restructure government and NGOs and community, stakeholder, and school strategies to effectively overcome these barriers. Additionally, the laxity of implementation of laws and ambiguous policies are in need of a redress. When implemented, the action plan will stimulate requisite policy reforms, system alignments, and funding strategies. The key recommendations and strategies are as follows:

1. The government should maintain data on PwDs up to the lowest administrative unit (village) to inform policy and planning. This will facilitate individualized education plans for determining the degree and types of adaptations needed in evaluating learners' progress and the demand for IE.
2. The government should provide an adequate budgetary allocation for IE with clear guidelines on the use of funds and to ensure an effective regular audit of the same.
3. Research on policy and practice at the micro-level (schools and communities), meso-level (educational systems and external agency support services), and macro-level (national and international policy and national legislation).
4. Establish a community philosophy and vision that all children can belong to and learn leadership skills from. This can be done through sensitization and mobilization of grassroots leadership (including chiefs) to ensure free compulsory education is a reality for all children. This will encourage the presentation and enrolment of all children regardless of disability.

5. Develop collaboration to support cooperative learning and the changing roles of all staff in an array of services like social services and the realms of physical and mental healthcare.
6. Initiate a partnership with parents to encourage them to present all children, including those with disabilities, for school admission, providing locally available resources for the LwDs to maximize their learning potential and increase overall parental participation in the education of these learners.
7. Create accessible and flexible learning environments in terms of pacing, timing, technology, and location. For instance, the government should establish more boarding schools that accommodate CwDs, especially for pastoralist communities.
8. The strategies established for the implementation of Article 24 of the Convention should be research-based and adopt best-practice methods.
9. An increase in curriculum organization and pedagogical perspectives for LwDs, particularly in the CBC, such as attention to pedagogy and curriculum adaptation, and development of standardized tests.
10. Transforming special schools into resource centres, as they typically provide training and courses for teachers and other professionals. This includes taking steps to ensure obligatory training for all teachers (beyond special education teachers) on how to teach CwDs and to include IE as an integral part of core teacher training curricula in universities. This will ensure that the values and principles of IE are instilled at the outset of teacher training and teaching careers. The government should increase the number of education assessment and resource centres (EARCs) and allocate adequate funds to them.
11. Develop and disseminate materials and methods that support mainstream schools and parents. Here, the government should provide adapted textbooks (and other teaching aids) for use by LwDs to counter the perceived discrimination when textbooks are availed to regular pupils.
12. Provide short-term or part-time help for individual learners to support them entering the labour market. The government can contribute to this by using affirmative action to improve transition rates to secondary schools

(and beyond) for LwDs. It can also provide vocational centres with more technical teachers to offer vocational skills to these learners when they cannot transit to higher levels of education.

13. Monitor the effectiveness of the implementation and sustainability of the CRPD in the research locale through:
    i) developing a country-/region-centred plan;
    ii) implementing inclusion reports;
    iii) developing an inclusive network for schools throughout Kenya.
14. Restructure the schools to offer IE and carry out research that will support the government to formulate inclusive standardized strategies to serve as indicators of knowledge, skills, and dispositions. The strategies will provide the impetus for a radical transformation of school programmes and systems, leading to the effective implementation of IE. Several strategies to involve the MoE in curriculum development and policy change include:
    i) involving the MoE staff in direct activities such as curriculum development and teacher training in the implementation of IE for LwDs;
    ii) providing policymakers and teachers with exposure to successful programmes and involving them in dialogue with both national and international professionals and experts on IE;
    iii) increasing the role of policymakers in IE programmes to enhance ownership in facilitating the implementation of inclusive programmes and strategies in the long run.

Above all, it is imperative for Kenya to have a clear definition of IE and to set smart objectives for the country to be able to comply with Article 24 of the CRPD. Moreover, IE 'cannot operate without acceptance, understanding and cooperation by community members and parents' (Ohba and Malenya, 2020: 15). Active inclusion of stakeholders at grassroots levels must be included in leadership and decision-making processes regarding the implementation of the Convention as captured by the MoE, which states that '[p]artners and/ or stakeholders need to be guided by a comprehensive policy framework to ensure effective coordination and implementation of special needs education programmes' (RoK, 2009: 46). Students, parents, teachers, administrators, and government officials need to collaborate within their local spaces to identify the strengths and barriers of their local educational systems. However, Randiki (2002) argues that bringing all these concerned parties together to implement IE in Kenya is a mammoth hurdle. Perhaps a comprehensive and stringent action plan to provide for the adoption of best practices and extraction of barriers and challenges for effective IE and inclusive communities at large is a worthwhile step in the right direction. This can be facilitated by increased governmental funding towards the successful implementation of Article 24 of the CRPD. However, it is crucial to set realistic and applicable strategies that can also be monitored within Kenya's local spaces of practice.

Bibliography

Baart, J., and Maarse, A. 2017. *I am EmployAble: Creating Access to Technical and Vocational Education for Young People with Disabilities*. Vienna: Light for the World.

Baboo, N. 2011. 'The Lives of Children with Disabilities in Africa: A Glimpse into a Hidden World' <https://www.africanchildforum.org/index.php/en/component/com_sobipro/Itemid,158/pid,2/sid,146/> [accessed 10 April 2021].

Bell, L., and Stevenson, S. 2015. 'Towards an Analysis of the Policies That Shape Public Education: Setting the Context for School Leadership', *Management in Education* 29(4):146–50.

Bii, C., and Taylor, L. 2013. *Inclusive Education in Kenya Assessment Report – Kenya/Somalia Program*. Handicap International (now known as Humanity and Inclusion).

Bunning K., Gona, J.K., Newton, C.R., and Hartley, S. 2017. 'The Perception of Disability by Community Groups: Stories of Local Understanding, Beliefs and Challenges in a Rural Part of Kenya', *PLoS ONE* 12(8): e0182214.

Carew, M. T., Deluca, M., Groce, N., and Kett, M. 2019. 'The Impact of an Inclusive Education Intervention on Teacher Preparedness to Educate Children with Disabilities within the Lakes Region of Kenya', *International Journal of Inclusive Education* 23(3): 229–44.

Department of Education (DoE). 2012. *A Policy Framework for Education – Aligning Education and Training to the Constitution of Kenya (2010) and Kenya Vision 2030 and Beyond*. Nairobi: Republic of Kenya.

Ireri, B.R., King'endo, M., Wangila, E., and Thuranira, S. 2020. 'Policy Strategies for Effective Implementation of Inclusive Education in

Kenya', *International Journal of Educational Administration and Policy Studies* 12(1): 28–42.

Kabare, K. 2018. *Social Protection and Disability in Kenya*. Development Pathways.

Kenya Institute of Special Education (KISE). 2018. *National Survey on Children with Disabilities and Special Needs in Education*. KISE.

Kenya National Commission on Human Rights (KNCHR). 2014. *From Norm to Practice: A Status Report on the Implementation of Rights of Persons with Disabilities in Kenya*. Nairobi: KNCHR <https://www.knchr.org/Portals/0/EcosocReports/From%20Norm%20to%20Practice_Status%20Report%20on%20the%20Implementation%20of%20the%20Rights%20of%20PWDs%20in%20Kenya.pdf?ver=2018-06-06-182335-003> [accessed 15 March 2022].

Kenya National Commission on Human Rights (KNCHR). 2016. *Compendium on Submissions to CRPD 2016: Compendium on Convention on the Rights of Persons with Disabilities* <https://www.globaldisabilityrightsnow.org/sites/default/files/related-files/260/Compendium%20on%20Submissions%20to%20CRPD_Vol%201.pdf> [accessed 15 April 2021].

Kiru, W.E. 2018. 'Special Education in Kenya: Intervention in School and Clinic', *Hammill Institute on Disabilities* 1–8 <https://journals.sagepub.com/doi/pdf/10.1177/1053451218767919> [accessed 10 April 2021].

Koech, D.K. 1999. *Commission of Inquiry into the Education System of Kenya*. Nairobi: Republic of Kenya.

Male, C., and Wodon, Q. 2017. 'The Price of Exclusion: Disability and Education. Disability Gaps in Educational Attainment and Literacy', *Global Partnership for Education and The World Bank* <https://www.edu-links.org/sites/default/files/media/file/Disability_gaps_in_educational_attainment_and_literacy.pdf> [accessed 12 April 2021].

Ministry of Education, Science, and Technology (MoE). 2005. *ICTs in Education Option Paper*. Nairobi: Ministry of Education, Science, and Technology.

Moodley, S. 2002. *Inclusive Education: Challenges for Distance Learning Policy and Practice*. Sydney: Technikon.

Moi University. 2015. *Moi University Procedures: The Procedure for Student Support – Special Needs Services*. Eldoret, Kenya: Moi University Press.

Moyi, P. 2017. 'School Participation for Children with Disabilities in Kenya', *Research in Comparative and International Education* 12(4): 497–511.

Mueke, R. 2014. *A Baseline Study on Areas of Successes and Barriers in Skills Development and Employment of Graduates with Disabilities*. ADDA Kenya and EmployAble Project Partners.

Mutisya, C.M.S. 2010. 'Factors Influencing Inclusion of Learners with Special Needs in Regular Primary Schools in Rachuonyo District'. A Thesis Submitted for the Degree of Master in Education (Special Needs Education) in the School of Education, Kenyatta University.

Mwangi, L. 2013. 'Special Needs Education (SNE) in Kenyan Public Primary Schools: Exploring Government Policy and Teachers' Understandings.' PhD thesis, Brunel University, London.

Mwangi, E.M., and Aluko, J. 2014. 'Challenges Facing Implementation of Inclusive Education in Public Primary Schools in Nyeri Town, Nyeri County, Kenya', *Journal of Education and Practice* 5(16): 118–25 <https://www.iiste.org/Journals/index.php/JEP/article/viewFile/13081/13662> [accessed 10 March 2022].

National Gender and Equality Commission (NGEC). 2016. *Access to Basic Education by Children with Disability in Kenya.* Ministry of Education, Higher Education, Science and Technology.

Ngugi, M. 2000. *Distance Learning: Introduction to Inclusive Education.* Nairobi: Kenya.

Njoroge, M.N.N. 1991. 'Factors Influencing Initiation of Successful Mainstreaming of Visually Handicapped Students in Kenya'. Unpublished PhD dissertation, University of Texas, Austin.

Ohba, A., and Malenya, F.L. 2020. 'Addressing Inclusive Education for Learners with Disabilities in the Integrated Education System: The Dilemma of Public Primary Schools in Kenya', *Compare: A Journal of Comparative and International Education* 52: 19–36.

Opini, B. 2009. 'Women Students with Disabilities in Kenyan University Education: Experiences, Challenges and Coping Strategies'. Unpublished doctoral dissertation, University of Toronto, Toronto.

Owino, E. 2020. *Status of Disability in Kenya – Statistics from the 2019 Census.* Development Initiatives.

Oyeng', S., and Kajilwa, G. 2020. 'Dilemma of Special Schools over Covid-19 Measures', 9 October 2020. *The Standard*, Nairobi.

Randiki, F. 2002. *Historical Development of Special Needs Education.* Nairobi: KISE.

Republic of Kenya (RoK). 1964. *Ominde Report.* Nairobi: Government Printers.

Republic of Kenya (RoK). 1976. *Gachathi Report.* Nairobi: Government Printers.

Republic of Kenya (RoK). 1988. *Kamunge Report.* Nairobi: Government Printers.

Republic of Kenya. (RoK). 2003. *Persons with Disabilities Act, 2003.* Nairobi: Government Printers <http://www.ilo.int/dyn/natlex/natlex4.detail?p_lang=en&p_isn=69444> [accessed 11 March 2022].

Republic of Kenya (RoK). 2005. *The Sessional Paper No1 of 2005.* Nairobi: Government Printers <https://academia-ke.org/library/download/mest-sessional-paper-no-1-of-2005-on-a-policy-framework-for-education-training-and-research/> [accessed 12 November 2020].

Republic of Kenya (RoK). 2008. *Kenya National Survey for PwDs.* Nairobi: Government Printers <https://www.afri-can.org/CBR%20Information/KNSPWD%20Prelim%20Report%20-%20Revised.pdf> [accessed 12 October 2020].

Republic of Kenya (RoK). 2009. *National Special Education Policy Framework.* Nairobi: Government Printers.

Republic of Kenya (RoK). 2010. *The Kenya Constitution, 2010.* Kenya Law Reports.

Republic of Kenya (RoK). 2013. *The Basic Education Act.* Nairobi: Government Printers.

Republic of Kenya (RoK). 2016a. *National Plan of Action: On Implementation of Recommendations Made by the Committee on the Rights of PwDs in Relation to the Initial Report of the Republic of Kenya, September 2015–June 2022.* Nairobi: Government Printers.

Republic of Kenya. 2016b. *SNE Policy Review Data Collection Report.* Nairobi: Government Printers.

Republic of Kenya (RoK). 2018. *Sector Policy for Learners and Trainees with Disabilities.* Nairobi: Government Printers.

Rohwerder, B. 2020. 'Kenya Situational Analysis. Disability Inclusive Development'. June 2020 update <https://opendocs.ids.ac.uk/opendocs/bitstream/handle/20.500.12413/15508/DID%20Kenya%20SITAN_June%202020.pdf?sequence=1> [accessed 10 April 2021].

Sightsavers. 2018. *An Analysis of the Status of Persons with Disability in Kenya.* Nairobi: Sightsavers Kenya.

United Nations Educational, Scientific and Cultural Organization (UNESCO). 1994. *The Salamanca Statement and Framework for Special Needs Education.* Paris: UNESCO.

United Nations Educational, Scientific and Cultural Organization (UNESCO). 2003. *Overcoming Exclusion through Inclusive Approaches in Education: A Challenge and a Vision.* Paris: UNESCO.

UNESCO. 2010. *Reaching the Marginalized: Education for All Global Monitoring Report.* Paris: UNESCO.

Van Reusen, A.K., Shoho, A.R., and Barker, K.S. 2001. 'High School Teacher Attitudes toward Inclusion', *The High School Journal 84(2)*: 7–20.

Wodon, Q., Male, C., Montenegro, C., and Nayihouba, A. 2018. *The Price of Exclusion:*

Disability and Education. 'The Challenge of Inclusive Education in Sub-Saharan Africa'. World Bank (WB) and USAID <http://documents1.worldbank.org/curated/en/171921543522923182/pdf/132586-WP-P168381-PUBLIC-WorldBank-SSAInclusive-Disability-v6-Web.pdf> [accessed 10 April 2021].

World Bank (WB) and International Monetary Fund (IMF). 2012. *Global Monitoring Report 2012* <https://elibrary.worldbank.org/doi/abs/10.1596/978-0-8213-9451-9> [accessed 12 November 2020].

World Health Organization (WHO). 2006. *International Classification of Functioning, Disability and Health*. Geneva: WHO.

Zandy, J. 2019. 'Universal Declaration of Human Rights', *Radical Teacher* 113: 56–57 <https://doi.org/10.5195/rt.2019.591>.

5

A Disabled Disability Movement: The Paradox of Participation in Uganda

HERBERT MUYINDA & SUSAN REYNOLDS WHYTE

Introduction

> When the disability movement does not move to disability, the disability moves to the disability movement, and this is what happened in Uganda – disability moved to the disability movement, and it is now disabled. In certain aspects, this disability movement is too deformed to be reformed ... (Disability representative, local council in Kampala)

This harsh assessment of the disability movement in Uganda extends the definition of disability from the functional abilities of individuals in their social environment to those of groups and an entire movement. The local council representative was no doubt speaking metaphorically, but his message is clear. The disability movement, with its commitment to activism, advocacy, and the realization of rights, is not functioning in a way that allows meaningful participation and change. As with any disability, this one must be understood in terms of socio-economic and political conditions that hinder ability.

The United Nations (UN) Convention on the Rights of Persons with Disabilities (CRPD) aims to apply the principle of non-discrimination to every human right in every context of a human being's existence. It is legally binding, and therefore its articles should pave the way to future political developments in the disability sector (Ferraina, 2012; Harpur, 2012). Uganda ratified the CRPD and its Optional Protocol on 25 September 2008 without reservations. In so doing, Uganda committed itself to accord the same rights to persons with disabilities (PwDs) as to all other citizens (National Union of Disabled Persons of Uganda [NUDIPU], 2017). But it is one thing to have rights in principle.

It is another to implement them in a way that is inclusive and participatory.

In this chapter, we address the paradox of participation: Uganda has a progressive policy of representation for PwDs, but political organization and participation have not yielded real improvement in the lives of most people and families with disabilities. We question the policies that are thought to be positive but that in practice are disabling by 'commission' or 'omission'.

Drawing on accounts by disability leaders, political representatives, bureaucrats, and professionals, disabled people themselves, and a close look at the disability movement in Uganda over more than ten years (2005 to 2019), this chapter elucidates the processes of implementing disability policy agendas in one exemplary African country. We examine the conditions, discourses, and practices, and the paradoxical outcomes that affect PwDs. We consider the (dis)connection between PwDs and processes of mobilization and organization, and how these influence the abilities and possibilities of PwDs, particularly in low-income settings. Our focus is on the disability movement itself.

The right to political participation and disability organization is enshrined in the CRPD Article 29 on Participation in Political and Public life, part (b), which obligates the State:

> To promote actively an environment in which persons with disabilities can effectively and fully participate in the conduct of public affairs, without discrimination and on an equal basis with others, and encourage their participation in public affairs, including: (i) Participation in non-governmental organizations and associations concerned with the public and political life of the country, and in the activities and administration of political parties; (ii) Forming and joining organizations of persons with disabilities to represent persons with disabilities at international, national, regional and local levels.

This right is advanced on the assumption that such organizations and participation would advance the cause of PwDs in many areas of life, indeed that they would promote all of the other rights set out in the CRPD (Mannan, MacLachlan, and McVeigh, 2012; Lang *et al.*, 2011; Malhotra, 2008; Russell, 2002; Young and Quibell, 2000). They should pursue a vision such as that of the NUDIPU: 'A Just and Fair Society Where Persons with Disabilities Live Prosperous and Dignified Lives'. Researchers and activists believe that Disabled Peoples Organizations (DPOs) have a key role to play:

> I would argue that we need to move beyond mere legal instruments, or the concept of legal empowerment, to achieve justice and rights for disabled persons in the majority world. One possibility would be to increase the capacity of DPOs to wage the political fight for disability rights and to take that fight to rural areas. Their actions could include, among other things, publicizing the CRPD and national disability legislation and supporting individuals at the grassroots level (Grischow, 2015: 111).

In Uganda and the world over, the mission of DPOs is to advance the civil and human rights of persons with disabilities (PwDs) through legal advocacy, training, education, and public policy and legislative development (NUDIPU, 2017; UN, 2006). Yet the capacity of the DPOs is called into question, even by some of their own members. One NUDIPU official cast doubt on the ability of the organization to help realize the rights to universal infrastructure, communication, assistive technology (AT), education, livelihood, and respect that are enshrined in the CRPD:

> Despite the political goodwill and our protracted efforts to fight for disability rights, there is hardly any evidence that those policies have had direct impact on facilitating access to the services needed, or in providing either financial or other assistance to households facing difficulties due to disability of their members. Our experiences as PWDs are characterized by infrastructure without disability inclusive designs, service delivery devoid of sign language, scarcity of assistive technologies, non-attendance and drop out of school by children, and increased poverty. Communities continue to be ignorant of the disability rights particularly relating to local beliefs and superstitions. Many PWDs are locked up in houses, tied on trees, denied shelter and food among other essential needs. This is because the disability movement here operates in perpetual scarcity, unending uncertainty – in other words [it is] functionally disabled (NUDIPU official when asked about the role of the disability movement in Uganda).

We argue that two conditions in Uganda are disabling for the disability movement and inhibit its capacity to help translate the rights of the CRPD into realities. One is what we term 'disabolitics': disability politics that are characterized by patronage, entanglement with national political parties, donor dependence, and elitism. The other is the condition of perpetual scarcity that affects very many Ugandans and makes it difficult for most people in the country, especially those with disabilities, to live 'Prosperous and Dignified Lives'.

The Disability Movement in Uganda

The disability movement in Uganda was well-established long before Uganda ratified the CRPD in 2008. After preliminary developments which were cut short by fifteen years of political unrest, the NUDIPU was formed in November 1987. As an indigenous umbrella non-governmental organization (NGO), it works in collaboration with the government, other NGOs, and the general public. Thus, the disability movement involves all the groups, social institutions, government departments, donors, and local and international organizations that are engaged in disability work. It is those socio-political networks and mechanisms that disabled people in Uganda engage with to ensure that the objectives of the intended policies are delivered.

After the National Resistance Movement (NRM) government took power in 1986, a new Constitution was adopted in 1995 that had specific provisions on disability. Article 35 specifies that PwDs have a right to respect and human dignity and that the State and society shall take appropriate measures to ensure that they realize their full mental and physical potential. The Constitution stipulates that a person shall not be discriminated against on grounds of disability –nor on other grounds such as race, sex, or religion (Government of Uganda, 1995). Against the framework of this Constitution, an impressive list of laws was adopted in favour of PwDs (see Abimanyi-Ochom and Mannan, 2014). The most important of them required political representation: five positions were reserved in parliament through the Parliamentary Elections Statute of 1996, and two seats (one male and one female) were earmarked on local councils at every level from village to district by the 1997 Local Government Act. Uganda's 47,000 representatives with disabilities represent one of the largest groups of politicians with disabilities in the world (NUDIPU, 2017). Thus, the disability movement is fed by, and feeds into, the political system.

These socio-political structures are initiated to facilitate the participation, decision-making, and development of disabled persons. However, the disability policies were designed with an assumption that they are appropriate for PwDs. Moreover, their implementation has often failed: 'Although Uganda has excelled in developing a comprehensive body of legislation that upholds disability rights particularly through affirmative action, many of these have not been implemented' (Abimanyi-Ochom and Mannan, 2014). When a policy is enacted, the policy should be materialized – and the materiality of the policy matters. The policy also lives its life, which means that it can change or diminish; a policy missing its targeted outcomes turns out to be paradoxical.

Patronage and Disabolitics

The adoption of disability-supportive legislation and the inclusion of disabled people as councillors and parliamentarians are positive outcomes of the politics of disability. We adopt the term 'disabolitics' to call attention to the fact that there are also negative effects of the particular ways in which disability and politics are entangled in Uganda – and in some other African countries as well. Disability politics can disable movement in some ways. In Uganda, this happens through an overly close association with political parties, through patronage, and through the elitism and corruption that characterize many facets of Ugandan political life.

According to the 2014 National Housing and Population Census, people with disabilities constituted nearly 14% of Uganda's total population of about thirty-five million people (Ugandan Bureau of Statistics [UBOS], 2014). In the view of politicians, this is support worth pursuing. The relation between the NRM (the ruling party) and the NUDIPU has been close since the establishment of the NUDIPU. Since 1997, when it became mandatory to include PwDs on local councils, the elections for these seats have been organized through the NUDIPU. For almost two decades of NRM rule, Uganda had a non-party system, or in effect a one-party system. Representatives of PwDs were automatically linked to the NRM. After the 2005 referendum that returned Uganda to a multiparty system, the NRM registered as a political party (the NRM Organization – NRMO) and instituted a party league for PwDs at all levels – from village to National Executive Committee – with two PwDs (a male and a female) at every level. Other political parties followed suit, including Forum for Democratic Change, Alliance for National Transformation, and other opposition parties. Yet the disability movement in Uganda as a whole is still perceived as an NRM structure, and as a constituency, disabled people are looked at as people who support the ruling party. Beckmann (2018: 171–2), writing about the history of deaf people during and after the Lord's Resistance Army war in Northern Uganda, makes the same point about the co-option of the disability movement by the NRM.

Benefits from having a voice with the ruling party notwithstanding, the disability movement suffers the costs of being compromised and having to conceal the weaknesses of the State, and being used to silence those who might wish to criticize them loudly. PwDs are often not free to comment on disability programmes that did not do well, lest they would be branded unappreciative and saboteurs of government programmes. A number of disability-related issues are political in nature, yet disabled people are not wholly free to complain about their conditions, and are even reluctant to discuss this aspect of not being able to complain:

> So many things go wrong, and we see them. Government officials, councillors, and other leaders often give excuses that are clearly inappropriate, and when we complain, some powerful people above keep silent – a clear message to us to conceal all that information. Sometimes they allow you to shout and they just ignore. This is because some of these local leaders are campaign managers for the big people who do not want to antagonize their political bases – it is all politics (Local council representative).

The political leaders use their official positions to fulfil their political obligations, without necessarily addressing the disability issues. This makes it difficult to effectively push disability programmes and to implement policies at different levels. Thus, the disability movement activities are more to do with protecting the political image of the government in power – being seen to be doing something – and less to do with solving the real problems of the disabled people. This pattern may not be unique to Uganda. De Silva (forthcoming) analyses the Ethiopian government's embrace of high-tech rehabilitative technology as a political move to present the State as modern and developmental. A person using a prosthesis is a 'model citizen', even though this technology is not particularly relevant for many persons with mobility disabilities.

In some cases, disability is used as a political instrument by certain individuals, groups, and organizations in their struggle to legitimize their own presence and representation as players in disability activities. During political campaigns, for instance, candidates and some organizations mobilize disabled people into groups as part of a process of organizing them to improve their lives. However, some informants complained about 'groupism', which does not necessarily help them improve their conditions, and after getting the votes, the politicians forget about the groups until the next campaign period. Politicians representing PwDs as well as 'able-bodied' politicians curry support by supplying mobility devices. In one of our previous studies, we heard how the sitting Minister of Agriculture provided a tricycle for a woman he saw marching on her knees in a World Food Day parade. Councillors campaigned for disability seats on the basis of how many devices they were able to give (Whyte and Muyinda, 2007: 297). The same pattern of supplying assistive devices or other material benefits in order to gain political favour is reported from Nigeria (Nwokorie and Devlieger, 2019). Where some assistance is extended, there is usually no follow-up to monitor progress and provide support.

The leadership is perceived to be out of touch with ordinary disabled people. Those who are chosen as representatives of PwDs receive opportunities to participate in training, often funded by donors, which takes them to urban areas and sometimes even to other countries. In addition to some financial benefits, they gain 'exposure' to disability activists and to international disability organizations. They learn advocacy skills and become more effective at lobbying for rights and influencing legislation. But such exposure also distances them from the everyday concerns of most PwDs. A gap opens between the 'disability elites' and people at the grassroots (Beckmann, 2018: 178).

Leadership is about problem-solving, and it needs much knowledge and concentrated detail about the targeted and concerned people. For a disability movement, there is need to effectively connect with the disabled persons themselves, the local populations. But the disability leadership appears alienated and isolated from the disabled people, and the realities of the PwDs' lives are inadequately appreciated. When the local PwDs try to challenge any decisions, the leadership just refers to the 'powers from above', which are the State institutions. This 'power from above' nurtures a mind of entitlement, with some of the disability leaders acting with impunity. These leaders conform facts about disability to their political opinions, as opposed to shaping their opinions and biases based on facts about the PwDs in their jurisdiction. The challenges of PwDs, their suffering and fears, are reported through sanitized language to portray a positive image to people in power but leaving the real challenges unattended to. 'That's why disability problems in schools, hospitals, on the roads ... still persist' (Official of Ministry of Gender, Labour, and Social Development).

The disability elites are more oriented to their political patrons than to their constituents. Representation is often manipulated by those in power to ensure that their positions sail through at various levels, regardless of the interests of the disabled persons (Ssengooba *et al.*, 2012; Harpur, 2012). The disability leadership is shaped by the demands of political representation inherent in the disabolitical patronage system. This disabolitics rests on a little-understood form of political reciprocity that links the patrons with their clients along the vertical socio-economic and political channels needed to deal with disability issues.

In the disabolitical patronage setup, the social, economic, and political fulfilment of the obligations of this disability movement hardly has anything to do with the disabled people. The positions of the patrons are perceived in terms of their ability to provide for their own (patronage) obligations – that is, to champion their own interests. The activities of Uganda's disability movement are thus largely conditioned by the need to satisfy the patronizing forces. Politicians use the disability movements for their own patronizing purposes. In this case, the disability leadership is not seen primarily as an independent advocate for disability, but as a link to the patronizing chain that connects the patrons with the phenomenon of disability. At the same time, PwDs at a local level seem to lack the skills necessary to hold their leadership accountable; this is due not only to a lack of education, but also to the uncertainty of what would come next, and fear of losing the little achieved.

The disability leader in one of the divisions[1] in Kampala attributed the dysfunction of the disability movement in Uganda to the differences in interests of the different actors:

[1] The city of Kampala is administratively divided into five divisions, each headed by a mayor. The whole city is in turn headed by the lord mayor.

> The disability movement creates different shades of disabled people: the very powerful and comfortable – the members of parliament, the district councillors, the cabinet ministers; the powerful but uncomfortable with the direction the disability movement is taking – NGOs and DPOs, academicians, the bureaucrats and professionals who are involuntary recruits in the disability movement; and the majority of the people who are neither powerful nor comfortable. What happens is that the very powerful and comfortable, and the powerless but comfortable through corruption, hoodwink the majority who are not powerful and not comfortable to vote 'properly', and after elections, it is over. Moreover, the disabled people are perceived as a 'small group of people' with negligible political impact, which leads to lack of political sensitivity to their conditions. This is translated into interventions that are ad hoc and quite far from addressing real disability problems.

These political, social, and economic inequities are beneficial neither to members of the disability movement nor to the leaders who intend to gain from them by serving their personal interests, because the negative outcomes that arise from such disconnections disadvantage the disabled community as a whole. This has been done through exploitation of the vulnerability of different categories of PwDs – women, youth, and local disability leaders – to promote the interests of the politicians. They give donations to individuals and particular groups instead of implementing the CRPD and the national policies for the benefit of all the disabled people.

Perpetual Scarcity

It is important to place the disability movement and the CRPD in the wider context of Ugandan development. Uganda is a predominantly agricultural country; although the rate of urbanization is increasing, about 80% of people live in rural areas with agriculture as a primary occupation. Unemployment is very high, if employment means having a monthly wage. Even well-educated people must participate in the informal economy of small business and trade. The country is poor, with insufficient tax revenue and dependence on loans and foreign investment for infrastructure development. Corruption is rampant in both the public and private sector. In particular, health and welfare are highly donor-dependent.

The Uganda National Population and Housing Census of 2014 (UBOS, 2016) estimates a disability prevalence rate of 13.6% among the population aged five years and above. The census estimates that the most prevalent forms of disability are: difficulty seeing (6.5% of the population); difficulty remembering (5.4%); difficulty walking (4.5%); and difficulty hearing (3.1%) (UBOS, 2014). In Northern Uganda, where the war with the Lord's Resistance Army continued for two decades, many have acquired conflict-related impairments (Muyinda, 2013), as have the people from South Sudan and the Democratic Republic of Congo who live as refugees in Uganda (Schuler, 2018). While older people constitute a small proportion of the population, many of them live with progressively worsening disabilities (Bavuma *et al.*, 2017). The category of PwDs encompasses a wide variety of problems and socio-economic situations. Adequate interventions would need to be tailored to different needs. Yet very many people feel that their actual needs are ignored (Muyinda and Whyte, 2011).

One of the main problems is that disability is a priority area for government only at a policy level. Disability has suffered serious inadequacies as far as government funding is concerned. Planners have pointed out that a lack of adequate resources to deal with the persistent and seemingly overwhelming problems of HIV/AIDS, in addition to entrenched poverty, makes disability seem less urgent. Apart from the national Disability Day celebrations, hardly anything else is funded, contrary to the government policy and the CRPD. The disability movement must rely on external donors: the NUDIPU website lists twelve 'partners' and notes that there are also others supporting activities for disability. A similar situation has been reported in other countries in sub-Saharan Africa (Hussey, MacLachlan, and Mji, 2016; Opini, 2010; Oduro, 2009; Nepveux, 2006).

The participation of DPOs in the formulation of poverty reduction and development policies of recent decades has been limited, despite good intentions. They did not have the economic resources to send representatives to consultative meetings, nor did they have adequate familiarity with the process of advocacy and policymaking. Nor, indeed, did the government ministries and donors supporting these policies and programmes appreciate the need to incorporate DPOs in a substantive way. So the interests of PwDs were not well integrated into policies of social protection and poverty eradication (Wazakili *et al.*, 2011).

In some instances, the government rhetoric of supporting disability through favourable policies makes potential donors to disability activities divert to other sectors because of the impression that the government is doing enough for disabled people. For instance, many micro-finance organizations in Northern Uganda did not lend money to disabled people because they thought that the Northern Uganda Social Action Fund had catered for PwDs. The donors also thought that the disabled people would not repay the loans, and some felt that disability rehabilitation was not a 'good investment': an indication of the weak impact of advocacy.

Some service delivery organizations perceived disabled people as incapable of making their own decisions and taking control of their lives; they were viewed as objects of pity and charity. Some organizations made 'contributions' that they knew very well would be inconsequential to the lives of the targeted disabled people, but went ahead with them because they perceived the disabled as desperate people who would take anything that was given to them. Some organizations provided what they called 'disability-appropriate technologies', which included agricultural implements and machine repair tools. However, the technologies were not different from the usual and were in many ways incompatible with the disabled people's conditions. Members of the Gulu Landmine Survivors Association were given ox-ploughs, hoes, and manual milling machines that required one to stand for long periods, although many of them were amputees. The disability leadership accepted the technologies, reasoning that inappropriate technologies were better than nothing.

There were hardly any indications of efforts to improve the life conditions of disabled people, particularly in the rural areas. The reason was usually 'lack of funds'. Most local authorities were waiting for plans and resources to be handed down from above (that is, from the leadership of the national disability movement) for them to implement. This undermined even the simple local measures that would not necessarily require high-level directives and large resources but would make a significant improvement in disabled peoples' lives. For instance, local government by-laws could be used to waive some taxes to create gazetted areas for disabled people to initiate small businesses so that they could stop begging. They could also be used to mandate special facilities such as wide doors, verandas, modified toilet and latrine facilities, ramps alongside steps, and other changes to accommodate the needs of the PwDs.

The understanding of PwDs was that the disability movement could not achieve everything, but they expected it to deliver what they considered to be the basics in the areas of accessibility, AT, education, and livelihood. In other words, they believed the movement should mobilize for the realization of the rights enshrined in the various articles of the CRPD.

The disability organizations were expected to deliver on inclusive architectural designs and access to water sources, public places, buildings, and other infrastructural facilities. Access to water was one of the basic needs in life that PwDs felt should never be overlooked by the disability leaders. However, the water supply system continues to marginalize PwDs' access to and utilization of water resources. Long distances to water points are a big challenge in both rural and urban areas. Disability-friendly facilities at the water points, such as drawing or pumping devices, ramps, wide entry ways and handrails or supports, are lacking. PwDs attributed this lack of attention to these needs to the lack of focus of the disability movement. Further, public transport remains inaccessible because there are no special provisions, especially for the wheelchair users.

In rural areas, wheelchairs are difficult to use on narrow, uneven, dusty or muddy paths (Bavuma *et al.*, 2017). In urban areas, where they could be useful, there is a general lack of appropriate road designs and weak enforcement of traffic regulations. Luwangula and colleagues (n.d.) provide a detailed description of the barriers to getting around Kampala as a person with mobility disabilities. Potholes, obstructed sidewalks, dense traffic, and lack of safe street crossing points were just some of the challenges they documented. There are concerns regarding the quality of road infrastructure, vehicles, road safety, and their impact on the lives of PwDs. The WHO Global Status Report on Road Safety 2013 named Uganda among the countries with alarmingly high road accident rates (WHO 2013), and traffic dangers are well recognized (Fallon, 2014; Kamoga *et al.*, 2015).

Most disabled people in Uganda face fundamental access challenges. They lack adequate ATs, such as wheelchairs, crutches, and calipers. Without these, it is difficult for the disabled people to organize themselves, to attend meetings, and to advocate for their rights. This also makes it difficult for disabled people to follow up disability programmes. Apart from tax exemptions on importation of a few assistive devices such as modified cars, not much has been achieved in terms of access to disability technologies. Transport, communication, agriculture, and other technologies important in the day-to-day activities of PwDs are still being taxed heavily. Communication technologies, such as sign language translation and access to electronic media for the deaf, are insufficient (Murangira *et al.*, n.d.), despite Uganda's early recognition of signing as an official language.

The (in)accessibility of assistive and appropriate transport technologies greatly affects access to services, including education. Only about 9% of children with disabilities (CwDs) of school going age attend primary school and 6% attend secondary school (UNICEF, 2014). This is despite the efforts that have been made, mainly at primary level and university level. The Statistical Abstract 2016 indicated that of all children enrolled for primary education in Uganda, only 2% were CwDs and other special needs (UBOS, 2016), and little has been done at secondary level.

It was also pointed out that the approach being used by the government is not clear. Its policy is inclusive education (IE), where CwDs are supposed to be mainstreamed in ordinary schools under the universal primary education programme, which provides free schooling. However, schools for people with hearing and sight impairments require children to board, and they are not free. Consequently, very few PwDs attain tertiary education despite the affirmative action[2] in place to provide government scholarships for PwDs at public universities. The lack of schooling means that persons with disabilities in Uganda have high illiteracy rates (NUDIPU, 2018).

Livelihood is a major concern for PwDs as for everyone else. Article 27(1) of the CRPD provides that States Parties must recognize the right of PwDs to work. Yet the programmes such as Special Grants for PwDs, started in 2009/2010, which are meant to support PwDs have not been followed up and supported by the disability leaders and the government. The Social Assistance Grants for Empowerment (SAGE), is a pilot social cash transfer scheme under the Ugandan government's Expanding Social Protection programmes (Abimanyi-Ochom and Mannan, 2014). It was meant to provide support to both the elderly and families

[2] PwDs need only two principle passes to get a government scholarship, which differs from the competitive performance regime applied when allocating scholarships to the rest of the students.

made vulnerable by disability. While cash payments to the elderly continue in selected districts, the activities aimed at disability have been discontinued.

Perpetual scarcity is not only a condition of government, which claims inadequate resources for implementing disability-supportive policies and programmes. It also characterizes the lives of very many, perhaps most, individuals and families living with disability. They have 'life projects' of subsistence, housing, and schooling – everyday concerns that sometimes intersect with donor-supported disability projects or opportunities to receive allowances for being representatives in government or party organizations. Whyte (2020) shows how an interest in material benefits often overshadows that in rights and policies for poor rural people: her interlocutors in rural eastern Uganda were keenly aware of allowances and refreshments when they were called to attend meetings for PwDs. Projects that provided livestock or other income-generating activities were most highly valued, and there was suspicion and criticism that benefits meant for them were being diverted. Beckmann (2018: 161ff.) goes so far as to argue that the older donor-development focus on basic needs was more relevant to many poor rural PwDs than the current rights-based approach. They are more concerned about resources than rights.

Conclusion

The deleterious effects of disabolitics and perpetual scarcity in Uganda have handicapped a disability movement that is progressive and promising in many ways. Many laws and policies have been adopted of which the government can be justly proud. Yet implementation is weak and the promise of 'prosperous and dignified lives' rings hollow. The movement is highly dependent on donor funding and is oriented towards the international disability movement, with its emphasis on rights rather than the realities of resource-poor settings. On the national scene, the disability representatives are heavily influenced by their political patrons and less concerned with the actual needs of PwDs on the ground. Paradoxically, representation does not mean participation with and by those being represented.

Yet one could argue that the political structures and awareness for which the disability movement advocated, together with new technologies and scattered donor interventions, have created potentials that are being realized at places on the ground. Grassroots initiatives are often responses to immediate needs rather than demands for rights. Such practical efforts may take on political dimensions, but they start with concrete problems and the implementation of activities.

People with disabilities join together locally in small informal groups to pursue a common interest. An excellent example of this is in the border town of Busia, where mobility-impaired people engaged in cross-border transport with hand-crank tricycles (Whyte and Muyinda, 2007). They had a joint interest in negotiating with customs officials and organized themselves in a group that eventually joined the NUDIPU, but they started with efforts to earn a living, not with training on their rights as PwDs. Devlieger (2018) has made a more extensive study of a similar development in the cross-border trade between Kinshasa and Brazzaville.

When the war against the Lord's Resistance Army ended in Northern Uganda, much of the donor support for PwDs was phased out. Small groups, sometimes consisting of only two or three persons, formed around income-generating activities and, in one case, efforts to teach people how to use assistive devices (Muyinda 2020). In Kampala, deaf people use messaging on mobile phones and get-togethers after church services to communicate all kinds of information through what they call the DBC, the Deaf Broadcasting Corporation, with a playful nod to the BBC's services for hearing people (Murangira *et al.*, n.d.). Informal and often small, these groups and activities are not part of the organized and structured disability movement, though they may develop connections. They emerge in response to perpetual scarcity, and they avoid many of the dangers of disabolitics.

The CRPD and Uganda's national legislation cannot in themselves bring about changes, much as they provide an enabling framework. Focus must shift from rights to resources and from policies to implementation. This means that promotion of inclusive environments to foster participation of different categories of PwDs and deal with the challenges that emerge should be identified along the way and dealt with as activities are being carried out. This calls for the reorientation of the current institutions and systems towards this new direction. All institutions, including roadworks and infrastructural construction, tertiary institutions, schools, health facilities, and all service organizations should initiate mechanisms that capture PwDs' diverse needs as policies are being implemented, rather than identifying them at the end, which sometimes is too late. In this way, the rights enshrined in the CRPD might be realized in practice.

To reform the disability movement in Uganda in order to change the paradoxical presentations that currently characterize it, entails reflecting on the statement made by the disability representative of the local council in Kampala – and quoted earlier in this chapter – to now state that the disability movement should move to disability, before the disability moves to the disability movement.

Bibliography

Abimanyi-Ochom, J., and Mannan, H. 2014. 'Uganda's Disability Journey: Progress and Challenges', *African Journal of Disability* 3(1): 1–6.

Bavuma, N.-R., Kyaddondo, D., Kiwuwa, S., and Kajja, I. 2017. '"I Am Not That Sick": The Use of Assistive Mobility Technologies among the Elderly', *Journal of Aging Research and Healthcare* 2(2):23–30.

Beckmann, G. 2018. 'Competence for Citizenship: Deaf People's (Re) Creation of Polities and Claim-Making Possibilities in Northern Uganda', PhD thesis, University of Zurich.

De Silva, V. Forthcoming. '"Its Name Is *Awetasc*": Devices and Everyday Life of People with Physical Disability in Ethiopia'.

Devlieger, C. 2018. 'Rome and the Romains: Laughter on the Border between Kinshasa and Brazzaville', *Africa* 88(1): 160–82.

Fallon, A. 2014. 'Uganda Pins Road Safety Hopes on New Traffic Authority', *Guardian*, Monday, 20 January 2014 <https://gulfnews.com/world/oceania/uganda-pins-road-safety-hopes-on-new-traffic-authority-1.1281004> [accessed 11 March 2022].

Ferraina, S. 2012. *Analysis of the Legal Meaning of Article 27 of the UN CRPD: Key Challenges for Adapted Work Settings*, BAG:WfbM and Unapei, EASPD, Brussels.

Government of Uganda. 1995. *Constitution of Uganda* <https://www.statehouse.go.ug/sites/default/files/attachments/Constitution_1995.pdf> [accessed 11 March 2022].

Grischow, J.D. 2015. '"I Nearly Lost My Work": Chance Encounters, Legal Empowerment and the Struggle for Disability Rights in Ghana', *Disability and Society* 30(1): 101–13.

Harpur, P. 2012. 'Embracing the New Disability Rights Paradigm: The Importance of the Convention on the Rights of PwDs', *Disability and Society* 27(1): 1–14.

Hussey, M., MacLachlan, M., and Mji, G. 2016. 'Barriers to the

Implementation of the Health and Rehabilitation Articles of the United Nations Convention on the Rights of PwDs in South Africa', *International Journal of Health Policy Management* 6(4): 207–18.

Kamoga, M., Bagarukayo, E., Kanani, R., Natugasha, D., and Arinda, Y. 2015. 'Vehicle Speed Tracking and Reporting System for Uganda', *International Journal of Computing and ICT Research* 9(1): 41–54 <http://ijcir.mak.ac.ug/volume9-issue1/article4.pdf> [accessed 10 April 2021].

Lang, R., Kett, M., Groce, N., and Trani, J.-F. 2011. 'Implementing the United Nations Convention on the Rights of PwDs: Principles, Implications, Practice and Limitations', *ALTER – European Journal of Disability Research* 5(2): 206–20.

Luwangula, R., Muyinda, H., Beckmann, G., and Kyaddondo, D. Unpublished Manuscript. 'Disability, Road Use Technologies, and Citizenship in Uganda'.

Malhotra, R. 2008. 'Expanding the Frontiers of Justice: Reflections on the Theory of Capabilities, Disability Rights, and the Politics of Global Inequality', *Socialism and Democracy* 22(1): 83–100.

Mannan, H., MacLachlan, M., and McVeigh, J. 2012. 'Core Concepts of Human Rights and Inclusion of Vulnerable Groups in the United Nations Convention on the Rights of PwDs', *ALTER – European Journal of Disability Research* 6(3): 159–77.

Murangira, A. Forthcoming. 'Deaf People Appropriating AIDS Eduacation Messages in Uganda'.

Muyinda, H. 2013. *Limbs and Lives: Disability, Violent Conflict and Embodied Sociality in Northern Uganda*. Saarbrücken: Lambert Academic.

Muyinda, H. 2020. 'The Skilling Journey: Disability, Technology, and Sociality in Postconflict Northern Uganda', *Current Anthropology* 61: S21.

Muyinda, H., and Whyte, S.R. 2011. 'Displacement, Mobility and Poverty in Northern Uganda'. In: B. Ingstad and A. Eide. Eds. *Disability and Poverty: A Global Challenge* (pp. 119–36). Bristol: Policy Press.

Nepveux, D.M. 2006. 'Reclaiming Agency, Ensuring Survival: Disabled Urban Ghanaian Women's Negotiations of Church and Family Belonging', *Disability Studies Quarterly* 26(4) <http://dsq-sds.org/article/view/814/989> [accessed 10 April 2021].

Nwokorie, O.V., and Devlieger, P.J. 2019. '"We only got Coca-Cola": Disability and the Paradox of (Dis)empowerment in Southeast Nigeria', *African Journal of Disability* 8(0): a444.

National Union of Disabled Persons of Uganda (NUDIPU). 2017. *Disability Demands: 2016–2021*. Kampala Uganda.

National Union of Disabled Persons of Uganda (NUDIPU). 2018. *Analysis of Inclusiveness of Teacher Education Policies in Uganda*. Kampala: NUDIPU.

Oduro, F. 2009. 'The Quest for Inclusion and Citizenship in Ghana:

Challenges and Prospects', *Citizenship Studies* 13(6): 621–39.
Opini, B.M. 2010. 'A Review of the Participation of Disabled Persons in the Labour Force: the Kenyan Context', *Disability and Society* 25(3): 271–87.
Russell, M. 2002. 'What Disability Civil Rights Cannot Do: Employment and Political Economy', *Disability and Society* 17(2): 118–30.
Schuler, M.-T. 2018. 'Disability and Logics of Distribution in a Ugandan Refugee Settlement', PhD thesis, University of Zurich.
Ssengooba, M., Rau Barriga, S., Dufka, C., Peligal, R., and Amon, J. 2012. '"Like a Death Sentence": Abuses against Persons with Mental Disabilities in Ghana', *Human Rights Watch Report* <https://www.refworld.org/docid/506e94752.html> [accessed 19 July 2014].
Uganda Bureau of Statistics (UBOS). 2016. *The Statistical Abstract 2016*. Kampala, Uganda
Uganda Bureau of Statistics (UBOS). 2014. *National Housing and Population Census*. Kampala, Uganda.
United Nations (UN). 2006. *Convention on the Rights of PwDs (CRPD)*. New York, Geneva <https://www.un.org/development/desa/disabilities/convention-on-the-rights-of-persons-with-disabilities/convention-on-the-rights-of-persons-with-disabilities-2.html> [accessed 11 April 2021].
Wazakili, M., Chataika, T., Mji, G., Dube, K., and MacLachlan, M. 2011. 'Social Inclusion of People with Disabilities in Poverty Reduction Policies and Instruments: Initial Impressions from Malawi and Uganda'. In: B. Ingstad and A. Eide. Eds. *Disability and Poverty: A Global Challenge* (pp. 15–29). Bristol: Policy Press.
Whyte, S.R., and Muyinda, H. 2007. 'Wheels and New Legs: Mobilization in Uganda'. In: B. Ingstad and S.R. Whyte. Eds. *Disability in Local and Global Worlds* (pp. 287–310). London: University of California Press.
Whyte, S.R. 2020. 'In the Long Run: Ugandans Living with Disability', *Current Anthropology* 61: S21.
Young, D.A., and Quibell, R. 2000. 'Why Rights Are Never Enough', *Disability and Society* 15(5): 747–64.

6

Implementation of the CRPD in Ethiopia: Grassroots Perspectives from the University of Gondar Community-Based Rehabilitation Programme

MIKYAS ABERA

Introduction

This chapter investigates whether community-based rehabilitation (CBR) has been a feasible and 'practical strategy for the implementation of the [Convention on the Rights of Persons with Disabilities, or] CRPD' in low-income countries (World Health Organization [WHO] *et al.*, 2010: 26), based on lessons drawn from the oldest higher-education-based CBR programme in Ethiopia: the University of Gondar's CBR (UoG-CBR) programme. As the name implies, CBR focuses on community-based initiatives to improve the lives and livelihoods of persons with disabilities (PwDs). Originally focused on rehabilitation programmes, CBR recently has moved towards a broader approach – rebranded as community-based inclusive development (CBID) – which encompasses health, education, livelihoods, social development, and empowerment. In the CBR/CBID approach, Disabled People's Organizations (DPOs) support local communities to create and implement disability programmes best suited to local needs and conditions. Grassroots approaches of this kind might be especially important for achieving disability rights under the CRPD, in light of a persistent lack of political will and inadequate institutional and technical capacities and resources in many countries in the Global South, which have rendered the CRPD and associated policy or legal frameworks ineffective in improving the lives of PwDs and supporting their families and communities. As a result, many families are left to their own devices to support their loved ones with disabilities. CBR/CBID seeks to help families and communities in three ways: by preparing PwDs to operate in an accessible environment, by making the environment more accessible for PwDs, and by creating and empowering DPOs to assist in the process.

The analysis that follows aims to contribute to bridging the perceived knowledge gap (Weber, Pollack, and Hartley, 2015) on the impact and contribution of CBR to creating opportunities for PwDs and promoting an inclusive society. Capturing the outcomes and impact of CBR on peoples' lives is very challenging conceptually and methodologically. The flexibility and adaptability of CBR – immense advantages in their own right – can make clear monitoring and evaluation guidelines on, and appropriate tools for, CBR programmes very difficult. CBR philosophy and principles are variously operationalized and contextualized in response to local and emerging realities. Hence, the evidence in this chapter on the impact of the University of Gondar's community-based rehabilitation programme (UoG-CBR) on PwDs, and their families and communities, will be necessarily anecdotal. The goal is to contribute to the conversation about, and nurture interest in, formulating a robust, systematic, and participatory approach to CBR monitoring and evaluation – in this case, to discuss promoting successful CRPD implementation. If CBR is presented as the best available strategy to support and empower PwDs by building capabilities and harnessing community resources and efforts, such discussions will be necessary to sensitize CBR administrators, practitioners, partners, and stakeholders to the strategic need of understanding and explaining clearly the how, why, and where it works, so that others can draw important lessons.

Using the example of the University of Gondar's CBR programme, the discussion below argues that CBR can be a valuable tool for implementing the CRPD in Ethiopia if there is an emphasis on collaboration, partnerships, and local ownership in removing barriers to disability rights. However, it also points to significant challenges, including the need for awareness-building at the community level, developing effective and culturally appropriate international partnerships and building the capacity of Ethiopian DPOs. The latter is especially important, because DPOs in Ethiopia have lacked effective leadership, resources, and goodwill from PwDs. The chapter therefore argues that CBR programmes must include capacity-building for DPOs in addition to programmes for PwDs. To build the argument, the chapter will survey the CRPD and CBR before presenting and assessing the University of Gondar (UoG) CBR programme as a tool for achieving the CRPD in Ethiopia.

The CRPD and the Situation of PwDs

Global statistics show that there is an urgent need for the CRPD in the Global South. While the WHO estimates that 15% of the world's population are PwDs, 80% of PwDs live in low- and middle-income countries (WHO and World Bank [WB], 2011). Due to multiple barriers, PwDs as a group are more likely to experience isolation, exclusion, and marginalization than persons without disabilities, and this is manifested in areas such as poor healthcare, unemployment, and barriers to education. PwDs are three times more likely to report being denied medical care and are four times more likely to report receiving sub-standard care (WHO, 2011). They are among the poorest members of a society, and have been referred to as 'the largest minority group'. They are often unemployed, underemployed, or paid less than their non-disabled counterparts. Youth with disabilities (YwDs) specifically are the last to be hired and the first to go at times of downsizing or economic slump (Lindsay, Hartman, and Fellin, 2015). Most are concentrated in informal and odd jobs with little or no prospect of advancement, personal development, or occupational safety. This is not the problem of only the less well-educated PwDs, however: well-educated PwDs also need to search for longer to find a job and, when hired, mostly find jobs with less security, reduced levels of occupational safety, and fewer prospects of promotion than their non-disabled colleagues with a similar education (Groce, 2004). A knowledge of this environment has discouraged many from even searching for a job (Lindsay, Hartman, and Fellin, 2015).

Women, minorities, and CwDs face the most challenging circumstances in their daily lives. Generally, women's participation in formal employment is significantly lower than men's in both developed and developing countries. Globally, the WHO's 2011 World Report on Disability estimated that the employment rate of women with disabilities (WwDs) was only 19.6%/29.9%, compared to 52.8%/64.9% for men with disabilities (WHO and WB, 2011). Women across Africa also receive lower pay and engage mostly in informal, odd jobs and low-level roles and positions – and these gender gaps in employment are widening.

In Ethiopia, only a quarter of PwDs rely on paid or self-employment. Around 95% of Ethiopian PwDs live in poverty (Seyoum, 2017) and 55% depend on the extended family (ILO, 2013), while the rest resort to begging and the help of neighbours and friends to support themselves. CwDs face violence four or five times more often than those without disabilities (Covell and Becker, 2011). Data from CBR programmes and their partners show neglect is the most reported form of violence against CwDs in Ethiopia (Boersma, 2013). CwDs are ten times less likely to enrol in schooling or progress past the lower levels (Kuper *et al.*, 2014), and overall only 3% of CwDs go to school due to attitudinal, institutional, and resource barriers (Humanity and Inclusion, 2020).

Disability and poverty are strongly related. The Joint Position Paper on CBR (ILO, UNDP, and WHO, 2004) underlines the strong correlation between disability and poverty: 'Poverty leads to increased disability, and disability in turn leads to increased poverty. Thus, a majority of PwDs live in poverty.' In a similar vein to Robert Chambers' 'deprivation trap' (Chambers, 2000), the position paper explains 'lack of access to healthcare and rehabilitation, education, skills training, and employment contributes to the vicious cycle of poverty and disability' (ILO, UNDP, and WHO, 2004). The WHO and WB (2011) identified the multiple barriers of PwDs in accessing opportunities and resources at the same level as everyone else in their communities/societies:

1. Multiple or aggravated forms of prejudice and discrimination;
2. Inaccessibility of facilities as well as unfavourable attitude and limited capacities of personnel therein to provide support and services;
3. Inadequate or non-existent rehabilitation centres and services with affordable assistive aids and devices;
4. Inadequate knowledge of disability inclusive development and service delivery or lack of motivation to learn about it.

These barriers and challenges that PwDs are faced with are part of the rationale for the UN General Assembly adopting the Convention on the Rights of PwDs (CRPD) in 2007 (UN General Assembly, 2007).

Currently ratified by 186 countries as well as the European Union (EU), the CRPD aims to 'promote, protect and ensure the full and equal enjoyment of all human rights and fundamental freedoms by all PwDs, and to promote respect for their inherent dignity'. In contrast to previous UN instruments on disability, the CRPD integrates the social model of disability into its framework.

Article 1, for example, states that PwDs 'include those who have long-term physical, mental, intellectual or sensory impairments which in interaction with various barriers may hinder their full and effective participation in society on an equal basis with others' (CRPD, 2007). This affirms the social construction of disability whereby limitations/hindrances arise in a person's interactions with environmental barriers rather than as the consequence of an individualized impairment or inherent limitation.

The CRPD is comprehensive in that it covers a range of human, civic, political, economic, cultural, and social rights of PwDs. It strongly underlines human rights as 'indivisible, interrelated and interconnected' (UN General Assembly, 1993). As a human rights treaty, it contains general and substantive provisions. Article 4(1) covers general provisions that oblige ratifying States to immediately implement the civic and political rights of PwDs – i.e. equal protection before the law, liberty and security of the person, right to life, protection of the integrity of the person and right to participation in public life. On the other hand, Article 4(2) recognizes the potency of robust institutions, capacities, and resources to bracket out economic, social, and cultural rights – including freedom of expression and rights to education, work, adequate standards of living, health, and participation in cultural life – for their gradual implementation over a reasonable period with the support of partners, submitting progress reports to the Committee on the Rights of Persons with Disabilities (CoRPD). Though at a glance the Convention seems to include 'newly created rights' applicable exclusively for PwDs, its 'articles on living independently, personal mobility and habitation and rehabilitation are intrinsic to the attainment of historically recognized human rights' and/or 'for the purpose of clarifying the means through which other CRPD rights are realized' (Stein and Lord, 2008: 20).

In terms of the topic of this chapter, the CRPD recognizes the role of international and local partners as well as grassroots participation and mobilization in supporting ratifying States towards effective implementation (Article 32). Concerning international cooperation to support the realization of disability rights and inclusion, this Article sets out four overarching modalities:

1. Inclusive and accessible international cooperation and development programmes for PwDs, both as participants and beneficiaries;

2. Capacity-building, including sharing and exchange of information, experience, training programmes, and best practices;
3. Cooperation in research and access to scientific and technical knowledge;
4. Technical and economic assistance, including access to, sharing and transfer of accessible and assistive technologies (ATs).

It adds,

> States Parties recognize the importance of international cooperation and its promotion, in support of national efforts for the realization of the purpose and objectives of the present Convention, and will undertake appropriate and effective measures in this regard, between and among States and, as appropriate, in partnership with relevant international and regional organizations and civil society, in particular organizations of PwDs (Article 32[1]).

As Article 32(1) underscores, grassroots mobilization and participation is given considerable significance in the implementation of the CRPD. Article 33(2) mentions this as well, stating that 'civil society, in particular PwDs and their representative organizations, shall be involved and participate fully in the monitoring process'. Cumulatively, these provisions support an ample scope and indispensable role for DPOs as partners in the States' national implementation of the CRPD (Article 32[1]) and the monitoring process (Article 32[2]).

The CRPD has also provided additional and specific prerogatives to promote the effective involvement of PwDs and their associations in designing, implementing, and monitoring policies, strategies, programmes, etc. on disability inclusion and sustainable development. For example, Article 4(3) obliges States to 'closely consult with and actively involve PwDs, including CwDs, through their representative organizations ... in the development and implementation of legislation and policies to implement the present Convention, and in other decision-making processes concerning issues relating to PwDs'. To promote this objective, ratifying States have agreed to ensure the rights of PwDs and provide support as required, to 'form and join organizations of PwDs to represent PwDs at international, national, regional and local levels' (Article 29[b.ii]) and 'recognize the right of PwDs to social protection programs and poverty reduction programs' (Article 28[2.c]).

Despite many countries swiftly ratifying the Convention, numerous low-income countries have struggled to align their domestic laws, systems, and institutions with its provisions. As the reality for PwDs remains far from what was envisaged in the Convention, CBR has entered the disability discourse and became promoted as an effective strategy to meet the challenges of these countries. In philosophy and priorities, the CRPD aligns closely with CBR programmes, especially since CBR reconfigured rehabilitation from a multisectoral human rights and equity orientation rather than the conventional biomedical model. Besides, the CRPD complements CBR programmes, which include robust international human rights frameworks in their strategies, engagement, and service delivery in order to promote and facilitate inclusive development and provide modalities for collaborations with international, national, and local partners. The WHO CBR guidelines clearly establish direct connections between CBR and the CRPD when it states its purpose as being to 'promote CBR as a strategy which can contribute to implementation of CRPD, and of disability inclusive national legislation, and which can support community-based inclusive development' (WHO *et al.*, 2010).

The Concept and Philosophy of CBR in Disability Movements

The rebranding of CBR as community-based inclusive development (CBID) to make it broad-based, multisectoral, and mainstream intervention as part of sustainable development agenda is a response to the daunting lessons that disability-specific services do not necessarily and/or automatically lead to the inclusion of PwDs in mainstream society. Societal, institutional, and physical barriers – stereotype, prejudice, and discrimination, inaccessible facilities, lack of knowledge about the abilities and contributions of PwDs – remain resilient, demanding robust strategies and programmes that target communities and institutions.

The concept of CBR was introduced by the WHO in the late 1970s as a strategy to enhance the quality of life of PwDs and their families in low-income countries. Over the decades, the concept has evolved, reflecting and adjusting to changing perspectives on disability and human rights priorities; recently, its focus has been increasingly geared towards 'achieving human rights, equality and inclusiveness for PwDs' (Wickenden, Cornielje, and Nkwenge, 2017: 25). In other words, it grew past its early focus on individual impairments to adopt a rights-based and development-oriented approach/strategy aimed at equal opportunities and the inclusion of all.

Since 2010, though, CBR officially has employed a multisectoral design with five interrelated components: health, education, livelihoods, social interaction, and empowerment. In other words, CBR openly acknowledges and integrates the contributions of families and communities in the holistic rehabilitation of PwDs. In sum, CBR programmes 'work for the benefit and development of the whole community, encouraging inclusive development, fostering empowerment and emphasizing the realization of human rights for all' (Finkenflugel *et al.*, 2008, cited in Post *et al.*, 2016: 9).

As a strategy, CBR promotes disability inclusion. But 'disability mainstreaming' depends upon the availability of disability-specific service delivery – the provision of specialized services to individuals with different types of impairments – in order to enable PwDs to achieve their full potential. Inclusion also requires 'disability adjustments' on the part of organizations and society as a whole, such as building modifications, accessible transportation, producing materials in braille, sign language interpretation, etc. These two sets of CBR engagements are represented by what is called the twin-track approach – one 'where efforts are made to prepare individuals and the environment at the same time so that by the time the people are ready to engage in activities the environment is favorable to enable them participate accordingly' (Nganwa, Sserunkuma, and Mbugua, 2017: 61).

Recently, a 'third track' has been recognized and emphasized as being indispensable to CBR programmes in achieving the inclusion, full participation, and rights of PwDs: the creation, empowerment, and support of PwD organizations (DPOs). DPOs are organizations of, and run by, PwDs, and also include parents of CwDs. Conventionally, planning, implementing, and evaluating government policies and programmes – as well as the delivery and evaluation of specialized and mainstream services – requires input from DPOs. The CRPD specifically requires governments and partners to involve, consult, with and include PwDs in all decisions that may affect them. 'Nothing about us without us' (Charlton, 1998) best sums up the importance of this 'third track' to disability, and the need to support the growth and development of strong DPOs at local, national, and international levels.

Let us underline the consensus on this matter here: no track is better or more important than the other. All three are important to ensure that the needs of children, youth, and adults with disabilities are met, and the equality of opportunity, inclusion, full participation, and respect of PwDs are ensured in society.

The Challenges and Prospects of CBR Practice in Ethiopia

As the reader may have realized already, the challenges, achievements, and prospects of CBR are interrelated, and they are linked to its philosophy, principles, and strategies – mainly in connection with its international and domestic partnership strategy. The main challenges of CBR programmes emanate from their integrated and community-based approach to disability. Most CBR programmes around the world approach disability as a social construct – with diverse and major components – and engage with disability as embedded in communities and their structures. Compared to the institutional model of rehabilitation, CBR requires more time and energy from committed and dedicated management and CBR workers. Besides, CBR's philosophy is to work in and with communities and impact individual, institutional, and community factors. A sound strategy of partnership between the main actors, including PwDs and their associations, is vital to its implementation and successes. Partnership is not just one of the strategies when it comes to CBR programmes: it is the strategy *par excellence*. As a result, it might strain the management of CBR programmes and it could be draining at times, especially when partners and stakeholders come with diverging interests and priorities.

For instance, Boersma (2013) reported how existing, mostly donor-driven child protection policies in Ethiopia failed to take into account the working conditions within CBR projects, especially among CBR fieldworkers. CBR projects understand disability as a social construct, and they underline the importance of environmental factors in addressing the challenges of disability. They adopt an integrated approach to rehabilitation, and they work towards mainstreaming disability and rehabilitation into community life and institutional cultures (WHO *et al.*, 2010). This means that some of the recommendations for individualistic child protection policies would be hard to follow within the philosophy of CBR or contextual realities in developing countries like Ethiopia. For instance, these policies make a unilateral recommendation that an agent has to remove the child victim from the violent environment, initiate legal procedures, and provide emotional and psychological support in an institutional setting and in the best interests of the child. But this might not work for CBR programmes in countries like Ethiopia, for three major reasons:

1. Work with communities – the core philosophy of CBR. CBR programmes engage with partners and key actors in communities to remove conditions that promote violence against children and limit access to legal protection and justice. This may involve replacing a child-centred approach that immediately removes children from their support system and communities in favour of working to transform the environment for the better. While theoretically better, this approach runs the risk of keeping children in abusive situations that are not easily improved (Boersema, 2013).
2. Non-existent, unwilling, or inadequate institutional structures. Low disability awareness and inadequate resources limit the development of facilities and institutions that could take victims after removal from a hostile environment. Boersma argued, 'the existing [institutional] facilities are often unsuitable for children with disabilities and traditional support systems like neighbors or family members are often reluctant to take such children into their care' (2013:118).
3. Specialized requirements of individualized supports on CBR practitioners. As in many developing countries, the recommended emotional and psychological support for child victims of violence or abuse under individualized approaches are too specialized for CBR workers in Ethiopia, especially at grassroots levels. Although there are traditional and religious sources of such supports for victims, they are still part of the society, and their attitudes towards disability and PwDs could affect whether, and how, they provide the needed support.

The causes of violence, discrimination, and stigma against PwDs are rooted in community members' and other key actors' attitudes, knowledge, and understanding of disability and PwDs (African Child Policy Forum, 2012; Jones, Presler-Marshall, and Stavropoulou, 2018). Consequently, CBR projects have worked to address these problems of PwDs through an interrelated set of activities i.e. raising disability awareness in the community about the challenges, abilities, and rights of PwDs and training key people in the community, including community representatives, religious leaders, and the police. In low-income contexts such as Ethiopia, the CBR approach of promoting positive attitudinal changes and breaking barriers for PwDs in societies and their structures has delivered well on desirable outcomes.

CBR does require time and committed personnel to build an integrated approach to its projects and interventions, but the partnership and networking it promotes are easily transferrable to other related initiatives. To put it another way, the synergistic outcomes of effective partnership under the CBR umbrella can be sustained for a prolonged time or scaled up as required, because its synergy implies partnership built through time and regulated interactions and communications that promote mutual trust and the development of common visions and goals.

Compared to institutional rehabilitation, CBR's integrated and participatory approach is more likely to create improved life conditions for PwDs. It engages partners, stakeholders, and PwDs and their associations meaningfully in the process of planning, implementing, and monitoring CBR projects, which generally promotes the sense of ownership among communities of actors and ensures the sustainability of concerted engagements. Ultimately, the CBR approach enables a framework that channels partners' efforts towards predefined and shared goals through their respective and consensually defined roles and responsibilities in the project. The dialogue and shared sense of mission that the CBR approach promotes among partners reduces the possible redundancy and duplication of efforts that may have occurred had they acted separately.

The CBR Programme at the University of Gondar

In 2005, the University of Gondar (UoG) established its CBR programme (UoG-CBR), the first ever CBR programme hosted by a higher educational institution (HEI) in Ethiopia. In its engagement with PwDs, their families, and communities, UoG-CBR partners with Light for the World – an Austrian-based, CBR-focused non-governmental organization (NGO) – Save the Children, the Mastercard Foundation, and the Austrian Development Agency. The programme employs the WHO CBR guidelines to inform its design and implement collaborative initiatives to benefit PwDs through CBR programmes, including provision of assistive devices, referral to advanced medical care, promotion of accessibility of schools, and delivery of different training and community awareness creation programmes.

Hosting the CBR programme in an HEI came with immense opportunities to inform and fruitfully integrate teaching with research and community engagement. Designed originally as a community service project accountable to the office of the vice president for research and community service, its broad-based and multisectoral approach has systematically linked UoG's three institutional pillars i.e., teaching, research, and community service. The university community – academicians, professionals, technicians, students, etc. – fed into the mission of UoG and have been contributing to the shared agenda of creating barrier-free environment for equal and inclusive participation of PwDs in education, employment, and service delivery.

Academicians and professionals in diverse disciplines – mainly health and social sciences, and humanities – have worked with the CBR staff to design and deliver tailored training and support for PwDs and their families as well as organize community awareness creation programmes. They also conducted research on disability and/or rehabilitation, with their findings invaluably refining further community intervention strategies and curricula. Under the fold of UoG-CBR, students of physiotherapy, sociology, psychology, law, and social work, among other areas, have been engaging in course-based placements and writing academic papers. These varied and active ways in which the university is involved with the community strengthen the culture of reflexive learning and practice at UoG, which help improve the quality and relevance of education as well as community engagement programmes. As an institution with a strong culture of and commitment to community service, the CBR programme added a further layer to UoG's efficacy and vibrancy in its organization, collaboration, and delivery of social, health, legal, etc. services to a variety of marginalized groups, including PwDs.

Initially, UoG-CBR's programmatic focus targeted selected districts of North Gondar Zone in the Amhara National Regional State (ANRS). But as collaborations with local, national, and international partners grew, its catchment areas expanded to include two districts in South Wollo Zone of ANRS, while it also provides its services and work to increasing numbers of districts in North Gondar Zone. It also increased its personnel from 8 in 2005 (1 coordinator, 6 fieldworkers, and 1 consultant) to 32 in 2014 (1 coordinator, 5 supervisors, an accountant, 24 fieldworkers, and a driver) and its services reaching 11 districts instead of just 2. As part of its sustainability strategy to reduce the programme's dependence on philanthropy and funding from donors and outside sources, it transformed its organizational structure, and the proposal to have its personnel on UoG's, rather than the donor's, payroll was approved by the UoG and the Ethiopian civil service commission in early 2019. Consequently, UoG-CBR now has 81 staff (1 director, 2 coordinators, 2 assistant coordinators, 15 senior and junior supervisors, 5 support staff [1 accountant, 1 driver, 3 office assistants] and 56 fieldworkers), and it reaches 16 *woredas*[1] in two zones of the ANRS.

UoG-CBR and Grassroots Disability Movements

UoG-CBR implements its strategies and programmes through the combined efforts of PwDs, their families and communities, non-governmental – national and international – organizations and the appropriate health, education, vocational, and social sectors of the government. At its inception, it informed its intervention strategies based on the 2004 Joint Position Paper on CBR by ILO, UNESCO, and WHO, which defined the objectives of CBR in terms of supporting PwDs to build their capacities, enabling their access to social services and resources, and activating and supporting communities to promote the well-being and welfare of PwDs. Since 2010, the CBR guidelines, which identified a

1 Ethiopia has a federal administrative system. From the highest to the lowest, the federal system is organized into five administrative units: federal, region, zone, *woreda,* and *kebele.*

matrix of five major CBR components – with each containing five sets of activities – became the hallmark of UoG-CBR.

Based on the Guidelines, UoG-CBR has been engaging in various activities that address the major components of CBR as per the matrix, including:

1. Providing health support, including making referrals to the University of Gondar hospital;
2. Providing assistive devices for PwDs;
3. Promoting access to schooling for CwDs;
4. Promoting independent living for PwDs through various kinds of livelihood support, including training on income-generating activities (IGAs);
5. Providing family and social support for PwDs;
6. Promoting empowerment by strengthening PwDs' self-help groups and DPOs;
7. Raising and creating community awareness on disability and the capabilities of PwDs.

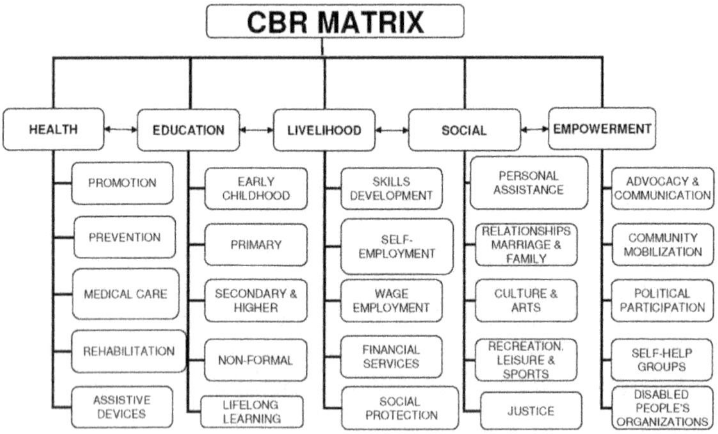

Figure 6.1 The CBR Matrix
(Source: Reproduced from Community-Based Rehabilitation: CBR Guidelines. Geneva: World Health Organization (WHO) <https://www.who.int/disabilities/cbr/cbr_matrix_11.10.pdf> [accessed 17 January 2022]).

In addition to the CBR guidelines, UoG-CBR has been informed by and geared towards achieving the CRPD. It has been repeatedly noted that CBR should be seen as a strategy to achieve the goal of CBID for PwDs by employing a twin-track approach, which has brought successes to its programmes over the years.

In Ethiopia, the disability movement involving DPOs has been a recent phenomenon. There have been institutions like Cheshire Services Ethiopia that have provided services to PwDs for several decades, but the centring of DPOs in disability programming started only in the late 1990s with the formation of such organizations as the Ethiopian Centre for Disability and Development (ECDD), Federation of Ethiopian Associations of Persons with Disabilities (FEAPD), etc. Since its formation at the turn of the century, UoG-CBR has been working with PwD self-help groups to create an environment and framework enabling them to grow into DPOs. The programme mostly focuses on delivering financial and social support to PwDs organized under self-help groups, as a way to promote their growth into DPOs. As the number of DPOs in the area in which UoG-CBR operates grew, it started delivering training mainly tailored to building the DPO leaders' capacities in organizational management, mass/resource mobilization, and advocacy. Until DPOs arrived, UoG-CBR had been focusing on encouraging various community-based organizations (and their leadership) to collaboratively campaign for the rights of PwDs.

As part of the grassroots movement to advocate for the rights of PwDs, CBR programmes are required to work with and involve DPOs (WHO, 2010). But, in Ethiopia, DPOs have to face several challenges from inception onwards. These start with attracting, recruiting, and retaining members, since, DPO leaders claim, the overriding motive for most joining DPOs is individualized gain, rather than promoting and advocating for the well-being and rights of all PwDs. As a consequence, according to many DPO leaders, most employed and thus relatively well-off PwDs shun membership or limit their involvement in DPOs, because they do not see value in membership. These leaders also suggest that PwDs who do join DPOs often cancel their membership if their fortunes improve. Conversely, PwDs themselves claim their main reasons for avoiding and/or quitting DPOs relate to the organizations' impotency or weak leadership, and their inability to effectively and fully involve all PwDs. However, in fairness to DPOs, many do not even have office spaces from which they can coordinate their works.

It is against this backdrop, and to activate DPOs as active collaborators in disability advocacy, that UoG-CBR has been providing training for DPO leaders on CRPD and other legal/ policy instruments that enshrine and/or promote the rights of PwDs. When leaders are aware of what instruments are available to them, this often improves their resolution and commitment to the agenda of inclusive and sustainable development. In fact, DPO leaders who went through the training sessions were able to identify loopholes in the legal instruments that make their implementation and desired outcomes on the rights and lives of PwDs ineffective or inadequate. For instance, they realized that the mere proclamation to ratify the CRPD does not automatically guarantee its implementation at the national level, because, although States Parties are mandated to implement the CRPD's provisions, they are not obliged to do so. As a result, the implementation of the CRPD is left to the will and wishes of people in power and those with control over scarce resources.

UoG-CBR administrators, on the other hand, judge that most DPOs they work are not at a level where active and effective participation of PwDs and sound monitory and evaluation plan can be expected. Most DPOs lack functional organizational systems (including general assemblies), robust rules and regulations, accounting systems, etc. It is also startling to note that several DPOs are not registered, legal entities, and that they operate without certification from the Ministry of Justice (MoJ) or relevant regional authorities. DPO leaders lament their own lack of knowledge and inability to meet the requirements. Financially, DPOs need to pay 450 ETB[2] as a registration fee.[3] Though Ethiopia ratified the CRPD and its Article 32 requires ratifying States to promote the establishment of DPOs and their active involvement in design, implementation, monitoring, and evaluation of policies that directly affect the well-being and welfare of PwDs, many DPOs feel the government is not removing existing barriers to their legalization and institutionalization.

It is obvious that registration with appropriate authorities is a requirement for DPOs to attain legality; but their financial and

2 ETB = 0.031 USD, as of 28 February 2020.

3 There is a variation in the amount to be paid for DPOs' registration by their regional location. Each regional state defines the appropriate amount of registration fee, considering the state's human, financial, and logistics factors as well as the catchment area of the proposed project.

technical limitations inhibit their registration, which makes their involvement in debates on public issues impossible. In other words, while focusing on whether DPOs meet registration requirements, the dialogue neglects the required national commitment to enabling the participation of DPOs in discussions on relevant public or disability-related policies, strategies, or projects. Consequently, most DPOs are not in the position to advocate for the rights of PwDs in development- or disability-related agendas.

UoG-CBR administrators reiterate how the programme does not plan for establishing DPOs from scratch. Instead, the programmatic focus is on strengthening the structure and leadership of existing DPOs. In this area, UoG-CBR is specifically supported by the Austrian Development Agency, with finance from the EU and Light for the World. The original programmatic intervention plan, developed and endorsed in consultation with relevant partners, including the two European institutions, did not budget for the formation of DPOs either, for there was a fear that it could become an unwarranted support to DPOs and slide them into dependency on external agencies in their operations.

Accordingly, UoG-CBR invites all DPOs operating in its catchment area to recruit and nominate leaders for various capacity-building training sessions. UoG-CBR's engagement with DPOs does not require the latter to be legal entities, as long as they act as an association of PwDs. With few registered DPOs, the viable option for UoG-CBR was to work with willing associations of PwDs and harness their potential to advance and advocate the rights of PwDs. The programme kept the requirement for nomination of trainees at a basic level: a letter bearing the association's seal was sufficient. UoG-CBR administrators and social workers are mostly aware of the fact that more than a few DPOs are unregistered and may not have proper documentation with the relevant authorities.

A few DPOs embraced under the UoG-CBR programme have attained legality courtesy of their strong leadership and support from UoG-CBR and other partners. But the general view among DPO leaders regarding the proclamation on Civil Society Organizations (CSOs) is unfavourable, for, they claim, it does not distinguish between associations established to advocate for marginal groups, including DPOs, and NGOs with resources and sources of funding. Consequently, several DPO leaders see the requirements to register under the CSO – including the registration fee – as unfair and usually refuse to follow procedures.

On a positive note, a directorate for disability was recently set up under the regional Bureau of Women and Social Affairs (BoWSA), and the hope among disability actors is that the directorate will address logistic, financial, and other limitations, as well as the DPOs' requests of relevant authorities, thereby promoting their contributions to disability mainstreaming in development-and disability-related policies, strategies, and practices. UoG-CBR has already started working on this area and robust engagement plans are under construction, while its current engagements focus on coordinating with BoLSA to waive or provide technical support for DPOs to meet the requirements of registration.

UoG-CBR administrators complain that the rhetoric on disability mainstreaming did not produce visible changes in existing policies, strategies, and practices in the habilitation and rehabilitation of PwDs in the two zones or the regional state. They mention a lack of public funds earmarked for disability-related activities at any level of the government as evidence of the lack of direct support to PwDs and DPOs. Even the FEAPD, the largest national consortium of associations of PwDs with regional chapters, does not have a budget allocated from the government and operates solely on funds from members and/or philanthropy.

Conclusion

With inadequate high-level commitment and weak grassroots organizations, UoG-CBR administrators are assessing where they stand against the CBR Guidelines, the CRPD, and CBID initiatives. A programme evaluation of UoG-CBR, for instance, shows that limited resources, technical capacity, etc., have affected the implementation of activities informed by the CBR Guidelines, especially on activities that revolve mainly around empowerment and the physical accessibility of schools. This means that even if UoG-CBR defines its strategies and implements activities using the CBR Guidelines, it has not sufficiently addressed the range of challenges required to remove the barriers to the full participation of PwDs. In short, CBR's engagement with DPOs has not been its strong area. This, coupled with weak community coalition platforms, means that DPOs remain ineffective in influencing policy and planning debates and that schools and training centres continue to exclude persons with various forms of disabilities. The partial and/or selective application of the CBR matrix – forced or otherwise – has not meant that PwDs are not fully integrated into their communities. This, however, should not be taken to mean they were irrelevant to the disability movement, where they could play compelling roles in mitigating community stereotypes and building the capacities of PwDs for effective community mobilization and participation.

On the other hand, UoG-CBR administrators and practitioners see positives in the recent shift within CBR towards CBID, since the CBR's earlier platform had proved inadequate to support and advance the CRPD. This is partly in relation to CBR's definition of the concept of rehabilitation primarily in health or health-related activities, though within a broader focus on the family and community. In addition, CBR's focus on community has had the unintended outcome of relegating the government's role – in budgeting and mainstreaming, primarily – to an auxiliary level. This has fed into the government's reluctance to budget for the promotion of the rights and well-being of PwDs through structuring and mainstreaming, in spite of ratifying the CRPD and supposedly incorporating it into the law of the land. CBID, on the other hand, has the potential to supply a much more progressive and inclusive framework for the effective empowerment and participation of PwDs.

Bibliography

African Child Policy Forum (ACPF). 2012. 'Breaking the Silence: Violence Against Children with Disabilities in Africa'. In: African Child Policy Forum. Ed. *Improving Children's Lives through Research Summaries from Presentations at the Monthly Seminar Series of the Child Research and Practice* (pp. 30–31). Addis Ababa: Child Research and Practice Forum.

Boersma, M. 2013. 'Protecting Children with Disabilities from Violence in CBR Projects: Why We Need to Work with a Different Form of Child Protection Policy for Children with Disabilities', *Disability CBR and Inclusive Development* 24(3):112–22.

Chambers, R. 2000. *Whose Reality Counts? Putting the First Last.* London: ITDG Publishing.

Covell, K., and Becker, J. 2011. *Five Years On: A Global Update on Violence against Children.* Report for NGO Advisory Council for the UN Secretary General's Study on Violence against Children. New York: United Nations.

Federal Democratic Republic of Ethiopia (FDRE). Organizations of Civil

Societies Proclamation. Proclamation No. 113/2019.

Groce, N.E. 2004. 'Adolescents and Youth with Disability: Issues and Challenges', *Asia Pacific Disability Rehabilitation Journal* 15(2):13–32.

Humanity and Inclusion. 2020. 'Ethiopia' <https://www.hi-us.org/Ethiopia> [accessed 12 January 2012].

International Disability Alliance (IDA). 2010. 'Overcoming Invisibility: Making the MDGs Inclusive of and Accessible for PwDs'. A Contribution to Informal Interactive Hearings of the General Assembly with Non-Governmental Organizations, Civil Society Organizations and the Private Sector. 14–15 June 2010 <https://docsbay.net/making-the-mdgs-inclusive-of-and-accessible> [accessed 11 March 2022].

International Labour Organization, United Nations Development Programme, and World Health Organization (ILO, UNDP, and WHO). 2004. *CBR – A Strategy for Rehabilitation, Equalization of Opportunities, Poverty Reduction and Social Inclusion of People with Disabilities*. Joint Position Paper 2004. Geneva: World Health Organization.

International Labour Organization (ILO). 2013. 'ILO Factsheet: Inclusion of People with Disabilities in Ethiopia', <http://www.ethiopianreview.com/pdf/001/wcms_112299.pdf> [accessed 12 October 2020].

Jones, N., Presler-Marshall, E., and Stavropoulou, M. 2018. *Adolescents with Disabilities: Enhancing Resilience and Delivering Inclusive Development*. London: GAGE Programme Office.

Kuper, H., Monteath van Dok, A., Wing, K., Danquah, L., Evans, J., Zuurmond, M., and Gallinetti, J. 2014. 'The Impact of Disability on the Lives of Children: Cross-Sectional Data Including 8,900 Children with Disabilities and 898,834 Children without Disabilities across 30 Countries', *PLoS ONE* 9(9): 1–11.

Lindsay S., Hartman, L.R., and Fellin, M. 2015. 'A Systematic Review of Mentorship Programs to Facilitate Transition to Post-Secondary Education and Employment for Youth and Young Adults with Disabilities', *Disability and Rehabilitation* 38(14): 1329–49.

Nganwa, A.B., Sserunkuma, M.C., and Mbugua, P.K. 2017. *CBR Guidelines: A Bridge to Inclusive Society Beyond the 2015 Development Framework*. Bangalore: National Printing Press.

Post, E., Cornielje, H., Andrae, K., Maarse, A., Schneider, M., and Wickenden, M. 2016. 'Participatory Inclusion Evaluation: A Flexible Approach to Building the Evidence Base on the Impact of Community-Based Rehabilitation and Inclusive Development Programs', *Knowledge Management for Development Journal* 11(2): 7–26.

Seyoum, Z. 2017. 'Employment Opportunities and Challenges of People with Disabilities in Dire-Dawa, Ethiopia: Policy and Practice', *Journal of Education, Society and Behavioral Science* 22(4): 1–11.

Stein, M.A., and Lord, J.E. 2008. 'Future Prospects for the United

Nations Convention on the Rights of PwDs'. In: O.M. Arnardóttir and G. Quinn. Eds. *The UN Convention on the Rights of PwDs: European and Scandinavian Perspectives* (pp. 17–40). Leiden: Martinus Nijhoff Publishers.

Stein, M.A., and Lord, J.E. 2010. 'Monitoring the Convention on the Rights of PwDs: Innovations, Lost Opportunities, and Future Potential', *Human Rights Quarterly* 32: 689–728.

United Nations (UN) General Assembly. 1993. *A Vienna Declaration and Program of Action* (UN Doc A/CONF 157/23. July 12 1993). New York: United Nations.

United Nations (UN) General Assembly. 2007. Convention on the Rights of PwDs. Resolution 61/106. New York: United Nations.

Weber, J., Pollack, S., and Hartley, S. 2015. 'An Online Survey on Identification of Evaluation Capacity, Needs and Current Practice of Program Evaluation in Community-based Rehabilitation', *Disability, CBR and Inclusive Development* 27(2): 5–19.

Wickenden, M., Cornielje, H., and Nkwenge, P. 2017. 'Chapter 4: The PIE Model and Tools: Meeting the Need for a Systematic and Participatory Approach to Evaluating the Impact of CBR'. In: A.B. Nganwa, M.C. Sserunkuma, and P.K. Mbugua. Eds. *CBR Guidelines: A Bridge to Inclusive Society beyond the 2015 Development Framework.* Bangalore: National Printing Press.

World Health Organization (WHO) and World Bank (WB). 2011. *World Report on Disability.* Geneva: World Health Organization.

World Health Organization United Nations Education, Science and Culture Organization, International Labour Organization, and International Disability and Development Consortium (WHO, UNESCO, ILO, and IDDC). 2010. *Community-based Rehabilitation: CBR Guidelines.* Geneva: World Health Organization.

7

Knowledge and Utilization of the CRPD and Persons with Disability Act 715 of Ghana among Deaf People

WISDOM KWADWO MPRAH & JUVENTUS DUORINAAH

Introduction

This chapter investigates the potential of the United Nations (UN) Convention of the Rights of Persons with Disabilities (CRPD) and Ghana's Persons with Disability Act (PwDA) as tools for achieving disability rights for deaf Ghanaians. Based on qualitative research in four field locations, the analysis focuses on awareness of the CRPD among deaf Ghanaians and the extent to which the participants have used the CRPD and PwDA as vehicles to promote deaf rights. The fieldwork reveals that deaf Ghanaians face significant barriers in both learning about the CRPD and utilizing it to promote their rights. This is particularly true for those with lower levels of education, including poor literacy in sign language. As a result, despite Ghana's implementation of the PwDA in 2006 and ratification of the CRPD in 2012, their implementation has been problematic for deaf Ghanaians. Improving this situation will require a heightened commitment from the government of Ghana to provide awareness-raising programmes, as well as capacity-building for Disabled People's Organizations (DPOs) such as the Ghana National Association of the Deaf (GNAD) to enable these organizations to support deaf Ghanaians in their struggle to achieve the rights enshrined in the CRPD and PwDA.

It is well known that 80% of the world's one billion PwDs live in the Global South and that 40% reside in Africa (World Health Organization [WHO], 2011). In Ghana, the government estimates that 3% of the total population, or about 893,000 people, live with some form of disability (Ghana Statistical Services, 2012; World Bank [WB], 2020). Of these, the estimate of the number of deaf persons in Ghana ranges between 110,625 and 211,712 (Owoo, 2019). Persons with disabilities (PwDs), including deaf persons, are often excluded from development projects. The majority lack access to social and economic services such as education, employment, and healthcare. Consequently, they experience widespread poverty, and many are unable to exercise their fundamental human rights. This exclusion from rights is underpinned by negative attitudes and prejudice towards PwDs, as well as a lack of understanding of the causes of disability, especially in Ghana and other countries in the Global South (Agbenyega, 2003; Filmer, 2008). In many societies, disability is considered a disadvantage or a curse, or it is viewed from a one-dimensional 'medical' perspective focused on individual impairments as deviations from 'normalcy'. This narrow and stereotypical view of disability, although challenged by disability advocates and activists, leads to discrimination against PwDs, as it does not recognize that they have the right to participate in socio-economic activities on an equal basis to others (Shakespeare, 2010).

In the Ghanaian context, these barriers to disability rights are gaining more attention than before. There are efforts by the government to promote and protect disability rights, most notably the passage of the PwDA (Act 715) in 2006 and the ratification of the CRPD in 2012. However, negative attitudes towards PwDs are still widespread, resulting in numerous barriers to their participation in socio-economic activities (Mprah, 2011; Slikker, 2009; Agbenyega, 2003).

On the other hand, civil activism among PwDs to combat rights abuses has been relatively low in Ghana. PwDs have not been as aggressive in their advocacy efforts as their counterparts in developed countries. This is probably due to Ghana's political system prior to constitutional rule, especially in the period before the beginning of the Fourth Republic in 1992, which witnessed a lot of political instability. A succession of military regimes, which characterized the period between 1967 to 1992, suppressed political activities in general (Abdulai, 2009), and this seems to have affected the ability of disability rights movements to develop the capacity needed to effectively utilize provisions in the PwDA and CRPD.

Among Ghanaians, deaf people arguably face the greatest barriers to disability rights due to a lack of understanding of their unique communication needs, which makes it difficult for them to access mainstream information and services (Mprah,

2011; Heuttel and Ronstein, 2001). For example, information disseminated to the general population is often not provided in an accessible format, as it is rarely translated into sign language for the deaf population. This is a serious issue, because the high illiteracy rate among deaf people in Ghana makes it difficult for them to access information from print sources (Mprah, 2011; Mprah, 2013). In addition, low literacy makes it difficult for deaf people to process and understand the volume and complexity of information on human rights, which is couched in formal legal jargon. Thus, deaf people are unlikely to understand their rights, and procedures for demanding those rights may be too complex and expensive for them to utilize.

These barriers could be addressed through promoting the PwDA and CRPD. However, awareness-raising has been very limited among deaf people in Ghana. According to the GNAD, the government only promoted the PwDA and CRPD once to deaf Ghanaians, and this was limited to only three out of more than 200 districts in Ghana. Some organizations have conducted workshops on the CRPD, but their activities have not targeted deaf people (Juventus Duorinaah, personal correspondence, 20 April 2021). As a result, deaf Ghanaians face enormous difficulties in accessing and utilizing information in the PwDA and the CRPD, depriving them of being knowledgeable of the content of the two documents. In one specific case, Mprah studied access and use of sexual and reproductive health (SRH) services among deaf people in Ghana. The study found that most participants lacked knowledge of SRH issues due to the inaccessibility of information, and therefore were unable to exercise their SRH rights (Mprah 2011; Mprah 2013).

While duty-bearers have the greatest responsibility to ensure that rights are safeguarded, beneficiaries of legal instruments must have a clear understanding of what their rights are in order to claim them (Department for International Development [DFID], 2000). In other words, it is important for PwDs to be well informed about the content of the PwDA and CRPD, to enable them to utilize the provisions of the two instruments. However, little is known about the level of knowledge of users of these documents and the barriers they encounter to using them to claim disability rights. Our chapter investigates these issues by assessing deaf persons' knowledge about the PwDA and CRPD, and the barriers they encounter in utilizing these documents to claim their rights.

Theoretical Framework and Methodology

The analysis that follows is grounded in the diffusion theory developed by Rogers (2003), which describes how ideas are spread and utilized among groups of people in socio-cultural settings. According to this theory, when a new idea or an innovation is introduced, it gains momentum over time and spreads throughout a specific population. The process highlights the significance of understanding not only the innovation, but also the social networks through which it spreads.

The ultimate aim of the diffusion process is the adoption of the new idea, which manifests itself in behavioural or attitudinal change. It should, however, be noted that the adoption of the new idea among the populace does not take place at the same time for all people. Instead, it is adopted in a chronological sequence based how long it takes an adopter to begin using the innovations. Rogers identified five categories of adopters: Innovators, Early Adopters, Early Majority, Late Majority, and Laggards. The Innovators are adventurous, willing to take risks, and the first to try a new idea. They begin the diffusion process, influenced by change agents to adopt the innovation. They, in turn, exert influence on the behaviours of others, and the innovation diffuses through the other categories. The Early Adopters are usually opinion leaders in the community, and by virtue of their role as leaders, are already aware of the need to change. They, therefore, do not have issues with adopting an innovation. The third category, the Early Majority, are normally not leaders, but they are willing to accept new ideas before the average person. The majority of the population falls within this category, and they typically want to see evidence that the innovation is working before accepting it. The Late Majority are sceptical of change and will only adopt an innovation if it has been tested by the majority. The last group, the Laggards, are very conservative, and, as result, the most resistant to accepting innovation. For change agents, it is important to identify which category an individual belongs to, so that the adoption of an innovation can be achieved most readily.

The diffusion theory sees information as critical to decision-making. The availability of reliable information on a new idea is vital in reducing doubts and enabling an adopter to make informed decisions on the innovation. Access to and use of information has the effect of changing one's state of knowledge and capacity to act (Stenmark, 2001; Rogers, 2003), but information and knowledge are also interrelated: information affects knowledge and vice versa. But the dissemination of information depends on communication, and the degree to which effective communication occurs between people – for instance, between a change agent and an adopter – is influenced by many different factors. These include levels of educational attainment, languages used, age, gender, culture, cognitive limitations, the way the information is presented, and power issues (Schiavo, 2007; Rogers, 2003). For example, the use of complex terminologies could make comprehension difficult for adopters. As such, by implication, it is critical to interpret information in a meaningful way so that it will be accepted easily by the receiver and then transformed into knowledge (Stenmark, 2001).

Rogers' (2003) theory is useful for this chapter for several reasons. First, deaf people's potential to secure disability rights is intimately connected to, and indeed based on, access to information. Second, in a process very similar to Rogers' diffusion theory, information flows within the deaf community through the 'deaf grapevine', which is a network of deaf people passing information to one another through close associates such as friends and family members (Hugh, 2016). Third, also echoing Rogers' theory, DPOs in Ghana collaborate with State institutions and Civil Society Organizations (CSOs) to educate their members on new programmes and policies through workshops. The trainees, acting as peer educators, disseminate what they learned to other members of the community. Fourth, communication barriers threaten to block the flow of information and, in turn, the diffusion of disability rights. Most importantly, the English language, in which the PwDA and CRPD are presented, presents serious challenges to deaf Ghanaians, because it is their second language, and literacy in English among deaf people is generally low (Lodi *et al.*, 2014). Following Rogers, it is therefore important to focus on interpreting information about disability rights in a way that is meaningful to deaf Ghanaians, to remove bottlenecks in the adoption of the PwDA and CRPD.

To assess deaf Ghanaians' knowledge of the PwDA and CRPD in relation to adopting disability rights, we conducted a study in three districts: Wa Municipality in the Upper West Region, Tamale Metropolis in the Northern Region, and Bolgatanga Metropolis in the Upper East Region. We also included the University of Education, Winneba Campus, which had the largest number of deaf students at the time of the study, to help compare the knowledge of deaf people with a higher education with that of those with lower educational attainment. The study was descriptive and used a mixed methods approach. We first utilized a quantitative method and, after analyzing the data, followed it up with a qualitative research instrument. The quantitative method was conducted to gain a broader understanding of deaf people's knowledge of the PwDA and CRPD, while the qualitative method was used to gain an in-depth understanding of the barriers encountered by deaf people trying to utilize the provisions in the two instruments. The two methods provided a better picture of the level of knowledge of and barriers to the utilization of the PwDA and the CRPD than either could have produced individually. Each method complemented the other and compensated for weaknesses, particularly in the quantitative surveys. Deaf people generally have challenges reading English and often struggle to answer items in questionnaires, especially open-ended items. The qualitative component therefore provided opportunities for participants to express their views more completely using sign language.

A total of 132 participants (74 males and 58 females) took part in the study. One hundred and two participants completed the survey, and the remaining thirty participants took part in focus group discussions (FGDs). Whereas the survey targeted the general members of GNAD, the FGDs targeted GNAD leaders in each selected region, as well as the association's national board members. Established in 1968, the GNAD is a national organization for those with hearing difficulties, with branches in all districts of Ghana. It is a member of the disability rights movement in Ghana and one of the three founding members of the Ghana Federation of Disability Organisations (GFD). The main objective of GNAD is to build a strong and productive deaf community and to advocate for their rights. Through over fifty years of advocacy, the GNAD has been able to create awareness about the communication needs of the deaf community in Ghana and advocate for the inclusion of sign language interpreting in many national activities. It was also instrumental in advocating for the passage of the PwDA in 2006.

When targeting GNAD members, a convenience sampling technique was employed to recruit participants for the survey, while purposive sampling was used when recruiting FGD participants. The choice of the districts was informed by their statuses in the region. As the regional capitals, they attracted many people, including deaf people, from the rural areas. Since deaf people do not live together in clusters, using these locations was the best way to find participants. Announcements were made in advance through the various regional presidents, to inform potential respondents of the study. We then scheduled meetings for the potential participants in each of the communities, during which volunteers were screened and taken through the informed consent process. Survey responses were collected from a total of 102 (N = 102) respondents from the three regions and the University of Education, Winneba Campus. Table 7.1 presents their regional and demographic distribution.

Table 7.1 Distribution of respondents by location.

	Males		Females		
	Adults	Youth	Adults	Youth	Total
District	N	N	N	N	N
Bolga Municipality	11	11	6	7	**35**
Tamale Metropolis	8	14	5	11	**38**
Wa Municipality	7	8	8	8	**31**
Winneba Campus	1	10	3	6	**20**
GNAD Board	4	--	4	--	**8**
Total	**31**	**43**	**26**	**32**	**132**

N = Number of participants
(Source: Field data, 2016.)

For this study, we targeted only deaf Ghanaians with formal education. In Ghana, formal education is required for a deaf person to acquire the Ghana Sign Language (GSL), because GSL is offered mainly in the deaf schools. Communicating with deaf Ghanaians not literate in GSL would have posed a serious challenge, because it would have required knowledge of multiple localized sign languages developed by deaf persons to communicate with members of their respective communities. In addition, the GSL users were those who often benefited from workshops organized by the GNAD and were in position to discuss their experiences in relation to the Disability Act and the CRPD.

As noted above, the survey was given to 102 respondents. In addition, 4 FGDs were held: one for deaf leaders in each of the 3 selected regions and another for GNAD's 8 board members. On average, each FGD for the regional leaders had 7 participants.

Five deaf research assistants were recruited to support with the data collection, after receiving pre-field orientation on how to conduct FGDs, administer surveys, and protect the privacy and confidentiality of respondents. The survey instrument was self-administered with support by the field assistants, who also conducted the FGDs using a written guide, which contained open-ended questions on broad issues related to the research subject. Each FGD was videotaped after all participants agreed to be recorded and signed an informed consent form.

The survey data were cleaned, entered into an SPSS file, and analysed using descriptive statistics to generate frequencies, percentages, and cross-tabulations. The data were then summarized in tables. Each of the three field assistants transcribed all of the FGD videos independently from sign language to Microsoft Word format in English. After transcribing, the researchers and the field assistants read the transcripts thoroughly to identify, address, and reconcile differences. The two lead researchers repeatedly read through the transcripts to identify the relevant themes. Based on the objectives of the study, we marked out concepts, phrases, and sentences that matched the objectives, using colours (each of the three objectives was given a unique colour). We then grouped together sections with similar colours to form broad themes. These broad themes were further refined to form the main themes of the study. Some of the themes were divided into sub-themes and supported with direct quotations from the participants. In addition, some of the responses were quantified to produce a fair idea of the percentage of participants holding a particular viewpoint.

Out of the 132 participants who participated in the study, 60.3% were males and 39.7% were females. The youngest participants were between fifteen and twenty years old, and the oldest were over thirty-six (see Table 7.2 below). More than half of the respondents (58.8%) were single at the time of the study, 39.2% were married, and 2.0% were divorced. Christians accounted for a little over half (52.9%) of the respondents, with the remainder being Muslims. Fewer than half of the respondents (47.1%) were employed. All had some form of formal education, but the largest group had completed senior high school (SHS) education (50%), while the smallest group had completed tertiary education (33.3%).

Table 7.2 Socio-demographic characteristics of respondents.

Variable	Adults: N = 57	Youth: N = 75	Total: N = 132
Gender	40.2	20.1	60.3
Male	13.2	26.5	39.7
Female			
Age	--	4.9	4.9
15–20	--	31.4	31.4
21–25	11.7	37.3	37.3
26–30	14.7	--	11.7
31–35		--	14.7
36+			
Marital status	26.1	13.1	39.2
Married	19.3	38.7	58.0
Unmarried	1.3	0.7	2.0
Separated			
Level of education	5.6	11.1	16.7
JHS	16.7	33.3	50.0
SHS	11.1	22.2	33.3
Tertiary			
Occupation			
Employed	31.3	15.7	47.0
Unemployed	8.3	16.7	25.0
Students	9.3	18.7	28.0

N = Number of participants
(Source: Field data, 2016.)

The State of Knowledge of Human Rights, the CRPD, and the PwDA among Deaf People in Ghana

This section presents the findings from our fieldwork. First, however, it is important to discuss the legal framework underpinning disability rights in Ghana. After 1992, when Ghana adopted constitutional rule following the inception of the Fourth Republican Constitution, PwDs and their activists were given some power to advocate for equal rights. The Constitution provides, for example, for the fundamental human rights of all Ghanaians and prohibits all forms of discrimination against any person regardless of socio-demographic and economic characteristics, including disability. Article 29 of the Constitution tasks parliament with making legislation to protect and promote the rights of PwDs (Government of Ghana, 1992). In 2000, the first National Disability Policy was formulated. This was followed by the passage of the PwDA in 2006 and the ratification of the CRPD in 2012.

The National Disability Policy provides a framework for implementing programmes to improve the welfare of PwDs, covering issues such as the rights to employment, education, transportation, and healthcare. The Ministry of Employment and Social Welfare (as it was called in 2000), which was responsible for disability issues, was tasked with taking steps to address the barriers hindering the participation of PwDs in activities in their communities (Government of Ghana, 2000). Six years after the National Disability Policy was formulated, the PwDA was passed. The Act gives a great deal of power to PwDs and activists, allowing them to engage with the government of Ghana to formulate and implement policies and programmes that ensure PwDs are treated as equal citizens. The Act prohibits all forms of discrimination against PwDs. Although discrimination persists, the Act's passage has prompted an increased interest in disability issues, and steps are being taken to achieve the integration of PwDs in mainstream society (Government of Ghana, 2006).

The CRPD and PwDA are supported by two State agencies – the Commission on Human Rights and Administrative Justice (CHRAJ) and the National Commission on Civic Education (NCCE) – which are responsible for educating the citizenry on their rights and ensuring that these rights are respected and protected (Asibuo, 2002; Government of Ghana, 1993a). For example, the Act that establishes CHRAJ (Act 456), enjoins it to '... educate the public as to human rights and freedoms by such means as the Commissioner may decide, including publications, lectures and symposia' (Government of Ghana, 1993b: 5). It is also responsible for dealing with human rights abuses. Victims of human rights abuses could seek redress and legal support from CHRAJ (Government of Ghana, 1993b). The NCCE is expected to design and implement programmes that will create awareness among the citizenry about their rights and civic responsibilities (NCCE, 1994).

The CHRAJ and NCCE are supposed to collaborate with DPOs to educate their members on their rights and provisions in the PwDA and CRPD. The extent to which this function has been performed is, however, unclear. It has been observed that national human rights institutions, which are supposed to assist poor people to access their rights and hold governments accountable, often do not perform this function, exposing the poor to human rights abuses (Department for International

Development [DFID], 2000). In the case of Ghana, anecdotal evidence suggests that some regional and district offices of the CHRAJ and NCCE have not even seen copies of the PwDA and CRPD. At the same time, however, a major achievement for deaf Ghanaians since the passage of the PwDA, in connection with the CHRAJ and NCCE, has been promoting the use of sign language. Among other things, sign language interpretation has been introduced to translate news on the national television, and all nursing and midwife training institutions have made sign language a core subject for all trainees. Sign language has also been introduced in parliament to make parliamentary proceedings accessible to deaf people. However, a major challenge regarding the implementation is the attitude and lack of political will on the part of government.

Keeping the above context in mind, we shall now move on to presenting the findings of our study, focusing on two themes: levels of knowledge of human rights and barriers faced by deaf Ghanaians when demanding and lobbying for their rights. Regarding the former, the responses indicated that most of the respondents had knowledge of their human rights, as more than 80% knew they were entitled to basic human rights such as the right to life and the rights to education, language, and equal treatment without discrimination. Interestingly, the level of education attainment had little influence on respondents' knowledge of their rights, although those with a basic education seemed to have slightly less knowledge than those with SHS and tertiary education. Table 7.3 below shows respondents' level of education and knowledge of their rights.

Table 7.3 Knowledge of human rights by educational attainment.

	Basic N = 17	**SHS** N = 51	**Tertiary** N = 34	**Total** N = 102
Statement	%	%	%	%
Deaf people have the same rights as hearing people	87	91	96	91
Deaf people have a right to life	85	89	98	91
Deaf people have a right to education	87	93	96	92

Table 7.3 continued.

Statement	Basic N = 17 %	SHS N = 51 %	Tertiary N = 34 %	Total N = 102 %
Deaf people have a right to language	90	94	98	94
Deaf children can demand that their teachers use sign language	78	81	87	82
Deaf people have a right to choose their spouses	53	51	68	57
Deaf children have a right to equal treatment by their parents	81	85	94	87
Deaf people have a right to access public services without additional cost	67	82	71	73
Deaf people have a right to health	56	67	72	65

(Source: Field data, 2016).

This finding is consistent with data from the FGDs, where the majority of respondents were able to list at least some of the human rights that deaf people are entitled to. For example, a male participant from the GNAD board mentioned that '... [t]o me, I think, deaf have the same rights as hearing people, and they are aware of their human rights ...' A female participant similarly indicated that 'deaf people are human beings and have all rights as other human beings. There must not be discrimination against deaf people.'

Among our participants, knowledge of their human rights in general was slightly higher than knowledge of the CRPD specifically. For example, a little over two-thirds (62.8%) of the respondents indicated that they had heard of the CRPD, 62% had seen it, 41% had a copy, 41% had participated in workshop on the CRPD, and 48% had read it. Table 7.4 below illustrates the findings.

Table 7.4 Knowledge of CRPD by educational attainment.

Statement	Basic N = 17 %	SHS N = 51 %	Tertiary N = 34 %	Total N = 102 %
I have heard of the UN	59	63	79	68
I have heard of the CRPD	47	49	88	62
I have seen the CRPD document	53	51	68	52
I have a copy of the CRPD	41	39	44	41
I have read the CRPD	41	45	56	48
I understand information/words in the CRPD	27	46	65	46
Participated in a training or workshop on CRPD	29	41	32	36
CRPD does not work for PwDs in Ghana	41	26	35	31
CRPD only works for hearing persons who have disabilities	41	26	44	34
CRPD protects deaf people's right to life	59	76	91	79
CRPD does not cover deaf people's right to education	47	31	32	34
CRPD can be used by deaf people to protect their right to education	65	71	91	77
CRPD protects deaf people's right to sign language	71	75	91	80
CRPD protects deaf people's right to culture	65	71	91	77
CRPD guarantees deaf people legal assistance	59	65	94	74

(Source: Field data, 2016.)

Knowledge of the purpose of the CRPD was also somewhat good. Overall, about 60% of the respondents knew what the CRPD could be used for. The level of educational attainment seems to have had some influence on respondents' knowledge of the CRPD, as those with tertiary education were the most knowledgeable compared to other respondents.

This finding contradicted the data from the FGDs, where most of the participants (87.3%) said they did not know about the

CRPD and that deaf people generally were not aware of it. One female FGD participant, for example, said that '... there are few deaf people who know Disability Act 715 and Ghana Constitution but not CRPD'. A male FGD participant also noted that, '... no, to me I don't think many deaf persons are aware of CRPD ... even myself, I do not know much about it'.

With regard to the PwDA, about two-thirds of the respondents said they were familiar with it. More than two-thirds had heard about it (62%) had seen it (61%), had a copy of it (68%), had asked someone to explain it to them (73%), and/or had attended a workshop on it (73%). However, although more than two-thirds (68%) said they had read the Act, less than half (48%) said they understood what they had read. As with the CRPD, educational attainment seemed to have some influence on the respondents' familiarity with the Act, as those with tertiary education were the most knowledgeable among the three groups. A higher percentage of FGD participants said they had seen it (81.4%) and read it (77.5%), undoubtedly because the FGD participants were leaders of GNAD. Generally, however, the participants were more likely to have read and understood the PwDA than the CRPD.

Table 7.5 Knowledge of PwDA by educational attainment.

Statement	Basic N = 17 %	SHS N = 51 %	Tertiary N = 34 %	N = 102 %
I have heard of Persons with Disability Act, 715	53	55	74	62
I have seen Persons with Disability Act, 715	47	67	59	61
I have a copy of Persons with Disability Act, 715	53	65	76	68
I have read the Persons with Disability Act, 715	63	60	80	68
I understand information in the Persons with Disability Act, Act 715	47	53	68	48

I understand the Persons with Disability Act, 715	29	55	79	59
I have asked someone to explain Persons with Disability Act, 715 for me	59	67	88	73
I have participated in training or a workshop on Persons with Disability Act, 715	60	72	88	73

(Source: Field data, 2016.)

Also, a majority (73%) of the respondents said they had attended workshops on the PwDA. Respondents with tertiary education had the highest attendance, whereas those with basic education had the lowest. This is not surprising, since GNAD often purposively selects people who have the most potential to benefit from such workshops, usually those with higher education and opinion leaders, so that they can transmit whatever they have learned to other members in the community (see Table 7.5).

Barriers to Demanding and Lobbying for Rights

Knowing one's rights is important, but demanding and lobbying for those rights is critical, because exercising rights cannot be achieved passively. As an example, from our fieldwork, Table 7.6 below presents information on respondents who had demanded sign language interpretation services when attending meetings with important stakeholders. Overall, approximately half the respondents said they had demanded such services. Demands for services were highest at meetings with officials of the district assembly (52%) and the department of social welfare (50%). This is probably because these two organizations were more likely to pay for sign language interpretation services than other organizations. Level of educational attainment did not seem to have any influence on respondents' decisions to demand for sign language interpreters.

Table 7.6 Percentage of participants who demanded services provided for in the PwDA and CRPD.

	Educational attainment			
	Basic N = 17	**SHS N = 51**	**Tertiary N = 34**	**Total N = 102**
Statement	%	%	%	%
I demanded an interpreter during a meeting at the district assembly	47	55	53	52
I demanded an interpreter during a meeting with the district chief executive	47	47	41	45
I demanded an interpreter during a meeting with the department for social welfare	47	47	56	50
I demanded an interpreter during a visit to the hospital/clinic	41	47	44	44
I demanded an interpreter during a meeting at the police station	24	53	35	42
I demanded an interpreter during a meeting with NCCE	10	55	34.	37
I mentioned provisions in the Act when demanding my rights	10	53	64	46

(Source: Field data, 2016).

The FGD participants discussed barriers to access to information, which possibly hindered their understanding and effective use of the PwDA and CRPD. The major barrier identified by the participants was difficulty getting access to quality information. For example, 78% of the FGD participants stated that they had challenges accessing information on their rights and, for that matter, that they had limited knowledge of the PwDA and the CRPD. The participants identified a number of factors hindering access to information about their rights: lack of accessible formats such as sign language (73.5%); high illiteracy among deaf people hindering access to printed information (63.7%); and the exclusion of deaf people from sensitization programmes on human rights (65.7%). To cite one example, responding to a question on whether deaf people have easy access to information they need, a participant in the focus group said:

> No, deaf people do not have access to information from where hearing people get information. For example, most deaf people get no benefit from viewing TV because of the absence of the interpreter. Currently, only the state TV station provides sign language interpretation services during news time and few programmes, but nowadays they have been off because they [the TV station] explained their equipment for sign language service has broken down. It's almost seven months now.

In addition, there was consensus among the participants that the language used in both the PwDA and UNCRPD was difficult for them to comprehend and that no one had explained the contents of the document in sign language. There was also agreement among FGD participants that deaf people did not have enough resources to pay for legal services and generally could not pursue cases regarding abuse of their human rights. For instance, a member of GNAD's board said that '... [t]he cost of legal services for a deaf person, which include the cost of providing sign language interpretation services, is borne by deaf people, since the state does not pay for such services'.

On whether any State institutions, such as the CHRAJ, non-governmental organizations (NGOs), or CSOs had ever provided legal support for deaf people, none of the participants in the FGD said they had received or knew of any deaf person who had received any such support. This finding contradicts responses from the survey findings, which indicated that some deaf people had received such support: 40.2% and 62.7% said NGOs/CSOs and GNAD, respectively, had provided legal support to deaf persons who needed it. The FGD participants also claimed that some of the organizations responsible for providing legal assistance did not understand deaf people: '[i]institutions responsible for justice delivery do not understand deaf people well whenever a deaf person visited them with no interpreter'. This suggests that some deaf people had attempted seeking redress for abuse of their human rights but were not satisfied with the support they received.

When asked whether there were professionals within the deaf community who could support them, one board member said, '[n]o, there aren't any recognized deaf lawyers in Ghana now'. Another participant agreed and stated that '... there is currently none in the deaf community with knowledge and training to assist deaf people'. That is, while hearing professionals could not help deaf people because they had little knowledge of deaf people's needs, there were no deaf persons with the requisite knowledge to assist their own members.

Conclusion

As this study has shown, deaf people in Ghana have struggled to utilize the two important human rights instruments available to address their exclusion. Many respondents were unfamiliar with the provisions in the two documents despite the fact that they have existed for about a decade. This suggests that there have been significant issues with the implementation of the PwDA and the CRPD. For deaf people, the main issue lies in accessing information, because virtually all of the major sources of information are inaccessible to them. While information from auditory sources cannot be accessed because of their disability and inadequate sign language interpretation services, low educational attainment and poor reading skills deprive them of accessing information in print.

While formulating laws to promote and protect the rights of PwDs is key to their empowerment, it is also critical that beneficiaries of these laws have adequate knowledge and a clear understanding of their rights to be able to benefit from them (DFID, 2000). This means that deaf people need to be made aware of their rights as enshrined in the PwDA and the CRPD, as a prerequisite for building their capacity to demand better recognition and treatment. However, for many reasons, this seems not to be available to many deaf people in Ghana. Access to relevant information on the PwDA and CRPD is necessary for deaf people to be able to adopt them and secure their human rights. Deaf people will only have the capacity to demand and utilize the provisions in the documents if they have adequate knowledge of the importance of the instruments and how they can use them (Stenmark, 2001). Since deaf people generally have difficulty reading and understanding English language (Mprah, 2011; Lodi *et al.*, 2014), many of them find it difficult to read and understand the information in the documents, especially because they are written in complicated language. Thus, although some deaf people may have read the documents, they may not have been able to develop a deeper understanding of how information in the documents can be used to safeguard their rights. To make information in the documents accessible to deaf people, intensive education must be given using GSL. As this provision has been lacking, it is doubtful if the government has carried out adequate awareness-raising and education on the documents. To make matters more challenging, even if there was a deeper commitment to providing translations into GSL, there are few professional sign language interpreters in Ghana who can accurately translate the texts.

In Ghana, DPOs – acting as representatives of their members – work with NGOs/CSOs to educate their members on new legal instruments such as the PwDA and CRPD. The DPOs act as the first adopters of new ideas such as disability rights, and in turn run workshops for selected representatives, who are then supposed to transmit this new knowledge to other members of their communities. This diffusion process is similar to Rogers' (2003) diffusion of innovation theory, in that not all members of the deaf community will adopt the new idea at the same time because of personal and external factors. The language used in the PwDA and the CRPD and the low level of education among deaf people tends to delay adoption of new ideas, but the operation of the 'deaf grapevine' also means that the information relayed during this system of diffusion is often inaccurate (Mprah, 2011; Heuttel and Ronstein, 2001). More fundamentally, the PwDA and CRPD are aimed at addressing challenges encountered by deaf people, but the documents are not available in accessible formats, rendering them ineffective in dealing with the problems for which they have been created. Making these documents accessible to deaf people will ensure that they are well informed about the content of the documents. This will motivate them to initiate actions against abusers, negotiate for better treatment, and maintain positive attitudes and behaviours that will increase their participation in socio-economic activities.

The findings suggest that more needs to be done by the CHRAJ and NCCE to make the PwDA and CRPD accessible to deaf people. These institutions have a greater role to perform to ensure that the content of the PwDA and CRPD reaches their intended audience. There must be practical measures, such as supporting advocacy efforts towards the recognition of the GSL as the native language for deaf people, and adequately training sign language interpreters on legal issues. The GNAD should also consider human rights training as a crucial aspect of its activities. To achieve this goal, it could enter into partnership with the CHRAJ and other advocacy groups to provide better training for its interpreters and members.

Bibliography

Abdulai, A.G. 2009. 'Political Context Study-Ghana', Leeds and Accra: Human Rights, Power and Civic Action Research Project 12(1): 26–41.

Agbenyega, J.S. 2003. 'The Power of Labeling Discourse in the Construction of Disability in Ghana'. Paper presented at the AARE/NZARE Conference Auckland <https://www.aare.edu.au/data/publications/2003/agb03245.pdf> [accessed 10 April 2021].

Asibuo, S.K. 2002. 'The Role of the Commission on Human Rights and Administrative Justice (CHRAJ) in Promoting Public Service Accountability Under Ghana's Fourth Republic', *African Administrative Studies* 58: 63–82.

Department for International Development. 2000. 'Realizing Human Rights for Poor People: Strategies for Achieving the International Development Targets' <https://www2.ohchr.org/english/issues/development/docs/human_rights_tsp.pdf> [accessed 12 April 2021].

Filmer, D. 2008. 'Disability, Poverty and Schooling in Developing Countries: Results from 14 Household Surveys.' *The World Bank Economic Review*, 22(1);141–163.

Government of Ghana. 1992. *The Constitution of the Republic of Ghana.* Art 29.

Government of Ghana. 1993a. *National Commission* for *Civil Education Act*, Act, 452. Section 2(d).

Government of Ghana. 1993b. *Commission of Human Rights Act*, Act 456 <http://www.unhcr.org/refworld/docid/44bf7f804.html> [accessed 12 April 2021].

Government of Ghana. 2000. *Ghana National Disability Policy Document.* Ministry of Employment and Social Welfare, Accra, Ghana: Delaram.

Government of Ghana. 2006. *Persons with Disability Act*, Act 715. Section 7.

Ghana Statistical Services, Noguchi Memorial Institute for Medical Research, and ORC Macro. 2004. *Ghana Demographic and Health Survey 2003.* Calverton, Maryland.

Heuttel, K.L., and Ronstein, W.G. 2001. 'HIV/AIDS Knowledge and Information Sources among the Deaf and Hearing College Students', *American Annals of the Deaf* 146(3): 280–86.

Harpur, P. 2012. '"Embracing the New Disability Rights Paradigm": The Importance of the Convention on the Rights of PwDs', *Disability and Society* 27(1): 1–14.

Hugh, D. 2016. 'What is the "Deaf Grapevine?"' <https://blogs.ucl.ac.uk/library-rnid/2016/02/09/what-is-the-deaf-grapevine/> [accessed 15 April 2021].

Lodi, A.C.B., Bortolotti, E.C., Cavalmoreti, M.J.Z. 2014. 'Letramentos de surdos: práticas sociais de linguagem entre duas línguas/culturas', *Bakhtiniana, Rev. Estud. Discurso* 9(2): 131–49.

National Commission on Civic Education (NCCE). 1994. *First Annual Report* <https://www.nccegh.org/publications/view/83-First+Annual+Report+1994.pdf> [accessed 10 April 2021].

Mprah, W.K. 2011. 'Sexual and Reproductive Needs Assessment with Deaf People in Ghana'. PhD dissertation, University of Illinois, Chicago.

Mprah, W.K. 2013. 'Perceptions about Barriers to Sexual and Reproductive Health Information and Services Among Deaf People in Ghana', *Disability, CBR and Inclusive Development* 20(3): 21–36.

Owoo, M.A.N. 2019. 'Sign Language Needs Policy Protection in Ghana', *The Conversation*, January 21 <https://theconversation.com/sign-language-needs-policy-protection-in-ghana-109774> [accessed 11 April 2021].

Rogers, M.E. 2003. *Diffusion of Innovation*. London: Free Press

Schiavo, S. 2007. *Health Communication: From Theory to Practice*. San Francisco, CA: Jossey-Bass.

Shakespeare, T. 2010. 'The Social Model of Disability'. In: L.J. Davis. Ed. *The Disability Studies Reader*. New York: Routledge.

Slikker, J. 2009. *Attitudes towards Persons with Disability in Ghana*. Accra: VSO Ghana.

Stenmark, D. 2001. 'The Relationship Between Information and Knowledge'. Proceedings of IRIS 24, Ulvik, Norway <https://pdfs.semanticscholar.org/8c8d/c68dd0854bba591847a74f2935d94efe5d5b.pdf> [accessed 15 April 2021].

World Bank (WB). 2020. 'Population total – Ghana' <https://data.worldbank.org/indicator/SP.POP.TOTL?end=2018andlocations=GHandstart=1960chart> [accessed 12 April 2021].

World Health Organization (WHO). 2011. *World Disability Report*. Geneva: WHO Press.

8

CRPD Article 6 – Vulnerabilities of Women with Disabilities: Recommendations for the Disability Movement and Other Stakeholders in Ghana

AUGUSTINA NAAMI & JOANA OKINE

Introduction

The 2010 census report estimates that about 3% of Ghanaians have disabilities, which translates into 737,743 (Ghana Statistical Services, 2012). The census data reveal that there were more women (52.5%) than men with disabilities (47.5%). However, the 2012 Human Rights Watch report shows a remarkable difference in the number of persons with disabilities (PwDs) (United States Department of State, 2012). The statistics indicate that about five million people in Ghana live with disabilities. The five million figure corroborates the World Health Organization (WHO)'s estimates that disability affects 15–20% of every country's population (WHO, 2016). Nevertheless, the Human Rights Watch report does not give gender-disaggregated data. Thus, the number of women with disabilities (WwDs) cannot be determined. But it can be deduced from the Ghana census report that WwDs are likely to outnumber their male counterparts.

Just like everyone, women and girls with disabilities (WGwDs) have inherent human rights which they should enjoy without impediment. The Convention on the Rights of Persons with Disabilities (CRPD) recognizes that WGwDs fall within the intersection of disability and gender, which predisposes them to multiple disadvantages and discrimination that could impact their lives. Hence, the CRPD makes specific provisions for WGwDs in Article 6, Section 1:

> States Parties recognize that women and girls with disabilities are subject to multiple discrimination, and shall take measures to

> ensure the full and equal enjoyment by them of all human rights and fundamental freedoms.

The concerns raised in the CRPD (Article 6[1]) are emphasized in the literature (Heymann, Stein, and Moreno, 2014; Mizunoya and Mitra, 2013; Mitra, Posarac, and Vick, 2011; Naami, 2014; WHO, 2020). Article 6(2), therefore, entreats States Parties to devise measures to ensure meaningful participation and inclusion of WGwDs in society and to fully enjoy their human rights:

> 2. States Parties shall take all appropriate measures to ensure the full development, advancement and empowerment of women, for the purpose of guaranteeing them the exercise and enjoyment of the human rights and fundamental freedoms set out in the present Convention.

Ghana signed and ratified the CRPD in 2007 and 2012, respectively. Earlier in 2006, the Ghanaian government promulgated its first ever legislation specifically targeting persons with disabilities (PwDs): the Persons with Disability Act (PwDA), Act 715. Ghana has yet to domesticate local policies to align with the CRPD. In 2015, the National Gender Policy was also passed. The policy seeks to mainstream gender equality issues into national development processes and to promote gender equality and freedom of women, men, girls and boys, and PwDs. The overall goal is to improve the social, legal, civic, political, economic, and socio-cultural conditions of these groups of people (Government of Ghana, 2015).

Further, on 25 September 2015, United Nations (UN) member countries, including Ghana, adopted seventeen goals which seek to end poverty and ensure prosperity for all globally. These Sustainable Development Goals (SDGs) are in the 2030 Agenda for Sustainable Development. The SDGs outlined in Agenda 2030 provide for the needs of women and girls. Goal 5 of the SDGs aims specifically at empowerment for women and girls in its call to 'achieve gender equality and empowerment for all women and girls'. It is equally important to note that the SDGs explicitly mention disability in 12 out of the 169 indicators. This is important for specific targeting of disability issues. The overarching goal of the UN SDGs is to 'leave no one behind'.

Despite these broad moves, the government of Ghana has not made any legislative provisions to protect the rights and address the concerns of WGwDs, who face multiple discrimination relating to both disability and gender. The intersection of disability and gender create distinct experiences for WGwDs from both men with disabilities and non-women with disabilities (e.g. transgender and non-binary persons with disabilities). The PwDA does not include any specific gender perspectives and the National Gender Policy entirely overlooks disability perspectives, ignoring the unique experiences of WGwDs. What are the life experiences of WGwDs in Ghana, given that there is no single policy provision specifically targeting their unique needs?

Disability- and gender-based discrimination and disadvantages are significantly underexplored in Ghana, leaving out the voices of WGwDs and their unique experiences and needs. This chapter explores some of the challenges WGwDs in Ghana encounter by reviewing existing literature. Since there is a dearth of Ghanaian studies on this topic, we examine existing literature about the intersection of disability and gender. Gender and disability perspectives are necessary for disability and gender policies respectively, to enable interventions to address these needs. We then draw implications for the government, the disability movement, and other stakeholders in disability, including non-governmental organizations (NGOs) and Civil Society Organizations (CSOs). Throughout the chapter, we use the theory of intersectionality as a guide.

The Theory of Intersectionality

The theory of intersectionality was first developed in 1989 by feminist legal scholar Kimberlé Crenshaw. In her work, Crenshaw challenged the single categorization of discrimination based on race or gender, arguing that such categorization systematically omits the experiences of Black women because it does not factor them into both anti-racist politics and activism and feminist theory. Basing her argument on the legal system where she worked as a barrister in Geneva, Crenshaw claimed that the court framed Black female employment cases around those of their Black male counterparts without considering their sex, even in situations where sex disparities were evident. She emphasized that a monolithic ideology about people's identity leads to overlooking identities outside the dominant framework, which can place the most vulnerable people in society at greater risk. Crenshaw further developed her arguments in 1991, when she stressed that historical conceptualizations of sex and racial discrimination marginalize the true scope of discrimination and argued that feminism and anti-racism can legitimate marginalization.

Crenshaw and other scholars such as Collins (1990) and Nash (2008) theorize that the intersection of systems and structures such as gender, race/ethnicity, class, age, religion, and other categories determine the experiences of people who fall within more than one of these categories. The proponents of intersectionality, therefore, called for a re-examination of the definition of oppression to include the experiences of those who fall within multiple categories of vulnerabilities. This, they believed, could lead to more effective policies and legislation to address the needs of the most at-risk populations. We contend that WwDs fall within the intersection of disability and gender, hence they are more likely to face multiple disadvantages and discrimination which could adversely impact their lives. Disability- and gender-based discrimination is the focus of the rest of this chapter.

Vulnerabilities of Women with Disabilities

WGwDs face multiple disadvantages and discrimination on account of disability and gender. Figure 8.1 summarizes the oppressions WGwDs encounter in society. Gender inequality in our societies is an age-old tradition. The feminist movement started in the seventeenth century to advocate against the patriarchal dogma which oppresses women and for the inclusion of women in mainstream society. However, the women's movement is criticized for considering women as a generic group and in so doing ignoring the issues and needs of WGwDs (Lather, 1991; Lonsdale, 1990; Rubin, 1997; Traustadottir, 1990). This scenario is represented in the outer circle of Figure 8.1.

The disability movement advocates for the inclusion of PwDs in society as social, physical, transportation, institutional, and information barriers continue to prevent them from having full access to resources and opportunities to maximize their potential. However, the disability movement, just like the feminist movement, is criticized for not including issues of WwDs in their main agenda (Lonsdale, 1990; Rubin, 1997; Traustadottir, 1990). This scenario is represented in the second circle.

Different forms of oppression exist within each of the circles to perpetuate the vulnerabilities of WGwDs. It is important to note that the interaction of disability and gender is more than just an addition to the impact of oppression on WGwDs. Gender, disability, and other factors (e.g. culture, geographic region, minority status) interact simultaneously to produce many and varied effects, all of which can have negative consequences for WGwDs. To be visible and have their needs and issues addressed, WGwDs have to overcome oppression and marginalization within the disability and women's movements and society. They must challenge all these structures that exist to create and maintain disability- and gender-based discrimination and other forms of oppression.

Although WGwDs are embedded within the disability and feminist movements, as illustrated in Figure 8.1, both marginalize WGwDs. These structures inadequately address the needs of WwDs, who are more likely to face multiple disadvantages and discrimination, as suggested in the theory of intersectionality. For example, the unique needs of WGwDs, such as reproductive health, pre-and post-natal, and maternal health issues, rarely get onto the agenda of the disability and women's movements. Cultural norms, beliefs, practices, stigma, poverty, and the geographic region could shape the experiences of WGwDs in Ghana (Kassah, 2008; Naami, 2014; Slikker, 2009).

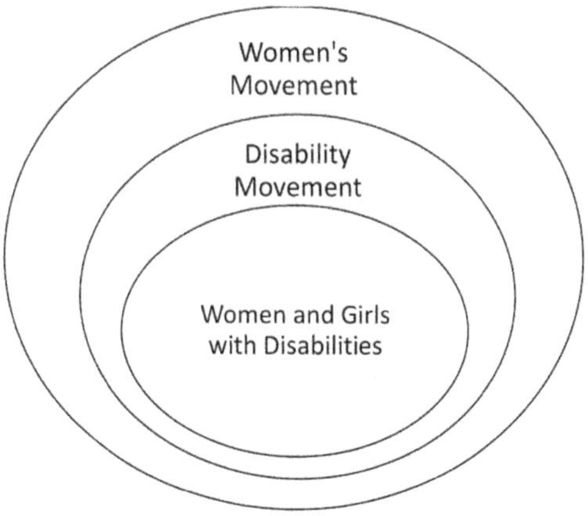

Figure 8.1 Vulnerabilities of women and girls with disabilites
(Source: Naami, Augustina 2010, 'The Impact of Unemployment on Women with Physical Disabilities in Tamale, Ghana'. PhD dissertation, University of Utah, USA).

Empirical Evidence

In this section, we use existing literature to demonstrate how disability–gender disparities manifest in education, employment, income, political participation, and violence against WGwDs. These issues are largely captured in SDG disability targets and indicators:

1. Education: Goal 4. Ensure inclusive and equitable quality education and promote lifelong learning opportunities for all.
2. Employment and income: Goal 8. Promote sustained, inclusive and sustainable economic growth, full and productive employment, and decent work for all.
3. Political Participation: Goal 10. Reduce inequality within and among countries.
4. Violence against WGwDs: Goal 3. Ensure healthy lives and promote well-being for all at all ages.

We also draw on the provisions in the CRPD to make a case for actions to address the outcomes of disability–gender disparities so that the experiences of WGwDs can be improved.

Employment of Women with Disabilities

Globally, a disability–employment gap exists (i.e. a gap in employment levels between persons with disabilities and others). Employment of PwDs is low, regardless of legislation in many countries to promote their participation in the labour market. However, WwDs are more disadvantaged because of the intersection of disability and gender. Statistics collected in 2011 for the *World Disability Report* (WHO, 2011), which surveyed fifty-one countries, including Ghana, indicate that men with disabilities are more than twice (52.8%) as likely to be employed compared to WwDs (19.6%). Other studies in both the developed and developing countries demonstrate persistent disability–gender employment disparities, in the sense of lower employment levels for women with disabilities compared to men with disabilities and women without disabilities (Dhungana, 2006; Emmett and Alant, 2006; Moodley and Graham, 2015; Smith, 2007; Traustadottir, 1999).

Not only do disability and gender create a double exclusion for WwDs in the labour market, but race and other demographic variables could worsen labour market exclusion for WwDs. In their study in South Africa, Moodley and Graham (2015) found that beyond the disability–employment gap, Black WwDs face triple jeopardy (on account of disability, gender, and race), which worsens their labour market outcomes.

Disability–gender income disparity also exists. PwDs earn less than their counterparts without disabilities, but WwDs earn the least among the former (Heymann, Stein, and Moreno, 2014; Kaye, 2009; Mitra and Sambamoorthi, 2006, 2009; Moodley and Graham, 2015; WHO, 2011). Moodley and Graham (2015) found that WwDs earned the least from work compared with men with and without disabilities and women without disabilities – a situation that is likely to propel PwDs into poverty. The association of disability and poverty is emphasized in the literature, with WwDs being overrepresented compared to their male counterparts (Mitra, Posarac, and Vick, 2011; Moodley and Graham, 2015; Mizunoya and Mitra, 2013; WHO, 2011). A study by Mitra, Posarac, and Vick (2011) shows a significant association of disability and multidimensional poverty in fourteen of the fifteen developing countries investigated. On a related issue, the literature also reports gender-disability-related discrimination concerning promotion conditions, access to training and retraining, and occupational segregation (Emmett and Alant, 2006; Naami, 2015; Smith, 2007; Barisin, Benjak, and Vuletic, 2011; Kaye, 2009). For instance, Naami (2015) found that, in Ghana, twice as many men with disabilities received training and promotions compared to WwDs.

Employment and disability–gender income disparities in Ghana could be similar to or worse than in other African countries (Moodley and Graham, 2015). This could be because of a combination of factors, including education, socio-cultural beliefs and practices, and physical and transportation inaccessibility. Lower educational outcomes for PwDs, especially in low-income countries, is clear in the literature. For example, WHO (2011) reported lower primary completion outcomes for PwDs in both developed (males without disabilities [72.3%] and males with disabilities [61.7%]) and developing countries (males without disabilities [55.6%] and males with disabilities [45.6%]). In the same study, lower educational rates were reported for WGwDs in both developed and developing countries respectively (59.3%; 32.9%) compared with those without disabilities (72.0; 42.0%). However, there is a dearth of literature to estimate the scope and trend of the employment of PwDs in Ghana.

Attitudinal barriers remain the major source of unemployment for PwDs. The World Report on Disability and several other studies cited discrimination as the major barrier to the hiring of PwDs (Heymann, Stein, and Moreno, 2014; Mizunoya and Mitra, 2013; Niehaus and Bauer, 2013; Prins, 2013; WHO, 2011). Attitudinal barriers on the job have also been documented, including negative perceptions about the capabilities of PwDs (Aromaa *et al.*, 2011; Naami, 2014; Prins, 2013). PwDs are also perceived as being unable to perform at the same levels as their counterparts without disabilities (Prins, 2013). Ghanaian' perceptions and attitudes towards PwDs are rooted in socio-cultural beliefs, traditions, and practices which marginalize PwDs (Kassah, 2008; Naami, 2015; Slikker, 2009) and could adversely affect WGwDs due to the intersection of disability and gender.

Women with disabilities are not only less likely to get jobs but also more likely to work in the informal sector, mostly in vulnerable employment. Vulnerable employment is characterized by marginal, seasonal, and menial jobs with a low income and lack of job security and job-related benefits (UN, 2013). The world's vulnerable employment gender gap is estimated at 2.3%: 50.4% of women were in vulnerable employment compared to 48.1% men (UN, 2013). Sub-Saharan Africa (of which Ghana is a part) had a rather high estimate, at 15%. PwDs are more likely to work in the informal sector compared to those without disabilities. Mizunoya and Mitra (2013), who sought to understand disability–employment disparities in 15 developing countries including 7 African countries, found that in 14 out of the 15 countries, a much greater proportion of PwDs work in that sector compared with those without disabilities. If many PwDs work in the informal sector, then we can conclude that the intersection of disability and gender could worsen the situation for WwDs. For example, in Ghana, a study by Naami (2015) revealed a gender–disability–vulnerable employment gap of 18.6%.

It could be argued that PwDs work in the informal sector due to flexibility of the sector (e.g. flexibility of working hours and times, the ability to work from home, minimal capital required in some instances). However, Mizunoya and Mitra (2013) argued that since many PwDs work in the informal sector, there is a need for further investigation to found out whether it is a choice or due to barriers to participation in the formal sector; physical, social, communication, information, transportation, and institutional barriers could all shape the employment experiences of PwDs.

Political Participation of WGwDs

On a global scale, female political participation is low for women with and without disabilities. UN Women (2019) estimates the global average percentage of women participating in politics as 24.3%, and that in some States fewer than 10% of parliamentarians are women. Low female political participation is also recorded in Ghana. Out of the 275 parliamentarians, only 35 (12.75%) were female (Media Foundation for West Africa, 2017).

Article 29a of the CRPD calls on States Parties to guarantee equal political rights to allow PwDs to participate fully in politics. Under the Article, States Parties are mandated:

> To ensure that persons with disabilities can effectively and fully participate in political and public life on an equal basis with others, directly or through freely chosen representatives, including the right and opportunity for persons with disabilities to vote and be elected.

Regardless of this provision, PwDs are currently underrepresented in politics and democratic processes. PwDs are less likely to take part in politics, although they are experts in their conditions and can provide valuable and relevant information about themselves, which could be useful to develop relevant interventions to address their issues. The literature attributes the low representation of PwDs in both developing and developed countries to several factors, including attitudinal barriers (Alvarez, 2012; Arthur, 2017; Prince, 2007; Sackey, 2015; Schur and Adya, 2013; Virendrakumar *et al.*, 2018), lack of resources to finance electoral procedures and regulations (Arthur, 2017; Sackey, 2015; Virendrakumar *et al.,* 2018), built environmental barriers (Arthur, 2017; Sackey, 2015), and low educational levels that impede understanding of informed decisions (Arthur, 2017; Virendrakumar *et al.,* 2018). However, there is insufficient literature on how females with disabilities experience political participation. Given that political participation for both women and PwDs is low, the experience of WwDs could be even worse, as they fall within the intersection of disability and gender.

Violence against Women and Girls with Disabilities

Gender-based violence is a global phenomenon, and women worldwide are more likely than men to experience economic, physical, sexual, and emotional violence. Global estimates indicate that about 1 in 3 (35%) women have experienced either physical and/or sexual violence in their lifetime, with some countries recording estimates of about 70% violence against women (UN Women, 2017). Women with disabilities are more vulnerable to violence because of the intersection of gender and disability. Recognizing that the world's largest minority group, PwDs – estimated at 1 billion by the WHO (2011) – are at risk of violence, the CRPD makes provisions to protect them in Article 16(1):

> States Parties shall take all appropriate legislative, administrative, social, educational and other measures to protect persons with disabilities, both within and outside the home, from all forms of exploitation, violence and abuse, including their gender-based aspects.

The UN followed this up with the Resolution (72/162), adopted by the General Assembly on 19 December 2017, which indicated that WGwDs continued to face more serious and varied forms of violence compared to other women and their male counterparts. Resolution 72/162 is related to implementing the CRPD and Optional Protocol regarding the situation of WGwDs.

Regarding gendered violence, the Resolution noted the increased risk face by WGwDs and called on States Parties to take action, in line with the CRPD's provisions. The Resolution expressed concerns,

> that stereotypes, stigmatization, and discrimination heightened the risk of violence exploitation and abuse, including sexual violence and abuse against women and girls with disabilities compared to women and girls without disabilities, as well as men and boys with disabilities (UN, 2018: 2).

The Resolution then called on States 'to take effective action to prevent and eliminate all forms of violence, exploitation and abuse, including sexual violence and abuse, against women and girls with disabilities without delay' (UN, 2018: 5). Concrete recommendations for States included: implementing legislation to protect WGwDs against violence; taking measures to ensure safe and equitable legal action to prosecute perpetrators; ensuring services and programmes to protect WGwDs are accessible, especially 'for those living in institutionalized settings, who are the most vulnerable to violence'; and ensuring that WGwDs and their families 'have access to a range of support services, information in accessible formats and education on how to prevent, recognize and report instances of exploitation, violence and abuse' (UN, 2018: 5).

The CRPD and Resolution 72/162 recognize that the intersection of gender and disability makes WGwDs more likely to be exposed to gender-based violence than women without disabilities and males with disabilities. WGwDs are at risk of several forms of abuse from different perpetrators, including family members, intimate partners, caregivers, healthcare providers, personal assistants, and peers (International Network of Women with Disabilities [INWWD], 2010; Nixon, 2009; Shah, Tsitsou, and Woodin. 2016; Women with Disabilities Australia, 2007). The study of Shah, Tsitsou, and Woodin further suggests that WGwDs are twice as likely to experience gender-based violence over a longer period and more likely to sustain severe injuries as a result of violence compared to their counterparts without disabilities.

There is also evidence of various barriers restricting WGwDs from reporting abuse against them, including barriers in transportation, information, finances, and physical access (Healey, 2013; INWWD, 2010; Shah, Tsitsou, and Woodin, 2016). The literature also reports barriers to accessing support services for the abused victims (Healey, 2013; INWWD, 2010). These occurrences could also worsen the experiences of WGwDs relating to violence compared to women without disabilities and men with disabilities.

The experiences of WGwDs in Africa are shaped by superstitious beliefs, stigma, and stereotypes about their sexuality (Opoku *et al.*, 2016; Van der Heijden, Abrahams, and Harries, 2016). Factors identified which could increase the risk of sexual abuse included disability, poverty, and rejection by family, as well as an inaccessible home environment. Regrettably, abuses resulted in unwanted pregnancy, fear, and trauma (Opoku *et al.*, 2016).

Conclusion

The vulnerabilities of WGwDs are clear from the preceding discussion. WGwDs experience violations of their rights from many angles because of the intersection of disability and gender. Ghana, a signatory to the CRPD, needs to develop measures that can eliminate barriers to the meaningful participation and inclusion of WGwDs in society to ensure that they can fully enjoy their human rights, as suggested in Article 6(2):

> States Parties shall take all appropriate measures to ensure the full development, advancement and empowerment of women, to guarantee them the exercise and enjoyment of the human rights and fundamental freedoms set out in the present Convention.

Addressing disability-specific gender discrimination and disadvantages, as proposed in the CRPD, could complement the achievement of the targets of the 2030 Agenda for Sustainable Development. These international frameworks set out the gender- and disability-related goals which have formed the themes discussed in this chapter. It is therefore imperative that the government and other stakeholders make conscientious efforts to ensure that WGwDs enjoy gender- and disability-based programmes equally. In addition to this, specific, stand-alone empowerment interventions targeting WGwDs will be imperative in addressing their unique needs, given that they are sidelined in both disability and feminist movements (Lather, 1991; Lonsdale, 1990; Rubin, 1997; Traustadottir, 1990). Here we recommend interventions for the thematic areas addressed in the chapter: education/skills development, employment, political participation and leadership for WwDs, ending violence against WGwDs, and implications for future research.

Education/Skills Development

Education is necessary for the employment and overall social participation of PwDs (WHO, 2011). Education contributes to human capital formation and thus is a key determinant of personal well-being and welfare. There is evidence that inadequate employable skills and formal education significantly impact the employment of PwDs (Mitra, Posarac, and Vick, 2011; Mizunoya and Mitra, 2013; WHO, 2011; Naami, 2015). Thus, the Ghanaian government and other stakeholders in disability should create more opportunities for WGwDs in terms of informal education and skills development to enable them to get jobs. We recommend disability–gender sensitive intervention to promote formal and vocational education for WGwDs, such as an accessible physical environment (including toilet facilities) and positive attitudes towards WGwDs (Gupta, 2021). Awareness-raising and strategies that change social behaviour, such as the use of the media, dance, drama, and showcasing success stories of WGwDs, could promote positive attitudes.

We suggest that the disability movement and CSOs support the use of female role models with disabilities to encourage and motivate WGwDs to pursue education and skills development. These individuals could share their success stories and how they managed with the odds against them. Role models could share their stories with WGwDs, their families, and communities to encourage the pursuit of education and skills development. Awareness-raising at all levels to promote respect for the dignity of WGwDs and the need for their inclusion in mainstream society is consistent with CRPD Article 8. The inclusion of female role models with disabilities in gender-disability-specific awareness-raising could empower both those sharing their stories and those who hear them. This approach could also help to create a positive image of WGwDs and hence change attitudes towards them.

In addition, the government should support those who want to learn vocational skills in their communities through a community-based rehabilitation approach. This programme should focus on teaching skills that apply to the job market, secretarial training, fashion design, cosmetology, and other relevant craftwork.

Employment

Concerning employment, we recommend inclusive labour market employment consistent with Article 27, Section 1(h) of the CRPD, which calls on States to 'promote the employment of persons with disabilities in the private sector through appropriate policies and measures, which may include affirmative action programmes, incentives and other measures'. Besides incentives, we suggest that the Ghana government consider punitive measures such as tax increases for firms that refuse to hire WwDs. The net positive effect on employment using this method is shown in Austria (Wuellrich, 2010: 175).

Another inclusive employment approach would require the government to work with organizations to create models that could address the specific needs of women with diverse forms of disabilities in mainstream organizations. An example would be a woman with a psychosocial disability who has challenges concentrating on a job for which she qualifies. Organizations could also employ qualified WwDs to train on the job (internship) to make them competitive for the job market, as stated in CRPD Article 27, Section 1(j), which instructs States to 'promote the acquisition by persons with disabilities of work experience in the open labour market'.

WGwDs who acquire vocational training should be given tools and start-up capital to equip them to work. There is evidence that WwDs are less likely than their male counterparts to access start-up capital due to a lack of collateral security (Naami, 2015; WHO, 2011). The government and CSOs should support females with disabilities who work in the informal sector to become competitive in the market. Female entrepreneurs with disabilities should be supported with training in business management and entrepreneurial skills to enable them to grow and sustain their businesses. This recommendation is consistent with CRPD Article 27, Section 1(f), which calls on States to 'promote opportunities for self-employment, entrepreneurship, the development of cooperatives and starting one's own business'.

Political Participation and Leadership for Women with Disabilities

The disability movement and CSOs should lobby, advocate for, and support the political participation of WwDs. WGwDs understand their unique experiences and can tell their own stories in ways that no one else can. These entities could best help develop appropriate interventions to address their needs. Including women's voices is therefore crucial in developing measures to address their needs.

The disability movement and CSOs could build the leadership capacities of WGwDs and provide mentorship support to those in leadership positions. The disability movement and CSOs could also lobby the government to ensure WwDs are appointed at various levels of government. Further, CSOs could pay for expenses relating to filing for political party candidacy and campaign expenses noted to hinder political participation for PwDs. They could also lobby political parties to reduce filing fees for WwDs.

Ending Violence against WGwDs

The literature suggests that violence against WGwDs is more pronounced than that against men with disabilities and women without disabilities. We recommend the disability movement and CSOs empower WGwDs, teaching them about their rights, what abuse is, and the different types of abuse. WGwDs also need to know what they should do when they are abused and where/how they can seek redress. Moreover, neither the PwDA nor the National Gender Policy addresses issues of WGwDs. This omission could affect interventions to address the unique needs of WGwDs. The disability movement and CSOs could lobby and advocate for the inclusion of disability–gender perspectives in these policies.

Implication for Future Research

We have discussed disability–gender-related gaps in the literature regarding employment and political participation. We have also indicated that WGwDs in Ghana could be worse off because of a combination of factors, including socio-cultural beliefs and practices, physical and transportation inaccessibility, and limited education. Empirical work is necessary to better understand the vulnerability and needs of WGwDs and inform appropriate interventions that could promote and enhance full enjoyment of their rights.

Bibliography

Alvarez, M.R. 2012. *Defining the Barriers to Political Participation for Individuals with Disabilities.* Working paper, # 001. Washington, DC: The Information Technology and Innovation Foundation.

Aromaa, E., Tolvanen, A., Tuulari, J., and Wahlbeck, K. 2011. 'Personal Stigma and Use of Mental Health Services among People with Depression in a General Population in Finland', *BMC Psychiatry* 11(1): 52.

Arthur, E.A. 2017. *Political Participation of Persons with Disability in Ghana.* Master's Thesis, University of Ghana, Accra.

Barisin, A., Benjak, T.M., and Vuletic, G. 2011. 'Health-related Quality of Life of Women with Disabilities in Relation to Their Employment Status', *Croatian Medical Journal* 52(4): 550–56.

Collins, P.H. 1990. *Black Feminist Thought: Knowledge, Consciousness, and the Politics of Empowerment.* Boston: Unwin Hyman.

Crenshaw, K.W. 1989. 'Demarginalizing the Intersection of Race and Sex: A Black Feminist Critique of Antidiscrimination Doctrine, Feminist Theory, and Antiracist Politics', *University of Chicago Legal Forum* 14: 538–54.

Crenshaw, K.W. 1991. 'Mapping the Margins: Intersectionality, Identity Politics, and Violence against Women of Color', *Stanford Law Review* 43(6): 1241–99.

Dhungana, M.B. 2006. 'The Lives of Disabled Women in Nepal: Vulnerability without Support', *Disability and Society* 21(2): 133–46.

Emmett, T., and Alant, E. 2006. Women and Disability: Exploring the Interface of Multiple Disadvantage', *Development Southern Africa* 23(4): 445–60.

Ghana Statistical Services. 2012. *2010 Population and Housing Census: Summary Report of Final Results.* Sakoa Press Ltd, Accra, Ghana <https://www.statsghana.gov.gh/gssmain/storage/img/marqueeupdater/Census2010_Summary_report_of_final_results.pdf> [accessed 10 April 2021].

Government of Ghana. 2015. *National Gender Policy* <https://www.ilo.org/dyn/natlex/docs/ELECTRONIC/103987/126660/F-515436150/GHA103987.pdf> [accessed 12 April 2021].

Gupta, R. 2021. 'Twin Tracking for Women with Disabilities in Disability' <http://www.disabilitystudiesnalsar.org/bcp-wwd.php> [accessed 9 April 2021].

Healey, L. 2013. *Voices against Violence: Paper 2: Current Issues in Understanding and Responding to Violence against Women with Disabilities.* Women with Disabilities Victoria, Office of the Public Advocate, Domestic Violence Resource Centre Victoria, Australia.

Heymann, J., Stein, M., and Moreno, G. Eds. 2013. *Disability and Equality at Work.* New York: Oxford University Press.

International Labour Organization (ILO). 2007. *Achieving Equal Employment Opportunities for People with Disabilities through Legislation Guidelines.* ILO Geneva (First published 2004).

International Network of Women with Disabilities (INWWD). 2010. 'Document on Violence against Women with Disabilities' <https://inwwd.wordpress.com/publications-of-the-inwwd/> [accessed 10 April 2021].

Kassah, A.K. 2008. 'Disabled People and Begging Justifications in Accra-Ghana', *Disability and Society* 23(2): 163–70.

Kaye, S. 2009. 'Stuck at the Bottom Rung: Occupational Characteristics of Workers with Disabilities', *Journal of Occupational Rehabilitation* 19: 115–28.

Lather, P. 1991. *Getting Smart: Feminist Research and Pedagogy within the Post-Modern.* New York: Routledge.

Lonsdale, S. 1990. *Women and Disability.* New York: St. Martin's Press.

Media Foundation for West Africa. 2017. 'Female MPs in Ghana's 7th Parliament' <https://www.fact-checkghana.com/female-mps-in-ghanas-7th-parliament/> [accessed 11 April 2021].

Mitra, S., and Sambamoorthi, U. 2009. 'Wage Differential by Disability Status in an Agrarian Labor Market In India', *Applied Economics Letters* 16(14): 1393–98.

Mitra, S., and Sambamoorthi, U. 2006. 'Government Programs to Promote Employment among Persons with Disabilities in India', *Indian Journal of Social Development* 6(2): 195–213.

Mitra, S., Posarac, A., and Vick, B. 2011. 'Disability and Poverty in Developing Countries: A Snapshot from the World Health Survey'. Discussion Paper Series. Social Protection and Labor: World Bank (WB) <https://openknowledge.worldbank.org/handle/10986/27369> [accessed 5 April 2021].

Mizunoya, S., and Mitra, S. 2013. 'Is There a Disability Gap in Employment Rates in Developing Countries?' *World Development* 42: 28–43.

Moodley, J., and Graham, L. 2015. 'The Importance of Intersectionality in Disability and Gender Studies', *Agenda* 29(2). DOI: 10.1080/10130950.2015.1041802.

Naami, A. 2015. 'Disability, Gender, and Employment Relationships in Africa: The Case of Ghana', *African Journal of Disability Studies* 4(1): 1–11.

Naami, A. 2014. 'Breaking the Barrier: Ghanaians Perceptions about the Social Model', *Disability, CBR and Inclusive Development* 25(1): 21–39.

Nash, J.C. 2008. 'Re-thinking Intersectionality', *Feminist Review* 89(1): 1–15.

Niehaus, M., and Bauer, J. 2013). *Opportunities and Barriers for Highly Qualified People with Disabilities: Transition to Employment That Is Subject to Social Insurance Contributions; Pilot Study on Professional Participation; Final Report.* Aktion Mensch.

Nixon, J. 2009. 'Domestic Violence and Women with Disabilities: Locating the Issue on the Periphery of Social Movements', *Disability and Society* 24(1): 77–89.

Opoku, P.M., Huyser, N., Mprah, W.K, Badu, E., and Alupo, A.B. 2016. 'Sexual Violence against Women with Disabilities in Ghana: Accounts of Women with Disabilities from Ashanti Region', *Disability CBR and Inclusive Development* 27(2): 91–111.

Prince, J.M. 2007. *The Electoral Participation of Persons with Special Needs.* Working Paper on Electoral Participation and Outreach Practices, Electoral Commission of Canada, Ontario.

Prins, R. 2013. 'Sickness Absence and Disability: An International Perspective'. In: P. Loisel and J.R. Anema. Eds. *Handbook of Work Disability: Prevention and Management* (pp. 3–14). New York: Springer.

Rubin, E. 1997. 'Rehabilitation Problems of Women Who Are Blind', *Sexuality and Disability* 15(1): 41–45.

Sackey, E. 2015. 'Disability and Political Participation in Ghana: An Alternative Perspective', *Scandinavian Journal of Disability Research* 17(4): 366–81. DOI: 10.1080/15017419.2014.941925.

Schur, L., and Adya, M. 2013. 'Sidelined or Mainstreamed? Political Participation and Attitudes of People with Disabilities in the United States', *Social Science Quarterly* 94(3): 811–39.

Shah, S., Tsitsou, L., and Woodin, S. 2016. 'Hidden Voices: Disabled Women's Experiences of Violence and Support over the Life Course', *Violence against Women* 22(10): 1189–1210.

Slikker, J. 2009. *Attitudes Towards Persons with Disability in Ghana.* Accra: VSO Ghana.

Smith, D.L. 2007. 'Employment Status of Women with Disabilities from the Behavioral Risk Factor Surveillance Survey (1995–2002)', *Work* 29(2): 127–35.

Tijm, M.M, Cornielje, H., Edusei, A.K. 2011. "Welcome to My Life!' Photovoice: Needs Assessment of and by Persons with Physical Disabilities in the Kumasi Metropolis, Ghana', *Disability, CBR and Inclusive Development* 22(1): 55–72.

Traustadottir, R. 1990. *Obstacles to Equality: The Double Discrimination of Women with Disabilities: Overview Paper.* DisAbled Women's Network Ontario.

United Nations (UN). 2006. *Convention on the Rights of Persons with Disabilities* <https://www.un.org/development/desa/disabilities/convention-on-the-rights-of-persons-with-disabilities/convention-on-the-rights-of-persons-with-disabilities-2.html> [accessed 15 April 2021].

United Nations (UN). 2013. 'Statistics and Indicators on Women and Men' <https://unstats.un.org/unsd/demographic/products/indwm> [accessed 15 March 2022].

United Nations (UN). 2018. 'Resolution Adopted by the General Assembly on 19 December 2017' <https://undocs.org/en/A/RES/72/162> [accessed 15 April 2021].

United States Department of State. 2012. *Ghana 2012 Human Rights Report* <https://2009-2017.state.gov/documents/organization/204336.pdf> [accessed 15 April 2021].

Van der Heijden, I., Abrahams, N., and Harries, J. 2016. 'Additional Layers of Violence: The Intersections of Gender and Disability in the Violence Experiences of Women with Physical Disabilities in South Africa', *Journal of Interpersonal Violence* 34(4): 1–22.

Virendrakumar, B., Jolley, E., Badu, E., and Schmidt, E. 2018. 'Disability Inclusive Elections in Africa: A Systematic Review of Published and Unpublished Literature', *Disability and Society* 33(4): 509–38.

Women with Disabilities Australia (WWDA). 2007. *Forgotten Sisters – A Global Review of Violence Against Women with Disabilities.* WWDA Resource Manual on Violence Against Women with Disabilities. Tasmania, Australia: WWDA.

World Health Organization (WHO). 2011. *World Report on Disability* <http://www.who.int/disabilities/world_report/2011/report.pdf> [accessed 10 April 2021].

World Health Organization (WHO). 2016. 'Disability and Health: Fact Sheet' <https://www.who.int/news-room/fact-sheets/detail/disability-and-health> [accessed 11 March 2022].

World Health Organization (WHO). 2020. '10 Facts on Disability' <https://www.who.int/news-room/facts-in-pictures/detail/disabilities> [accessed 12 April 2021].

Wuellrich, J.P. 2010. 'The Effects of Increasing Financial Incentives for Firms to Promote Employment of Disabled Workers', *Economics Letters* 107: 173–76.

9

Assessing the Benefits of the CRPD in Cameroon: The Experience of Persons with Disabilities in the Buea Municipality

WISDOM KWADWO MPRAH, MAXWELL PEPRAH OPOKU, & BERNARD NSAIDZEDZE SAKAH

Introduction

Persons with disabilities (PwDs) are indisputably one of the most marginalized groups in all societies around the world. The majority of them are poor and record low outcomes in education, employment, health, and political participation (World Health Organization [WHO], 2011). There is a positive correlation between disability and poverty: each can be a cause and a consequence of the other (Braithwaite and Mont, 2009; Filmer, 2008; Mitra, 2006; Trani and Loeb, 2010). Although the challenges faced by PwDs are global phenomena, they are worse for those in the Global South than the Global North, including countries in Africa (WHO, 2011). In Cameroon, PwDs encounter discrimination in all spheres of life, and their access to socio-economic resources, such as education, employment and healthcare, is limited. They often start school at older ages than their colleagues without disabilities, and they have a much higher tendency to drop out. The majority of children with disabilities (CwDs) who manage to access education do so in special schools, which are often poorly resourced and have weak capacities to meet their needs (WHO, 2011). As a result, PwDs have fewer educational qualifications and are more likely to be unemployed. When employed, they usually perform menial jobs with meagre wages.

These issues are true globally, but they are especially stark in the Global South, as (for example) Mitra and Sambamoorthi (2009) show in their 2009 study on India, and as Trani and Loeb (2012) demonstrate in an interesting comparison of Afghanistan and Zambia. Other evidence from Africa includes, to name a few studies, Cramm, Lorenzo, and Nieboer's (2014) comparison of education and employment among South African YwDs and their peers and Échevin's (2013) analysis of discrimination in education and employment among PwDs in Cape Verde. The main factors leading to exclusion from mainstream activities include prejudice and stereotypical attitudes arising from misconceptions about disability, as well as beliefs that PwDs are less human than their counterparts without disabilities (Shier, Graham, and Jones, 2009). It is in recognition of the vulnerability of PwDs that the Convention on the Rights of Persons with Disabilities (CRPD) was adopted by the United Nations (UN) in 2006. The CRPD provides the framework for the legal protection of the rights of PwDs. As a human rights-based instrument, it is aimed at empowering PwDs by providing them with their rights, while at the same time removing societal barriers to enable them to exercise these rights on an equal basis with others. The ultimate aim of the CRPD is therefore the inclusion of PwDs in mainstream society (Lang *et al.*, 2011).

The provisions in the CRPD contain a set of universal rights, including (for example) the rights to legal capacity, support in decision-making processes, accessible environments, reasonable accommodation, and freely choosing one's way of life (Lang *et al.*, 2011; Silecchia, 2013). The approach adopted by the CRPD is consistent with the social model of disability, which rejects the medical model that equates disability with individual impairments and calls for expert medical 'fixes'. In contrast, the social model defines disability as the outcome of disabling conditions, such as inaccessible physical structures, and negative societal attitudes, which create barriers for disabled persons and thus limit their potential to participate in their communities (Oliver and Barnes, 1998; Palacios, 2015). The human rights approach adopted by the CRPD is also a departure from the charity model and views PwDs as subjects who have rights instead of objects of charity (Katsui, 2008; Silecchia, 2013).

The CRPD is based on a set of overarching and fundamental principles that are aimed at guiding the interpretation and implementation of its provisions. The guiding principles form 'the starting point for understanding and interpreting the rights of disabled persons, providing benchmarks against which each right is measured' (UN, 2010: 17). These principles, contained in nine articles, include respect for inherent dignity, individual autonomy, non-discrimination, full and effective participation and inclusion in society, equal opportunity, and accessibility (Lang *et al.*, 2011). They are interrelated and form the foundation of all the Convention's provisions, and they are expected to guide the formulation of disability legislation and policies and how their implementation is monitored at the country level (UN, 2010).

The rights-based approach adopted by the CRPD has received much positive feedback globally, but it also has triggered a backlash in some quarters. For example, some critics observe that rights-based frameworks in poorer nations often involve prioritizing some rights over others, to the exclusion of disability rights. In the context of limited resources, particularly in the Global South, where poverty is widespread and PwDs form a large section of the poor, disability rights may be denied. This is because, although all rights are deemed equally important, some rights may be considered more urgent than others and be prioritized over others, since it is often impossible to fulfil all rights at the same time (Office of the High Commissioner for Human Rights [OHCHR], 2006). Power plays a role as well. The general strategy is to give priority to those who are most vulnerable in the society. However, in reality, the well-off and most powerful in society have often benefited because they are better placed. This is true of human rights and humanitarianism in general (Alston, 2005; Kennedy, 2004), and it is certainly true of disability rights (Silecchia, 2013).

It has also been argued that human rights can often be vague and culturally insensitive (Seppänen, 2005). Human rights approaches are usually planned from the top and designed (albeit necessarily) as 'one size fits all' tools (Alston, 2005), neglecting to consider contexts such as social, political, and historical conditions in specific countries (Kennedy, 2004; Batliwala, 2007). Their implementation therefore might not meet the diverse characteristics and interests of PwDs. At the very least, local contexts must be taken into account in the process of operationalizing human rights (OHCHR, 2006).

The Case of Cameroon

Cameroon is a Central African country with a unique colonial past. A German colony (Kamerun) from 1884 to 1916, the territory was then divided between France and Britain in 1919, with France receiving a much larger share (80%). The French territory gained independence from France in 1960 as the Republic of Cameroon under President Ahmadou Ahidjo. In 1961, the Republic gained new territory after a referendum that divided the British Cameroons between Nigeria and Cameroon. The country became a centralized, unitary State in 1972. In 1982, Ahidjo was succeeded by Paul Biya, who remains in power to this day. Although Cameroon has not experienced military regimes like its neighbouring countries, it was a one-party State under Biya until the early 1990s, when the enactment of the 'freedom laws' allowed multiparty political activities. However, Biya has held onto power as an autocratic leader despite the transition to democracy. Cameroon, therefore, has been under the leadership of autocratic executive presidents since independence, and these have exercised absolute control over the other arms of government (Mbuagbo and Akoko, 2004; Schraeder, 2004). Not surprisingly, this has had a negative impact on freedom of speech and association. For instance, President Biya, who has ruled Cameroon for more than three decades, has been ruthless in suppressing opposing viewpoints, and civil activism has been severely stifled as a consequence (Mbuagbo and Akoko, 2004). These developments seem to have greatly curtailed the participation of minority groups, including PwDs, in civil rights movements.

Apart from a political system that has hindered the development of civil rights activism among PwDs in Cameroon, PwDs face additional barriers to participation in socio-economic and political activities (Opoku *et al.*, 2016) and in fact constitute one of the country's most vulnerable groups (International Centre for Evidence in Disability [ICED], 2014). Poverty and socio-economic exclusion are major problems, as many PwDs have limited access to education and employment and have turned to begging as a means to survive (Mayer, 2007; Mbibeh, 2013, Opoku *et al.*, 2016).

Cameroon signed the CRPD and its Optional Protocols in 2008, and since then the government has also undertaken some legal reforms ostensibly to meet its obligations under the CRPD. Notable among them are the implementation in 2010 of a National Policy Paper on the Protection and Promotion of Persons with Disabilities in Cameroon, and the National Employment Pact (Republic of Cameroon, 2019). In 2018, the government followed this legislation with a decree setting out measures for implementing the National Policy Paper. The decree establishes procedures for assuring disability rights in the areas of education and vocational training, employment, and healthcare, as well as access to physical infrastructure (including housing), social activities, and political participation (Republic of Cameroon, 2018). Although the steps taken by the government since ratifying the CRPD in 2008 are significant, the impact these have had on PwDs has not been adequately evaluated. Some studies have been conducted to assess the impact of the CRPD (for example, Opoku *et al.*, 2016), but they have not closely examined the impact of the government's activities as aligned with the approach adopted by the Convention. This chapter addresses the knowledge gap by investigating the impact of the CRPD on PwDs in Cameroon from the perspective of the approach adopted by the Convention.

Methodology

The Buea municipality is the capital of the south-west region of Cameroon. It is a rural community located on the slopes of the Cameroon Mountains. It is a relatively remote municipality with an estimated population of about 200,000 inhabitants and few social amenities compared to other municipalities. The study design was descriptive, driven by the assumption that each individual ascribes a unique meaning to the same situation, because reality is subjective. Our aim, therefore, was to explore the meanings that participants with disabilities assigned to conditions in the Buea municipality (Smith, Flowers, and Larkin, 2009). Each participant had different experiences and interpreted these experiences differently. This approach allowed participants to share and explain their subjective experiences.

We used a convenience sampling technique to recruit participants for the study, choosing them based on certain practical conditions, such as their accessibility, proximity, availability at the time of recruiting, or willingness to participate (Etikan, 2016). We considered all PwDs as having important experiences and being capable of explaining issues affecting them in their own way. Our interview pool therefore was limited only by availability; we interviewed all participants who were available and ready to participate in the study. Prospective contributors were contacted through local Disabled People's Organizations (DPOs). We first met with the leaders of the three main DPOs in the community, representing deaf and blind people and those with physical disabilities. At our first meeting, we introduced the members to the study and explained its purpose, the eligibility criteria, and the role of the DPOs. We then had a second meeting with our assistants, to provide training in qualitative data collection procedures. Finally, we chose a representative from each DPO to help recruit participants.

Through WhatsApp messages, prospective participants from each group were invited to an interview location. After explaining the purpose of the study and the inclusion criteria, participants were asked to volunteer to participate. Those who agreed were taken through the informed consent process, and interview dates were fixed for each group. In total, 36 participants, made up of 12 participants from each disability category, participated in the focus group discussions (FGDs).

As explained above, three separate FGDs were organized, one with each disability group. A focus group guide, containing questions covering broad themes on the topic, was prepared to guide the group discussions. The main topics included knowledge of the CRPD, the extent of the participation of PwDs in decision-making, and barriers to participation. For the hearing participants – blind people and those with physical disabilities – the discussions were audio-recorded, while deaf participants were videotaped. Permission was sought from all participants before recording the interviews. Except for deaf participants, who used Cameroonian Sign Language, Pidgin English (the main language spoken by people in Buea) was used for the focus groups. An interpreter translated sign language by speaking into an audio recorder. Before the discussions, the research team set ground rules for the group discussions to facilitate equal participation. They were asked to respect the views, privacy, and confidentiality of other participants and to wait for their turn to talk, and they were told that no answers were to be considered right or wrong.

The researchers analysed the data by performing inductive content analysis. This involved transcribing the responses, reading through the transcripts, identifying ideas or comments that were relevant to the research objectives, grouping these ideas into broad themes, and linking them together to formulate the final themes. The recorded responses of all the discussions (audio-recorded and videotaped) were transcribed verbatim and separately by three of the researchers. After transcribing, we read through the transcripts several times to familiarize ourselves with the responses and gain more insight into the responses. We then compared transcripts to identify possible differences, addressing these in discussions among the research team. As we read through the transcripts, we made marginal notes identifying initial broad themes, listing these as they occurred. The next step was to make sense of the notes and identify connections between the emerging themes from the three groups. We then merged similar themes to form the main themes, which also form the subheadings of the findings section, to wit: negative labelling; equality and non-discrimination; and participation and inclusion. We decided to combine accessibility, participation, and inclusion into one theme because their contents were closely related.

To ensure proper ethics, the researchers first sought permission from the DPOs in Buea before the data were collected. With the permissions in hand, we obtained ethical clearance from the Kwame Nkrumah University of Science and Technology in Ghana (the home university of the first and second authors of this chapter, Wisdom K. Mprah and Maxwell O. Peprah). Written informed consent, translated from English to Pidgin and sign language for the hearing and deaf participants respectively, was used in the recruiting process. All participants signed the informed consent form before they participated in the study. In order to protect identities in publications, we assigned pseudonyms to the participants.

Findings: Barriers to Disability Rights in Cameroon

Our fieldwork revealed significant barriers to disability rights, relating to most provisions in the CRPD. Participants reported a lack of rights in the areas of political and social inclusion, healthcare, education, and employment. Many of them connected their lack of rights to pervasive stigma and discrimination. For example, participants described how ignorance about the causes of disability has led to negative labelling and treating PwDs in the area as less than human. All the participants in the three focus groups said they had experienced negative treatment on this level, including exclusion from decision-making and being shunned, stared at, or abandoned because of their disability.

In response to a question regarding whether people in the area considered PwDs less than human, Peter, who is physically disabled, responded: 'That is what people think and this has gotten into the heads of people. We are not valued, and neither are we considered when it comes to making of decisions.' Another participant described how the perception that PwDs were cursed made people avoid them wherever they went: 'The more you try to go close to people, the more they distance themselves. This has made us to fear trying to get closer to those in authorities' (Betty, woman with physical disabilities). John, a man with visual impairment, stated that:

> Everyone has abandoned me because they are saying my father stole someone's goat and the person cursed him ... It hurts when I hear that I have been cursed. Anytime I offend someone, that's what they tell me, and it makes me cry a lot when I'm alone.

Peter and James, both men with physical disabilities, shared their experiences of how even children stared at them because of their condition, which was embarrassing and made it difficult for them to interact with members of their community. According to Peter, he does not often go out because people stare at him too much. He stated that: 'I get a lot of attention since I crawl on the floor. Whenever I want to cross the road almost everyone stares at me. It is embarrassing so I don't go out.' John, another man with physical disabilities, said it was 'hard to live here [in his community] as a disabled person' because everyone would 'stop whatever they are doing and stare. So many people will be looking at me and gossiping. Even children would be following me and watching how I am walking with my hands.'

Adams, a person with visual impairment, and James, a deaf person, lamented that they had never been valued or treated like human beings by their own family members. According to Adams, he 'suffered a lot' in his own house. His own family did not value his capabilities: 'They doubt what I can do and always don't see me as a valuable person.' James' story was not different: 'It is very sad that our own people don't believe in us. They see us as worthless persons who can't support the family in anyway ... It hurts my soul to hear people say, "what can he do?"'

The treatment meted out to PwDs in the Buea municipality, as indicated in the responses, is not surprising in light of similar experiences reported elsewhere in Africa. Traditionally, disability has been viewed in many African societies from religious and cultural perspectives, often leading to it being interpreted as a curse or punishment for sins committed by a family member (Agbenyega, 2003; Nyangweso, 2021). As a consequence of these misconceptions, many PwDs are not treated as equal citizens who have rights. Thus, although denying individuals their rights because of perceived differences is a gross violation of the human rights principle that all human beings are equal, many PwDs in Africa are deprived of their basic human rights, such as the right to marriage, to education, to healthcare, and to employment (Nyangweso, 2021; Shannon, Schoen, and Tansey, 2009; Goreczny *et al.*, 2011)

This narrow representation of disability pushes the blame onto the individual with the condition, instead of African societies. Although all human beings are supposed to have inherent human rights and be treated with dignity, PwDs have often been denied these rights due to this misrepresentation and thus are treated differently and negatively. According to Nyangweso (2021), 'the assumption that disability is a personal or family problem rather than a matter of social responsibility absolves the society from their moral responsibility to treat these people as fully human' (p. 129). As a rights-based instrument which is rooted in the social model of disability, the CRPD recognizes that negative perceptions are the major cause of disability-based discrimination and seeks to eliminate them (Palacios, 2015). Our findings provide evidence of one local context where the elimination of discriminatory attitudes is indeed an important and necessary precursor to the achievement of disability rights under the CRPD.

A related issue that was extensively discussed in all the groups was that of being treated equally without discrimination. Many participants complained of not being treated as equal members of society. In some cases, this manifested itself in a lack of equal educational opportunities. According to the participants there were few schools for CwDs, so PwDs had fewer opportunities to attain higher education than non-disabled children. For example, Janet, a visually impaired woman, and Kofi, a deaf man, were both denied education by their parents because of their disabilities.

> My father took all his children to school except me. I now understand he left me home because of my disability. This shouldn't be the case. The fact that I'm disabled doesn't mean I can't learn but that is how I was treated (Janet).

> I don't get any support from my family ever since I started going to school. I beg for money during holidays to support my education.

> My church too has been helpful as they give me money when I'm in need. All my brothers are in school and they are being supported by my family, but they don't want to help me (Kofi).

Mateow, a blind person, further elaborated:

> Look, in Cameroon, there are few government schools for the blind and it is only few private individuals who have vocational schools which are very expensive to attend. Even if you attend such schools, that is the end and no university or polytechnic will give you admission. We have limited access to education and that is our main problem.

Kofi (see above) also described the importance of education and how the lack of schooling limits opportunities for PwDs:

> Education is important and people look at that when appointing people into office but disabled people in this country have no access to quality education. We only go to school so as to read and write and that is all. I want to go to school so as to become somebody, but the chance is not there. So, we can't compete with others. We have access to few jobs and other employment opportunities.

Low educational attainment has led to unequal access to employment for PwDs. Janet, mentioned previously, explained that: 'I'm always home because I can't find any job to do because of my disability.' She added that because, 'I couldn't go to school and I have not learnt any trade that is why I have not been able to get a job.'

Beyond education and job prospects, other participants spoke of the lack of specific laws in Cameroon to protect and promote the rights of PwDs: 'The laws do not respect us disabled people as equals as non-disabled persons so when it comes to access to services, we are highly excluded, and no one comes to our aid' [Peter, a person with physical disability]. John, a person with visual impairment, concurred:

> There is no legislation in place in the country to safeguard the rights of persons with disabilities. In such a society, they are bound to be excluded from national discussions of affairs or to have their rights to access basic services denied.

The principle of equality and non-discrimination implies that by virtue of being human, PwDs should have equal rights with others. They should not be treated differently, excluded, or discriminated against based on their disabilities (UN, 2010). However, our findings indicate that the participants experienced serious discrimination, and that compared to their non-disabled counterparts, they had limited access to socio-economic activities such as education and employment. Although the government ratified the CRPD and passed several decrees on disability rights, as John pointed out, there appear to be no national laws in Cameroon to protect the rights of PwDs. But even if those laws existed, participants felt that they would not be effective. This claim by the contributors may be correct, because Cameroon has apparently undertaken some legal reforms to meet its international obligations under the CRPD. However, the impact of these laws on the lives of PwDs is low, largely because the level of awareness on disability issues has been found to be generally low (Opuku *et al.*, 2016).

Stigma and discrimination made it very difficult for our participants to enjoy the rights enshrined in the CRPD, including political and social inclusion and the rights to education, healthcare, and employment. As expected, participants with physical disabilities were more concerned with physical barriers, while blind and deaf persons had issues with communication and information. In relation to political rights, many participants were concerned with their inability to exercise their political and civic rights because of inaccessible physical environments. Peter, a person with physical disability, said that although participating in political activities was '... one of the most important things disabled persons in the area wanted to do', he could not participate in it because, 'I crawl on the floor and in this town, it is always raining, so I can't move through the rain and go and vote for someone who will not help me in anyway.' John further elaborated:

> I'm in a wheelchair and I cannot move freely to go and vote. It would have been different if I could walk but my inability to walk doesn't allow me to go and vote. It would have been good that everyone gets the opportunity to vote but the way our environment is limited my ability to vote during any elections.

Although blind persons had difficulties with physical infrastructure, including open drains, a major concern voiced in the focus group related to barriers to participation in elections. Most significantly, although they felt strongly about voting independently to ensure that their privacy was assured, they were unable to do so because of a lack of information in braille. Comments from two of the participants illustrated this concern very clearly:

> I don't like a situation where I will go to the polling station and somebody has to hold my hand and help me vote. What if the person didn't vote for my preferred candidate? We have to respect privacy so until ballot papers are also provided in braille, I will never vote in any elections (Jane).

> I can't vote in any of our elections because I don't know what is written on the ballot paper. It is secret balloting and I want to vote without anyone assisting me. If we are practising democracy, then everybody should be given the chance to participate equally (Betty).

Jonas, another man with visual impairment, added that PwDs were not considered '... equal humans who have the capacity to reason and offer ideas, so they have limited our [PwDs'] ability to participate in [the] politics of this country'. For deaf persons, the absence of sign language interpreters adversely affected their ability to understand what was happening in the country. Pascal, a deaf person, shared his experiences:

> I don't follow anything that goes on in this country. Right now, I don't know what is going on in government or this town. There are no interpreters so I'm not able to understand whatever the government or local authorities are doing.

Mary, a deaf woman, described her desire to participate actively in the national decision-making process, but thought it was not 'safe' [i.e. one could be treated inhumanly] for PwDs in Cameroon, because one is pushed back whenever one makes such efforts:

> I would have loved to be active in national issues, but it is not safe to do so in Cameroon. At every step, you try to go closer [and] somebody pushes you back. They don't think we also have good ideas that can help in building of the country. Our culture limits our ability to participate in national affairs.

Even though PwDs have developed nationally recognized associations, they were not given representation at stakeholders' meetings held at the national level. Alhassni, a man with physical disabilities, was very sad that the 'disabled have no opportunity to be part of national issues'. Peter and Ama elaborated:

> Our association has been in existence for a long time, but they don't recognize us as people who could make our views known on national issues. We have registered and they know us, but they don't seek our opinions on national issues as they do for others (Peter, a physically disabled man).

> Let's not talk about national on this issue. Just at the local assembly, they don't involve our representatives to participate in stakeholders' meetings. They are with us and should know that we exist. At times I go there but they will tell me when they need us, they will call us, but they never did (Ama, person with visual disability).

In addition to being excluded from political activities, our participants reported social exclusion, especially at the level of family life. All participants reported that they were barred from participating in activities or decision-making in their families; even their own family members, including their wives and children, did not involve them when making decisions. Social exclusion occurred because they had difficulties being physically productive, which in the eyes of community and family members meant that they could not make meaningful contributions. Anthony, a person with physical disability, whose views were previously valued but who lost this respect after acquiring his disability, narrated:

> Since I became disabled, I can't work so people don't value my opinion anymore. My own wife and children don't ask or discuss issues with me. She is the one working and taking care of the family, so the children listen to her more and not me.

Daniel, a person with visual impairment, and Mark, a deaf person, had similar experiences of being excluded from decision-making by their families:

> They don't call me whenever the family is making a decision. Even when somebody dies in the family, they don't invite me. They are my family and I often expect them to involve me in whatever they do but that is never the case. They often call everyone except me (Daniel).

> I'm not working so they don't count me as an equal member of the family. They only invite those who are working whenever they are taking decisions in the family. I stay in the family house, but they have never discussed or asked about my opinion over issues (Mark).

Our participants also could not access the right to health, because healthcare centres were similarly inaccessible. The main accessibility issues were in the design of the buildings, equipment, and communication barriers. Maame, a person with physical disability, indicated that PwDs were not considered when the health centres were being built. Therefore, she had to hire someone to support her: 'It's hard to move with my wheelchair so I have to pay someone to carry me whenever I'm going for treatment. If I'm not very sick, I don't go to the hospital.' Gideon, another physically disabled person, complained of the nature of the hospital beds. He said: '[t]he beds are high for me to climb and they have not made any arrangement to protect us from getting hurt'.

Jean, a deaf person, was not happy with the communication barriers deaf people encounter at the hospital:

> It is hard to communicate with doctors and nurses whenever I'm sick. They don't know the sign language, so it makes it difficult to tell them my problem. At times, there is something that I need but there is no one to talk due to communication problem.

In terms of education, participants complained that schools are inadequate to cater for the needs of CwDs, thus limiting their access to education. Abdul, a participant with physical disabilities, and James, a participant with visual impairment, shared their thoughts on the issue:

> There is no school for disabled children in my community. The government has failed to provide us with schools that cater for us. The public schools are not accessible. I didn't get admission to public schools because they say those schools don't admit disabled children. Although I wanted to go to school, I couldn't go because of lack of schools [Abdul].

> The government of Cameroon did not build schools for physically impaired in this town and also many towns in Cameroon, so there are no schools for us. Going to school is not easy because the schools are not there, and the general schools are not accessible to us. I tried going to the public school, but it was hard for me. Their environment is inaccessible [James].

Jean, a deaf woman, lamented about the communication barriers deaf people face in the educational system because teachers cannot communicate in the sign language.

> Our teachers struggle to teach during classes. They can't sign most

> of the things to us, so at times we find it difficult to understand them. Every year, most of the students fail because we don't have the right teachers at our school.

Employment rights were also unattainable for most participants. Almost all the participants were of the view that getting a good job in Cameroon was difficult for PwDs. Recounting his experiences during a job search, Daniels, a person with physical disability, said, 'it was hell because, everywhere in the community was inaccessible' as he had to 'crawl up to the third floors of story buildings.' Ababa, a person with a hearing impairment, concurred that it was not easy getting a job in Cameroon, but attributed the situation to lack of education among PwDs: 'I agreed that disabled persons do not have access to jobs in this country. One must have education for one to get a job, but we don't have good certificates, so it is hard for us.' James also blamed the situation on lack of qualification among PwDs:

> There are no jobs in this country. Even non-disabled persons have difficulty getting jobs, so being a disabled, who has no good qualification means that you can't get any job. Wherever u go, they will ask for certificate which most of us don't have. Not even the government will give us jobs (James, a person with visual impairment).

Full and effective participation, inclusion, and accessibility are interrelated, and participation and inclusion are the end goals of disability-related policies and advocacy. However, to achieve full inclusion, barriers, both physical and social, need to be removed. This also means that PwDs must be valued as equal human beings who can contribute meaningfully to their communities and be allowed to do so without discrimination. Participation and inclusion are thus linked to universal design principles, which is defined in the Convention as the 'design of products, environments, programmes and services that should be usable by all people, to the greatest extent possible, without the need for adaptation or specialized design' (Article 2). It also means mainstreaming the needs of PwDs in developmental programmes. This would require valuing diversity and creating opportunities for everyone, irrespective of one's ability and need. If this is done, people with diverse needs, abilities, and preferences, including PwDs, can participate in activities in their communities on an equal basis with others.

However, as our findings indicate, PwDs in the Buea municipality could not participate effectively in socio-economic activities, most likely due to disability-related exclusion and the hostile political and economic conditions in Cameroon.

Conclusion

The findings from this study provide insights into the effectiveness of the CRPD as a framework for changing societal attitudes and empowering PwDs to take control over their lives. Disability studies and activism are relatively new to most governments and disability activists in the Global South. Most of the policies and laws on disability are designed for people in the Global North, where socio-economic and political conditions are completely different from those in the South. A rights-based instrument may work well in the North but not in the South because of specific local conditions, as in Cameroon, where civil activism and minority rights are regularly suppressed (Mbuagbo and Akoko, 2004). As Katsui (2008) observes, this problem reflects the fact that the CRPD adopts a top-down approach, and its provisions tend to be insensitive to local conditions, especially in the Global South. Our participants' experiences show that country-level nuances cannot be ignored in the implementation of the CRPD.

By adopting a rights-based approach, the CRPD seeks to respect and celebrate human diversity by implementing measures that would permit effective participation by a wide range of persons; a rights-based model also requires that PwDs are aware of and able to articulate their rights. However, this may be difficult for most PwDs in many countries in the Global South, including Cameroon. To protect and promote their rights, it is crucial to create awareness about those rights and to adopt measures to eliminate negative attitudes and behaviours that stigmatize and marginalize PwDs (UN, 2010). In fact, Article 5 of the CRPD calls on States Parties to undertake positive measures to promote and protect the rights of PwDs as contained in the Convention. However, little has been done in our study area, as these conditions are almost completely absent.

To achieve its intended purpose of ensuring meaningful participation of PwDs in all spheres of life, the CRPD should be able to help PwDs move beyond psychological empowerment. In other words, they should not only have a sense of control or worth, but also be able to set goals and take initiatives to achieve these goals. This can be achieved through creating awareness among PwDs about the CRPD's provisions, building their capacity to lobby for and demand the implementation of these provisions, and removing barriers that create impediments to exercising these rights. However, although participants were aware of their rights and appeared to be assertive, they were unable to translate this perceived sense of control into reality because of barriers they were encountering. Thus, providing rights without eliminating barriers to exercising these rights is not enough to increase the participation of PwDs in mainstream activities; rights-based approaches must equally tackle the barriers faced by PwDs.

It should also be noted that rights are not automatically given. PwDs and their activists must lobby for these rights. In the words of Meekosha and Soldatic (2011),

> Thus far, we have argued, human rights are not simply a set of international laws; they are formed in the process of struggle and debate. Human rights are a discursive process, not a static set of prescriptive values. In the area of disability rights, State legislation has been the focus of long and protracted struggle (p. 1387).

However, PwDs, especially those in the Global South, are often unable to lobby their respective governments for their rights, because they lack the means to do so and do not understand the complexity of the rights-based agenda. Therefore, the exclusive reliance on a human rights model for protecting the rights of PwDs without adaptation may be more beneficial to some people than others. It is thus important to adapt the CRPD to fit local conditions so that it can meet the needs of PwDs within specific contexts.

Although it may not necessarily lead to economic empowerment, having a say in making decisions on issues affecting their lives is important to PwDs; it is not often available to them, however. Enabling PwDs to participate in the decision-making process requires a more constructive dialogue between political parties, on the one hand, and PwDs and their activists, on the other. This will create opportunities for stakeholders to understand each other's worldview and eliminate misconceptions and doubts about the capabilities of PwDs. If this can be accomplished, then the CRPD stands a better chance of becoming a reality in Cameroon and across the Global South.

Bibliography

Agbenyega, J.S. 2003. 'The Power of Labeling Discourse in the Construction of Disability in Ghana'. Auckland, New Zealand: International Conference of the Australian Association for Research in Education 2003: Educational Research, Risks and Dilemmas <https://www.researchgate.net/publication/266866626_The_power_of_labeling_discourse_in_the_construction_of_disability_in_Ghana> [accessed 5 April 2021].

Alston, P. 2005. 'Ships Passing in the Night: The Current State of the Human Rights and Development Debate Seen Through the Lens of the Millennium Development Goals', *Human Rights Quarterly* 27: 755–829.

Batliwala, S. 2007. 'When Rights Go Wrong', *Seminar, Annual Issue* 569: 89–94.

Braithwaite, J., and Mont, D. 2009. 'Disability and Poverty: A Survey of World Bank Poverty Assessments and Implications', *Alter, European Journal of Disability Research* 3(3): 219–32.

Cramm, J.M., Lorenzo, T., and Nieboer, A.P. 2014. 'Comparing Education, Employment, Social Support and Well-being among Youth with Disabilities and Their Peers in South Africa', *Applied Research Quality Life* 9: 517–24.

Échevin, D. 2013. 'Employment and Education Discrimination against Disabled People in Cape Verde', *Applied Economics* 45: 857–75.

Etikan, I. 2016. 'Comparison of Convenience Sampling and Purposive Sampling', *American Journal of Theoretical and Applied Statistics* 5(1): 1–4.

Filmer, D. 2008. 'Disability, Poverty, and Schooling in Developing Countries: Results from 14 Household Surveys', *World Bank Economic Review* 22: 41–163

Goreczny, A.J., Bender, E.E., Caruso, G., and. Feinstein, S.C. 2011. 'Attitudes toward Individuals with Disabilities: Results of a Recent Survey and Implications of Those Results', *Research in Developmental Disabilities* 32(5): 1596–609.

Harpur, P.D. 2010. 'The Positive Impact of the Convention on the Rights of Persons with Disabilities: A Case Study on the South Pacific and Lessons from the US Experience', *Northern Kentucky Law Review* 37: 363–98.

International Centre for Evidence in Disability (ICED). 2014. *The North West Cameroon Disability Study Country Report*, London School of Hygiene and Tropical Medicine (LSHTM) <https://www.lshtm.ac.uk/sites/default/files/2019-06/Cameroon-Country-Report.pdf> [accessed 5 April 2021].

Katsui, H. 2008. *Downside of the Human Rights-Based Approach to Disability in Development*. Working Paper 2/2008, Institute of Development Studies Helsinki University, Finland <https://www.

sylff.org/wp-content/uploads/2008/12/downside_of_hrba_katsui_hisayo.pdf> [accessed 5 April 2021].

Kennedy, D. 2004. *The Dark Sides of Virtue: Reassessing International Humanitarianism.* Princeton: Princeton University Press.

Lang, R., Kett, M., Groce, N., Trani, J.-F. 2011. 'Implementing the United Nations Convention on the Rights of Persons with Disabilities: Principles, Implications, Practice and Limitations', *ALTER, European Journal of Disability Research* 5: 206–20.

Mayer, E.J.E. 2007. *Study on the Rights of Persons with Disabilities in Cameroon.* Report presented to York University <https://www.yorku.ca/drpi/files/DRPICameroonRepEn.pdf> [accessed 6 April 2021].

Mbibeh, L. 2013. 'Implementing Inclusive Education in Cameroon: Evidence from the Cameroon Baptist Convention Health Board', *International Journal of Education* 5(1): 52–56.

Mbuagbo, O.T., and Akoko, R.M. 2004. 'Roll-Back: Democratization and Social Fragmentation in Cameroon', *Nordic Journal of African Studies* 13(3): 1–12.

Meekosha, H., and Soldatic, K. 2011. 'Human Rights and the Global South: The Case of Disability', *Third World Quarterly* 32(8): 1383–97.

Mitra, S. 2006. 'The Capability Approach and Disability', *Journal of Disability Policy Studies* 16(4): 236–47.

Mitra S., and Sambamoorthi, U. 2009. 'Disability and the Rural Labor Market in India: Evidence for Males in Tamil Nadu', *World Development* 36(5): 943–52.

Nyangweso, M. 2021. 'Disability in Africa: A Cultural/Religious Perspective'. In: T. Falola and N. Hamel. Eds. *Disability in Africa: Inclusion, Care, and the Ethics of Humanity* (pp. 115–136). Rochester: University of Rochester Press <https://www.researchgate.net/publication/325642373_Disability_in_Africa_A_CulturalReligious_Perspective> [accessed 6 April 2021].

Office of the High Commissioner for Human Rights (OHCHR). 2006. *Annual Report* <https://www.ohchr.org/Documents/AboutUs/annualreport2006.pdf> [accessed 10 April 2021].

Oliver, M., and Barnes, C. 1998. *Disabled People and Social Policy: From Exclusion to Inclusion.* London: Longman.

Opoku, M.P., Mprah, W.K., and Sakah, B.N. 2016. 'Participation of PwDs in Political Activities in Cameroon', *Disability and the Global South* 3(2): 980–99.

Palacios, A. 2015. 'The Social Model in the International Convention on the Rights of PwDs', *The Age of Human Rights Journal* 4: 91–110.

Republic of Cameroon. 2018. 'Decree No 2018/6233 Fixing the Procedures for the Application of the Law No 201/002 of 13 April 2010 on the Protection and Promotion of PwDs in Cameroon' <https://www.un.org/development/desa/disabilities/wp-content/uploads/sites/15/2019/11/Cameroon_DECREE-OF-APPLICATION-2010-LAW-ENGLISH-VERSION.pdf> [accessed 12 April 2021].

Republic of Cameroon. 2019. 'Protection of the PwDs'. Yaoundé: Ministere Des Affaires Sociales.

Schraeder P. 2004. *African Politics and Society: A Mosaic in Transformation*. California: Woodsworth.

Seppänen, S. 2005. *Possibilities and Challenges of the Human Approach to Development.* The Erik Castrén Institute Research Reports, No. 17/2005. Helsinki: The Erik Castrén Institute of International Law and Human Rights.

Shannon, C.D., Schoen, B., Tansey, T.N. 2009. 'The Effect of Contact, Context, and Social Power on Undergraduate Attitudes Toward PwDs', *Journal of Rehabilitation* 75(4): 11–18.

Shier, M., Graham, J.R., and Jones, M.E. 2009. 'Barriers to Employment as Experienced by Disabled People: A Qualitative Analysis in Calgary and Regina, Canada', *Disability and Society* 24(1): 63–75.

Silecchia. L.A. 2013. 'The Convention on the Rights of PwDs: Reflections on Four Flaws that Tarnish its Promise', *Journal of Contemporary Health Law and Policy* 30: 96–130.

Smith, J.A., Flowers, P., Larkin, M. 2009. *Interpretative Phenomenological Analysis: Theory, Method and Research.* Los Angeles: SAGE.

Trani, J.F., and Loeb, M. 2012. 'Poverty and Disability: A Vicious Circle? Evidence from Afghanistan and Zambia', *Journal of International Development* 12(S1): S19–S52.

United Nations (UN). 2010. *Monitoring the Convention on the Rights of PwDs.* Guidance for Human Rights Monitors Professional Training Series No. 17. New York and Geneva: United Nations.

World Health Organization (WHO). 2011. *World Report on Disability.* Available at < https://www.who.int/teams/noncommunicable-diseases/sensory-functions-disability-and-rehabilitation/world-report-on-disability> [accessed 11 March 2022].

10

African Ontology, Albinism, and Human Rights

ELVIS IMAFIDON

Introduction

I am a person with albinism. I have lived with my family and worked in a small town in Southern Nigeria for nearly a decade. My wife is a coloured (Black) woman and my kids are too. As an individual, I have lived in this space for decades. I had my childhood and my education in this small town. I only left this town for my graduate studies and then returned to work in the university. So I am quite well known in this town. But when I move around town with my family, there is always this gaze of awe from people who know me quite well and those who do not. They wonder how a person with albinism could have a wife and children with melanin. Some tell me right to my face that I am fortunate not only to have a coloured woman as my wife – they are often in awe that she agreed to marry me – but to have children who do not have albinism as I do. What is responsible for the attitude of community members to what they see about me and my family? In one word: representation. These lived experiences just described show how powerful deeply entrenched representations of a group made manifest in beliefs can be. How a group of persons are presented and represented over time to a community of selves, which becomes codified as forms of beliefs, determines largely how members of such a community of selves understand, relate with, and perceive members of such a represented group. As Richard Dyer aptly puts it in *The Matter of Images* (1993: 1),

> How a group is represented, presented over again in cultural forms, how an image of a member of a group is taken as representative of that group, how that group is represented in terms of spoke for and on behalf of (whether they represent, speak for themselves or not), these all have to do with how members of

> groups see themselves and others like themselves, how they see their place in society, their right to the rights a society claims to ensure its citizens. Equally re-presentation, representativeness, representing have to do also with how others see members of a group and their place and rights, others who have the power to affect that place and those rights. How we are seen determine in part how we are treated; how we treat others is based on how we see them; such seeing comes from representation.

The representation of albinism as a form of disability in African communities is so deeply rooted in African ontology or understanding of being that it determines the way other members of the community view and treat such persons. Such representations of albinism in Africa are largely inimical to the health and well-being of persons with albinism and deprive them of the enjoyment of fundamental human rights. In what follows, I begin by exploring and analyzing how albinism is often negatively represented as a radically different in African ontology. I then proceed to examine how such deeply entrenched representations of persons with albinism in African ontology deprive them of the enjoyment of fundamental human rights as contained, for instance, in the Universal Declaration of Human Rights (UDHR) in general and the Convention on the Rights of Persons with Disabilities (CRPD) in particular, primarily because the enjoyment of such rights depends in the first place on being human, and in African communities persons with albinism are perceived as not human enough to enjoy such rights. I further discuss two levels of hopes that need to be explored to overcome these deeply entrenched yet negative representation of persons with albinism: the individual level and the social level. I conclude by highlighting the importance of critiquing representations by members of a community to ensure the enjoyment of rights by persons with disabilities (PwDs).

African Ontology and Albinism

African ontology consists of an analysis of African conceptions of the nature of being, of what 'is' or exists and, by implication, what does not exist. Such conceptions have been so interwoven into the African cultural fabric that persons within African communities accept them uncritically as objective and factual and live their lives on the basis of such conceptions. African ontology conceives of 'being' as consisting of a lively and active interaction between visible and invisible entities and forces. Visible entities cannot be conceived of as independent or separate from invisible entities and forces, and vice versa. An African ontology also consists of a study of the hierarchical categorization of beings or entities predominant in African thought systems. It can be deduced from many African cultures that from the apex to the bottom of this hierarchy, there are the Supreme Being, the divinities (primordial and deified), the ancestors, manipular spirits, the human person, animals, and plants and natural resources. These beings interact and their interaction is made possible due to the presence of vital force. Hence the theory of being that has become popular in scholarly literature about African ontology is the vital force theory (Imafidon, 2019b: 29). The sorts of interactions and relations that take place among beings in this hierarchy are such that higher beings are believed to have higher forces than lower beings and are thus able to manipulate and influence the well-being of lower beings. But a just and fair interaction is made possible because the highest beings in the hierarchy – the Supreme Being and the divinities – are believed to be ultimately good in their dealings with humans and have the power to protect lesser beings from the evil manipulations of manipular forces.

In the category of the human being, different African cultures have quite detailed and specific characterizations of both the descriptive and normative features of the human person. But a general consensus among African theorists of personhood is that a human being is only regarded as a person if they possess the ontological and normative qualities required of a person by the community (see, for example, Gyekye, 1984; 1992; Menkiti, 1984; Oladipo, 1992; Ndubuisi, 2004; and Oyeshile, 2006). The ontological or descriptive qualities consist of bodily normality and the structure or descriptive features of the body as conceptualized by the community. The normative qualities consist of socially expected behavioural patterns that a human being must exhibit. It involves living a lifestyle accepted by the community and exhibiting social behaviours endorsed by the community. The lack of the ontological and normative qualities of a person calls the personhood of a human being into question in various ways. Interestingly, with particular reference to the normative qualities, a human being can be a person at a given point in time and fail to be so at another, based on the extent to which they have failed to adopt a lifestyle accepted by the community. To be sure, this calls into question the extent to which an African person is allowed to exert his or her freewill, autonomy, and authenticity. This is, however, not our primary concern in this chapter. Our focus here is the extent to which a lack of ontological qualities or failure to fit into the bodily norm of the community leads to the denial of personhood for a human being. A case in point is albinism.

Albinism as the lack of, or presence of very little, pigmentation is a form of disability common in a number of African communities. In African conceptions of being, persons with albinism may in all respects appear to be human except, of course, for the lack of pigmentation, but they are, in fact, excluded from the category of human beings. Rather, persons with albinism are viewed as strange, unusual beings. Understanding persons with albinism as strange, unusual beings in these senses is very common in African societies. Their unusual nature stems not only from their visible physical difference but also from the ideas about the nature of their being presented and represented down the ages in the worldviews of African traditional societies (Imafidon, 2019a: 39).

What the evidence from African ontology shows is that persons with albinism do not fulfil all the requirements to be called a human being. Hence, in African societies, the linguistic connotations of persons with albinism are like those of every other connoting word, although the fact that they are naming a person clearly suggests otherwise. Among the Yoruba people, for instance, persons with albinism are called *afin*, which means 'horrible'. It is common among people in South Africa to refer to a person with albinism with the isiZulu expression *isishawa*, which means 'cursed'. In Zimbabwe, persons with albinism are referred to in isiXhosa as *sope*, a word used to indicate that such persons are possessed with evil spirits. In Tanzania, persons with albinism are referred to as *zeruzeru*, a Swahili word meaning 'ghost people'. Hence a person with albinism is not viewed in the same way a human being is viewed – that is, as possessing certain essential ontological qualities such as coming into being with a destiny chosen before the Supreme Being. Rather, the coming into being of a person with albinism is viewed as an outcome of a curse placed on the child-bearer, the husband of the child-bearer, or the family at large due to some wrongdoing, or the result of the punishment received by child-bearer, the husband of the child-bearer, or the family at large from a higher force (such as an ancestor or divinity) due to some wrongdoing. Hence a family that gives birth to a person with albinism is seen as unfavoured by some higher forces and faces ridicule from within the community of selves. For this reason, persons with albinism are conceived as a human other, *something* different from the approved and accepted notion of a human being (Imafidon, 2019a: 40). By implication, if persons with albinism are not considered as being human in the way melanin-privileged Africans are, then it logically follows that such persons would struggle to enjoy the same rights that melanin-privileged Africans or humans in general enjoy. And this leads us to the challenges that the coinage 'human rights' could face.

Human Rights and Albinism

After the Second World War and particularly since 1945, there has been a shift in legislative focus from natural rights to human rights, for quite obvious reasons. The concept of natural rights was ultimately linked to the concept of natural law, which became an issue of great controversy after the ugly experiences of the world wars and the ensuing controversies about the nature of the human being and what is by nature entitled to him or her. Peter C. Myers explains that

> The transition has ... been called the 'rights revolution' of the 20th and 21st centuries, and so, too, it is aptly named: 'Natural' and 'human' rights ... [and] signifies a radical change in the understanding of rights (2017: 2).

He explains that this radical shift was necessitated partly because of the limitations of the natural rights perspective, particularly its specific account of human nature.

> According to that account, human beings by nature possess certain specific faculties that entitle us to rights because they render us capable of responsible action ... [But] human rights are conceived not as the exercise of human faculties but as the fulfilment of human needs. The transition from natural rights to human rights is a transition from a *faculties*-based to a *needs*-based account of the basis of rights (Myers, 2017: 2).

Similarly, a popular phrase prior to the twentieth century, 'the rights of man', became anachronistic and stale because views on gender had moved on (Weston, 1984: 257). Hence, 'human rights' became the best denotation for the rights to be enjoyed by humans, although not without difficulties. For instance, since enjoying such rights is intrinsically linked to being human, and since being human is yet another essentially contested concept in different spheres and contexts, it would follow that if within the community of selves in which I live, I am not for whatever reasons considered as a human being, I would most likely be denied the opportunity to enjoy such rights. At best, I would most likely have to put up a fight to enjoy such rights, as we are doing right now. In most human societies, when a human being clearly shows that they have become un-human – say, a rapist or a serial killer – the system denies such a person some rights, such as the right to freedom of movement (Article 13 of the UDHR), and those rights are not restored until they prove that they are human enough again to enjoy such rights. So what exactly does it mean to be human? At what point do humans decide that a fellow human is no longer human enough to be treated as such? Persons with albinism are denied the enjoyment of many human rights in African societies simply because the socio-cultural system does not see them as human enough to enjoy such rights. And we shall return to this point shortly.

According to the Global Citizenship Commission (2016: 81), 'the framers of the UDHR led by Eleanor Roosevelt, envisaged three parts to the post-war human rights enterprise: a set of general principles; the codification of these principles into law; and practical means of implementation'. I believe the first two parts are not the major problems. The general principles are pretty much in order, face only minor difficulties, and can be revised, as has been done in recent decades. For instance, the core principles of equality and non-discrimination which prohibit any form of harmful distinction made on the basis of race, sex, religion, colour, political opinion, and, I dare add, bodily norms, are widely accepted as fundamental principles in international human rights law. These core principles have also been fundamental in, and have formed a basis for, the fight and agitation for the rights of persons with albinism. Human rights advocacy such as that being done by the former UN Independent Expert on the Enjoyment of Human Rights by Persons with Albinism, Ikponwosa Ero, is an advocacy and agitation, for instance, for non-discrimination and equality. This and similar advocacy is yielding some fruits today.

The pursuance of the acceptability of such principles in the legal systems of societies has also been achieved to a reasonable extent, and more can be achieved. Compared to what was happening in many nation states and societies in, say, the 1950s and 1960s, we could say with some sense of conviction that the core principles of human rights have been entrenched in the legal framework of human societies today more than before. For instance, many African nation states have now clearly codified in their legal systems laws that protect the rights of persons with albinism, although implementation remains a problem. For instance, the National Policy on Albinism in Nigeria was developed by the Nigerian government as a response to the many challenges faced by persons with albinism and is meant to improve the status, well-being, and rights of persons with albinism. And this, of course, owes a great deal to the agitations by The Albino Foundation (TAF) in Nigeria for the rights of persons with albinism.

However, the third part of the post-war human rights enterprise – means of implementation – is the one I find daunting and very challenging to achieve. It is very difficult to implement laws concerning the human rights of persons with albinism in a society where people have the seeming conviction that such persons are not really persons. A lot of coercion would be required in such circumstances to make people treat persons with albinism in ways that do not deprive them of their rights. And this has mostly been the case in many African societies: law-enforcement agencies have been used to *compel* people to do what is right. The problem with this approach is that it shouldn't even be the case in the first place. Persons with albinism should be able to enjoy human rights in a social context where many if not all are convinced that they should, and where people deliberately support such an arrangement by their action or inaction.

The problem of the implementation of human rights, for PwDs in general and for persons with albinism in particular, is also the major challenge confronting the CRPD and its applicability in African societies. Since it took effect in 2008, the CRPD has become one of the most important United Nations (UN) treaties and advocacy tools used for promoting the rights of PwDs and persons with albinism. As expected, the contents of the treaty are quite impressive and comprehensive; the general principles guiding the treaty, such as principles of non-discrimination, equality of opportunity, accessibility, equality between men and women, full and effective participation and inclusion, respect for inherent human dignity and autonomy, and respect for the evolving capacities of children and the preservation of their identities (UN, 2008) are all essential in enshrining the respect for, and preventing the abuse of, the rights of PwDs. But the challenge remains implementation in African States. Lord and Stein (2013: 97) put this aptly,

> African states strongly embraced the adoption of the CRPD, along with its Optional Protocol. The Working Group that developed the foundational text of the treaty included delegations from seven African nations. Likewise, the lone seat allocated within the Working Group to represent national human rights institutions was held by a South African Human Rights Commissioner. Sixteen African countries signed the CRPD on the first day it opened for signature, and 34 have ratified it, contributing to a rapid entry into force. In addition, 18 African states are party to the Optional Protocol to the CRPD, thereby assenting to its complaint procedure and procedure of inquiry. The Committee on the Rights of Persons with Disabilities has included experts from the continent, and the current Special Rapporteur on Disability is South African. Also significant is the declaration by the African Union of 1999–2009 and 2010–2019 as African Decades for Persons with Disabilities. The CRPD has therefore been enthusiastically embraced on the African continent, but so too have prior human rights treaties, with uneven subsequent progress. By the same token, the CRPD challenges Africa's states parties – as it does states parties from all regions of the world – to ensure treaty implementation in a manner that responds to broad obligations while being duly consonant to domestic social and legal norms.

In all fairness to the CRPD, it does establish a system of monitoring and implementation which incorporates PwDs in Articles 31 to 40. It anticipates several hindrances to implementation and addresses them (Lord and Stein, 2013). However, cultural beliefs, ontologies, and interpretation of disabilities, which continue to prohibit implementation of the CRPD, are not directly addressed. Hussey, MacLachlan, and Mji (2017) rightly explain attitudinal barriers as a major hindrance to the implementation of the CRPD, and advocate the need for a mindset change around disability in Africa. In their words, 'a challenge to the practical implementation of the CRPD, therefore, lies in overcoming barriers of attitude, which may also be associated with culturally based beliefs. Some of the attitudinal barriers indicated by participants [in their study] clearly illustrated the importance of cultural interpretations of disability.' For example, they quote one of the participants, who explained one of such culturally based beliefs about disability that could hinder the successful implementation of the CRPD thus: 'It is a cultural thing to hide your child with a disability. You do not want people to see this because in some cultures, it is seen as, you know, "the gods, the forefathers are frowning upon the family", and you know, cursing you.'

With specific reference to albinism, it is true that African States and non-governmental organizations (NGOs) and advocacy groups for persons with albinism are working hard to implement and secure rights for persons with albinism. Take, for instance, the right to education in Nigeria. The right to education is a universal human right for all persons enshrined in several UN treaties, such as the Convention on the Rights of the Child (UNCRC), the CRPD, and the World Declaration on Education for All. The Nigerian government makes it possible for all, including persons with albinism, to attain, at the very least, basic education for all. TAF, the Nigerian advocacy non-governmental organization (NGO), also works hard to ensure that persons with albinism secure the rights to education. The TAF website shows clearly that it set up the Education Trust Fund in 2017 to help ensure that persons with albinism, especially children with albinism, who are not in school for one reason or another, have access to quality education, with the goals of reducing the number of out-of-school children with albinism in Nigeria, improving school enrolment among children with albinism, and reducing illiteracy levels among the vulnerable population of persons with albinism.[1] TAF also shows in its website that it has a Scholarship Education Grant that is aimed at providing scholarship grants for persons with albinism to cover tertiary and post-tertiary opportunities).[2] These are no doubt fine initiatives in pursuance of the right to education for persons with albinism. But according to the lived experiences of persons with albinism in Nigeria today, these efforts have not combatted the social exclusion, prejudice, discrimination, and maltreatment that persons with albinism

1 <https://albinofoundation.org/donation/ihvntaf-ovc-project-for-vulnerable-children-in-fct/> [accessed 15 March 2022].

2 https://albinofoundation.org/donation/scholarship-education-grant-project/ [accessed 15 March 2022].

face in the Nigerian society. In fact, accessing education is still difficult, because although in theory the enjoyment of the right to education has been made possible, this has not taken away the challenges of exclusion and discrimination that children with albinism, for example, would face in classrooms, such as name-calling by fellow classmates, isolation by children with albinism, and maltreatment and insults from class teachers due to the inherent deeply entrenched beliefs about albinism that such teachers and students hold. Hence, the approach thus far for securing the rights of persons with albinism have largely ignored the important roles cultural interpretations and beliefs play in stalling effective implementation.

Therefore, attitudes emerging from cultural beliefs, interpretations, and ontologies of disabilities remain among the most important factors to consider in implementing the CRPD. In fact, as the study conducted by Hussey, MacLachlan, and Mji (2017) shows, such culturally based attitudinal barriers are either a direct cause of or an influential factor in all of the other types, including political, financial, health system, communication, and accurate data barriers. This is because cultural interpretations of disability perpetuate and deeply entrench social exclusion, since it is what most community members, including PwDs, believe in and accept to be the truth about disabilities. It is not only non-disabled members of the community that accept and live by these beliefs – even PwDs in such communities do; they see themselves as, for example, the curse of the ancestors or a lesser human being, and this makes it even more difficult to assist such persons to recognize and fight for their rights. Take, for example, the cultural belief mentioned above that persons with albinism are not human beings. This culturally influenced belief about the being and ontology of persons with albinism makes it difficult for community members to understand and accept the need to respect the 'human' rights of such persons. It also makes it difficult for a person with albinism to accept her rightful place in human society.

So, beyond the advocacy taking place in legal and political circles, which I believe is very important, there is also the need to pay careful and close attention to culturally influential factors that are very important in overcoming the false ontological representation of disability in general and albinism in particular in African societies, factors and beliefs that have become so deeply entrenched. We need to explore options to make implementation easier and more productive. And this is important not just for albinism issues but for disability issues in general. The next section discusses two such options,

Two Levels of Hope

In this section, I explore what I call two levels of hope in overcoming deeply entrenched cultural but false representations and beliefs about albinism that label the nature of the being of persons with albinism as less than human. By implication, these make implementation of the core human rights principles as they affect persons with albinism in many African societies difficult to attain. There are: (i) the individual level; and (ii) the social level.

The Individual Level

From our discussion of African ontology, we can deduce the difficulties a person with albinism will be confronted with in enjoying basic human rights, since in the first place, they are not considered a person, both ontologically and normatively speaking, in the same way melanin-privileged Africans are. They already lack the intrinsic worth or value that a melanin-privileged African enjoys simply because the latter fits within the community-accepted structure of being (Imafidon, 2019b: 1–16). As I have explained elsewhere,

> A human being in an African community lacking some features of personhood expected of her in the community would therefore be denied the intrinsic worth of a person who has the required features for being a person. In African cultures, persons with different forms of disability; a foreigner; a terminally, contagiously, mentally, or visibly ill person; and an immoral person who fails to live by the ethos and ethical standards of the community would make the list of persons whose worth will be called into question in African communities. Such persons will be seen as have lesser or no worth compared to African persons with intrinsic worth living within such communities. A person with albinism or a person with angular kyphosis, for instance, would not be regarded as persons understood in the ontological and normative senses discussed above. Rather, they would be seen ontologically as a queer human other, providing varying theorizations as to the nature and features of such othering (Imafidon, 2019b: 8).

Hence, overcoming the cultural representation of their being is essential for earning communal acceptance and recognition, overcoming the representation and, by implication, breaking down the barriers that inhibit their enjoyment of fundamental human rights. Put differently, a person with albinism living in an African place needs to deliberately earn their worth and value within the community of selves. What is obvious from our discourse so far is that with reference to persons with albinism, there are two categories of persons within an African community: the melanin-privileged Black African who has an intrinsic value because he is Black and enjoys the privileges and rights that result from being recognized within the cultural framework as a full human being ontologically speaking, and the person with albinism, who is denied such privileges and rights. The worst that could happen to a person with albinism – and it does happen – is that they imbibe, accept, and live by such representations and ideologies. They must rise above such categorization and earn their worth and respect in the society they are part of:

> It would involve a determined and consistent effort to ignore the mocking and jesting, name-calling, hatred and discrimination; it would involve developing a positive outlook and being around those who encourage that positive outlook; it would consist of going against all odds to keep oneself safe and unharmed, educated and enlightened, healthy and beautiful. Like every other quest to find a meaningful existence, getting these done will not be easy. It would require perseverance and determination (Imafidon, 2019a: 105).

Many persons with albinism have done it successfully through a deliberate and consistent effort:

> Today we know of Salif Keita, the Malian artist who was once ostracized by his family and his community because of his albinism, which is considered bad luck in the Mandinka culture, but still made his way to stardom. We know of his adopted daughter, Nantenin Keita, a Paralympian athlete with albinism who has also done very well for herself. Ikponwosa Ero, a young Nigerian girl, has risen beyond all challenges and stigmatization to become the current independent expert on albinism for the United Nations. Beyond these examples of persons with albinism that have risen to stardom, every community in Africa with persons with albinism has a few examples of such persons rising above the peculiar challenges faced by persons with albinism to

become successful medical doctors, tutors, journalists and the like (Imafidon, 2019: 106).

To be sure, not everyone with albinism in particular, or disability in general, would or should become notable persons in the respective communities in which they live. But simply challenging these representations and living outside of usual expectations is sufficient. To be honest, it doesn't make all the stigma and discrimination go away, but it does make authentic and meaningful existence possible. The end result of such efforts by individual persons with albinism is that they provide instances and some solid grounds for others in the community to question and become sceptical of the truthfulness and factualness of cultural representations and stereotypes of albinism. The more persons within a community challenge these representations of albinism in African places, the more likely these enabling environments are to flourish, and in turn the more assured persons with albinism can be of their fundamental human rights. Therefore, individual persons with albinism have important roles to play in making implementation of the core principles of human rights possible, and they should deliberately do so.

The Social Level

At the social level, the State needs to prioritize the pursuit of enlightenment for its members. Enlightenment is the key to making clear the falsehood of the representations of albinism in African to the public. From personal experience, I notice that when I interact with an enlightened person, we both forget about the fact that I am a person with albinism. It does not even come up in the first place. If African societies had more enlightened persons, it would be easier for persons with albinism to enjoy human rights. But what do we really mean by enlightenment or being enlightened? Despite Immanuel Kant's racist representation of Africa, I beg to borrow here his apt description of the term in his 1784 lecture, as I find it very useful in making the point:

> Enlightenment is man's emergence from his self-imposed immaturity. Immaturity is the inability to use one's understanding without guidance from another. This immaturity is self-imposed when its cause lies not in lack of understanding, but in lack of resolve and courage to use it without guidance from another. Sapere Aude 'Have courage to use your own understanding!' – that is the motto of enlightenment.

Kant adds,

> Laziness and cowardice are the reasons why so great a proportion of men, long after nature has released them from alien guidance (*natura-liter maiorennes*) nonetheless gladly remain in lifelong immaturity, and why it is so easy for others to establish themselves as their guardians. It is so easy to be immature. If I have a book to serve as my understanding, a pastor to serve as my conscience, a physician to determine my diet for me, and so on, I need not exert myself at all. I need not think, if only I can pay: others will readily undertake the irksome work for me. The guardians who have so benevolently taken over the supervision of men have carefully seen to it that the far greatest part of them ... regard taking the step to maturity as very dangerous, not to mention difficult.

Hence, an enlightened person refuses to believe things or accept any claim for which they have no evidence or which they cannot validate. This in no way means that every enlightened person becomes a social deviant or rejects every social norm for reason of not wanting to do things or believe things merely because others do or believe them. Rather, it implies having a grasp of the manifest and latent reasons for a belief or claim and holding on to it not because others do but because we have a strong basis for doing so and rejecting those that are not rationally defensible.

To make enlightenment possible in this sense, there is a need to explore the education system, both formal and informal, in African societies as a means of enlightening the public. An education and training exercise in reconstruction and awareness is strongly needed for personnel in key social institutions as well as for persons with albinism. This will reduce some of the false beliefs and ideologies about albinism in such spaces. Reconstruction education, often attributed to the twentieth-century philosopher of education, Theodore Brameld, holds that

> the goal of education is to assist the educated to address social questions through a curriculum that focuses on social reforms and a constructive criticism of ideologies and beliefs inherent in societies ... Awareness education on the other hand consists of education targeted at providing reliable and current information and knowledge to the educated. It is not just about providing information, but the information must be factual, current, reliable and heuristic (Imafidon, 2019a: 114–15).

Hence, reconstruction and awareness education would facilitate the overcoming of a false representation of albinism in African societies and provide an enabling environment for the enjoyment of rights by persons with albinism. Stakeholders in public education, such as formal schools, religion, town hall meetings, governmental and NGOs, media houses and the like, must take the lead in providing such enlightening education. Continuous and consistent advocacy and policymaking can make this possible.

Conclusion

From the foregoing, the implementation of human rights remains one of the major challenges that well-theorized human rights treaties such as the UDHR and the CRPD face due to various barriers in different spaces and contexts. Such barriers include political, financial, health-related, and gender-related barriers. But, as argued in this chapter, a common denominator of these other barriers, a factor that tends to ignite other barriers and is key in hindering the enjoyment of human rights by PwDs in African cultures, is the cultural factor resulting from cultural norms and interpretations, beliefs, representations, and cultural ontologies. The treatment of persons with albinism in African places as not deserving of the rights and privileges enjoyed by those defined by the cultural norm as persons without disabilities is simply a case in point. What is clear from the discourse thus far is that the challenges faced by persons considered unusual in different social contexts around the globe are more often than not socially and culturally defined and ignited. The need to publicly and actively challenge, question, and interrogate these culturally defined norms, interpretations, and representations of the disabled and the unusual in different social contexts by those individually affected and by various interested stakeholders and social groups is indeed imperative. Exploring the two levels of hope discussed above is essential for ensuring that the dignity and human rights of persons with albinism and with disability are deeply entrenched in society.

Bibliography

Dyer, R. 1993. *The Matter of Images: Essays on Representations.* London: Routledge.

Global Citizenship Commission. 2016. *The Universal Declaration of*

Human Rights in the 21st Century: A Living Document in a Changing World, ed. G. Brown. Cambridge: Open Book Publishers.

Gyekye, K. 1984. 'The Akan Concept of a Person'. In: R.A. Wright. Ed. *African Philosophy: An Introduction* (pp. 277–87). Lanham, MD: University Press of America.

Gyekye, K. 1992. 'Person and Community in African Thought'. In: K. Wiredu and K. Gyekye. Eds. *Person and Community: Ghanaian Philosophical Studies 1* (pp. 101–122), Washington: Council for Research in Values and Philosophy.

Hussey, M., MacLachlan, M., and Mji, G. 2017. 'Barriers to the Implementation of the Health and Rehabilitation Articles of the United Nations Convention on the Rights of PwDs in South Africa', *International Journal of Health Policy and Management* 6(4): 207–18.

Imafidon, E. 2019a. *African Philosophy and the Otherness of Albinism: White Skin, Black Race*. London and New York: Routledge.

Imafidon, E. 2019b. 'Intrinsic versus Earned Worth in African Conception of Personhood'. In: E. Imafidon. Ed. *Handbook of African Philosophy of Difference* (pp. 1–16). Dordrecht: Springer.

Kant, I. 1784. *What is Enlightenment?* <http://www.columbia.edu/acis/ets/CCREAD/etscc/kant.html> [accessed 12 August 2017].

Lord, J.E., and Stein, M.A. 2013. 'Prospects and Practices for CRPD Implementation in Africa', *African Disability Rights Yearbook* 1: 97–113.

Menkiti, I.A. 1984. 'Person and Community in African Traditional Thought'. In: R.A. Wright. Ed. *African Philosophy: An Introduction* (pp. 171–81). Lanham, MD: University Press of America.

Myers, P.C. 2017. *From Natural Rights to Human Rights and Beyond.* The Heritage Foundation: Special Report, No. 197.

Ndubuisi, F.N. 2004. 'A Conception of Man in an African Communalism'. In: J.I. Unah. Ed. *Metaphysics, Phenomenology and African Philosophy* (pp. 239–54). Lagos: FADEC Publishers.

Oladipo, O. 1992. 'The Yoruba Concept of a Person: An Analytico-Philosophical Study', *International Studies in Philosophy* 34(3): 15–24.

Oyeshile, O. 2006. 'The Individual-Community Relationship as an Issue in Social and Political Philosophy'. In: Olusegun Oladipo, Ed. *Core Issues in African Philosophy* (pp. 102–19). Ibadan-Nigeria: Hope Publications.

United Nations (UN). 2008. *Convention on the Rights of Persons with Disabilities and Optional Protocol* <https://www.un.org/development/desa/disabilities/convention-on-the-rights-of-persons-with-disabilities.html> [accessed 5 May 2021].

Weston, B. 1984. 'Human Rights', *Human Rights Quarterly* 6(3): 257–83.

Conclusion

JEFF D. GRISCHOW & MAGNUS MFOAFO-M'CARTHY

The United Nations (UN) Convention on the Rights of Persons with Disabilities (CRPD) signalled a paradigm shift in the international regime of human rights, promising 'to become a transformative international legal instrument' (Lewis, 2010: 98) for persons with disabilities (PwDs). As the UN's first legally enforceable disability rights instrument, the CRPD has the potential to transform disability policies and programmes in Africa. This is especially the case because the Convention is underpinned by the social model of disability, which directs attention to the responsibility of States and societies rather than individual PwDs for upholding disability rights (Corsi, 2018; Kanter, 2014). As Ibhawoh observes in Chapter 1, it also opens up the possibility of a holistic approach to disability rights, because the rights enshrined in the CRPD are universal, indivisible, and interdependent. However, there remain significant barriers to the implementation of the CRPD in many African countries. Where advancements have been made in areas such as advocacy and policymaking, the implementation of the Convention has focused on welfare programmes rather than economic, civil, and political rights per se (Ibhawoh, Chapter 1). With these issues in mind, this conclusion offers a synthesis of the contributors' findings, organized on the basis of the rights and duties enshrined in the Convention, as well as reflections on potential ways forward to achieve disability rights in Africa.

Rights of Persons with Disabilities

The contributors offer valuable assessments of the potential for achieving the CRPD's rights provisions in Africa. This section synthesizes the highlights, taking the rights Articles in the order in which they appear in the Convention. Beginning with Articles 12 (equal recognition before the law) and 13 (access to justice), Chapter 2 points to the importance of equitable access to the justice system for persons with intellectual disabilities (IDs) in South Africa. Accessing justice is especially important for persons with IDs, because they face higher risks of stigma, discrimination, and abuse, including sexual exploitation. The problem, however, is that the onus of proving legal capacity falls on victims themselves rather than the court. For this reason, supported decision-making – in which decisions are supported by third-party agents who are not disabled – is centrally important to accessing justice for persons with IDs in South Africa. This will be a challenging task, however, because the CRPD does not provide guidelines to help stakeholders negotiate the decision-making process (Werner, 2012), even though it is an important part of the Convention.

Chapter 9 on deafness in Ghana also discusses Articles 12 and 13 but shifts the ground to issues of communication and infrastructure. The chapter reports that none of the deaf Ghanaians surveyed received any form of legal support, even if they had requested it. Apart from the lack of supported decision-making, a lack of legal redress for human rights abuses resulted from the lack of sign language interpreters in the courts. They also reported a complete absence of deaf lawyers in Ghana, and no hearing lawyers who had adequate knowledge or training to work with deaf persons. So even if supported decision-making is possible, it will be effective only if deaf Ghanaians themselves find sign language interpreters. Similar barriers have been found in other African research, including Cameroon (Opuku *et al.*, 2016). Supported decision-making also applies to Articles 15 and 16, which guarantee freedom from torture, violence, abuse, and exploitation. These rights are particularly relevant with respect to the cross-cutting issues of IDs and gender. In Chapter 2, for instance, Capri argues that people with ID face significant risks in the absence of supportive decision-making. One of the most severe risks is sexual abuse, which is more common among WwDs than women without disabilities, largely because of beliefs and stereotypes about their sexuality. Naami argues that the same is true in Ghana, which other scholars have confirmed (Opoku *et al.*, 2016), as well as in the Global South generally (Dowse, Frohmader, and Didi, 2016).

With respect to the right to inclusive education (IE) as established in Article 24, our contributors show that it is particularly important for PwDs, because they constitute the largest marginalized group on a global level. IE can provide a pathway out of impoverishment by opening doors to education, healthcare, and other services. In this sense, in the words of Chataika and Hlatywayo in Chapter 3, it is an 'enabling right'. However, in Zimbabwe, despite the ratification of the CRPD and the provision for IE in the Constitution, very little progress has been realized. This is largely because the Constitution sets out the right to IE 'within the limits of the resources'. This language creates a major barrier to achieving IE. Another significant barrier is the lack of proper assistive technologies (ATs), worsened by a lack of commitment on the part of the government to providing them. Given that there is relatively little research on ATs in relation to the CRPD in the Global South (Borg, Lindstrom, and Larsson, 2011), Chataika and Hlatywayo's chapter is especially important in raising the issue as a matter of urgency.

In Chapter 4, Otundo reports a similar situation in Kenya: despite the State's full commitment to IE through the CRPD as well as a Disability Act, many learners with disabilities (LwDs) do not have access to inclusive schools. As a result, the majority of LwDs who are in school attend one of the country's 300 special schools. While this can improve their life chances, there are relatively few special schools relative to the total population of students with disabilities. The resulting low levels of literacy mean that PwDs in Kenya are confronted with limited chances of obtaining employment and sustainable livelihoods. There are numerous other barriers as well, including pervasive stigma and discrimination, generalized poverty, a lack of accessibility in supposedly inclusive schools, inadequate funding, poorly designed curricula, and a lack of clarity and rigour in government policies for IE. The situation is even more challenging in Cameroon, where Mprah *et al.* (Chapter 9) report a complete absence of government policies for IE, leading to classes where teachers are not equipped to teach students with disabilities, as well as a lack of special schools. Poor government policy is worsened by a lack of reliable data on disability, which Otundu observes is a major problem in Kenya. The lack of disability statistics is a significantly under-researched issue, but some work has been done to show that the problem is generalizable to the Global South (Eide and Loeb, 2016), and Jerven's research on African statistics shows that African national development statistics tend to be unreliable generally (Jerven, 2013).

Gender also affects IE in Africa. For instance, Chapter 4 reports that, although the number of WwDs is 50% higher than the number of men in Kenya, girls are less likely to go to school and their dropout rates are higher. Furthermore, girls in school are less likely to receive education than boys, especially in the areas of sex education, life skills, and health (particularly HIV/AIDs). A large part of the problem is the pervasive stigma and discrimination towards girls with disabilities in the Kenyan cultural context. In contrast, Nigeria has gone a long way towards improving educational access for PwDs, including albinism (Chapter 10). The Nigerian government has committed itself to making it possible for all children to receive basic education. To move this goal forward, The Albino Foundation (TAF) established the Education Trust Fund in 2017 to improve school enrolments of children with albinism, including the provision of scholarships. However, while this is a very positive development, children with albinism in Nigeria continue to find it very difficult to access education, and those who are able to go to school face intense stigma and maltreatment from teachers as well as students. The little research that has been done on this topic suggests that mistreatment of persons with albinism in schools is common across the African continent (Hong, Zeeb, and Repacholi, 2006).

Several chapters discuss health and well-being as set out in Article 25. Focusing on the experience of ID in South Africa, Chapter 2 argues that the right to healthcare is especially important, because family and relatives are rarely willing to support persons with intellectual disabilities, and there are very few facilities at the community level. Yet access to formal care is hampered by shortages of professionals, medications, and efficient referral networks. Training is often inadequate as well, especially in cases where persons with intellectual disability (PwID) also have other challenges, such as behavioural or mental health issues. PwDs in Cameroon (Chapter 9) also reported that it was very difficult for them to access healthcare because inaccessible infrastructure made it difficult for them to get to hospitals, and because the hospitals themselves are inaccessible (including beds). As noted above, deaf persons in Cameroon face the additional barrier of communication with doctors and nurses (Opuku *et al.*, 2016).

The extent to which Article 27, the right to work and employment, has been implemented is a key indicator of discrimination against the disabled, in Africa as elsewhere. Chapter 9 reports numerous barriers to employment for PwDs in Cameroon, including inaccessible job sites and a lack of educational opportunities, which make it difficult to obtain qualifications. It is even more difficult for WwDs to find employment. In Chapter 8, Naami and Okine observe that WwDs in Ghana are not only less likely to obtain employment, but also more likely to work in the informal sector when they do find jobs. As such, the employment gap among WwDs is worsened by the fact that they are more likely to fall into vulnerable employment. This reality has been confirmed for other countries in sub-Saharan Africa, as well as across the Global South (Mizunoya and Mitra, 2013).

As set out in Article 29, the right to participation in political and public life is another significant part of the CRPD. This is another enabling right, and it includes not only formal politics but also civil society, including Disabled People's Organizations (DPOs). Regarding the latter, our contributors show that there can be significant barriers to their effective operation. In Uganda (see Chapter 5), barriers include a lack of capacity, as well as the problem of patronage, where the leadership of DPOs can be tied too closely to the government and political office. As much as there is a benefit in having the ear of the ruling party, it also complicates lobbying efforts for disability rights, in that DPO leaders with close ties to the ruling party might refuse to criticize government policy. Also, the disability movement in Uganda sometimes protects the image of the government rather than advocating for disability rights. On the other hand, the government might use the disability movement to present itself as supportive of human rights and progressive on disability issues. Disability programmes might also be used by the government during elections to put a positive spin on candidates. More generally, close ties between disability leaders and the government create a gap between 'disability elites' and ordinary members of DPOs. Muyinda and Whyte used the very insightful term 'disabolitics' to describe this phenomenon in Uganda. The lack of real cooperation between the government and the disability movement, and the lack of public funding and support for disability programmes, means that most DPOs in Uganda rely on foreign donor funding and partnerships with international organizations. However, Muyinda and Whyte argue that the international disability movement, with its focus on human rights, often neglects the grassroots realities of areas marked by serious poverty and a lack of resources. This perspective provides a much-needed corrective to the rather uncritical optimism of some scholars over disability advocacy and the CRPD (e.g. Harpur, 2012).

Two other chapters discuss political rights. Chapter 9 on Cameroon reports that PwDs face challenges in exercising their political and civic rights because of the lack of accessibility in the built environment, including physical infrastructure, such as wheelchair ramps, and a lack of accessible supplies, such as braille voting ballots. Chapter 8 puts a gender lens on the conversation about political participation and the CRPD. Naami and Bekoe point out that there is little literature on political participation among WwDs in the Global South. However, it is known that women generally have lower rates of political participation than men in the Global South, and that PwDs are less likely to take part in politics then persons without disabilities. By extension, WwDs would be less likely to participate in politics than their male counterparts, as evidenced by Sackey's research on Ghana (Sackey, 2015).

Duties of States Parties

Shifting to the CRPD's provisions for duties, the chapters in this volume focus especially on the general obligations contained in Article 4. Of these, the duty of States Parties to enact national disability legislation is particularly important. Chapter 10, for instance, notes that Nigeria has developed a National Policy on albinism to improve the status and rights of persons with albinism. Chapter 2 discusses the need for legislation in relation to ID in South Africa. The most significant contribution of this chapter can be found in the observation that national disability rights legislation, even if consistent with the CRPD, may be inadequate in the absence of subsidiary legislation providing for the rights of specific groups. In the case of South Africa, Capri argues that the lack of legislation for persons with ID leaves a glaring gap in South Africa's framework for public policy, which leaves the door open to continued stigma and discrimination. The argument is supported by first-hand snapshots from the experience of two persons with ID, Mike and Cheryl, whose stories illustrate the problems of the gap between general disability legislation and specific legislation targeting ID.

Our contributors also assess Article 4, which obliges States Parties to work with disability associations to implement the provisions in the CRPD. Focusing on community-based rehabilitation (CBR) in Ethiopia, Chapter 6 foregrounds the duty of States Parties to work with DPOs in the interests of securing specific rights. In Ethiopia, the government has taken the positive step of inviting DPO leaders to capacity-building training sessions, in order to train them to carry out CBR initiatives. However, their participation has been constrained by the government's tight control over Civil Society Organizations (CSOs). Chapter 5 on Uganda also highlights challenges facing DPO participation in formulating public policies, but for a different reason. This is largely because the DPOs lack the resources to send members to consultative meetings or to educate members on advocacy and policymaking. On the other hand, the government of Uganda does not have the political will or see the need to partner with DPOs in the development of policy. Meanwhile, government rhetoric implying strong support for disability programmes has diverted international NGOs from supporting disability projects in Uganda, despite the fact that the government has not followed up with resources or programmes. Chapter 9 echoes this finding for Cameroon. The government ratified the CRPD in 2008, implemented a National Policy Paper in 2010, and announced a decree in 2018 containing measures for implementing the National Policy Paper. However, the government's autocratic character has made it very difficult for disability activists to hold policymakers to account in translating legislation into policy actions. Disability organizations are therefore unable to exert a voice, because civil society is not allowed to act freely. Taken as a whole, the experiences of DPOs narrated in this volume temper the optimism of some commentators who believe in the transformative power of DPO–government collaborations in achieving the rights enshrined in the CRPD (Mahomed, Lord, and Stein, 2019).

Article 4 also mandates States Parties to provide information about disability issues to facilitate achieving disability rights in the real world. Information must be provided to citizens in general, in order to increase the understanding of disability issues at a national level. It also must be provided to PwDs themselves in order to equip them to lobby for their rights. In the case of deaf persons in Ghana (Chapter 7), Mprah and Duorinaah's research found that the vast majority of deaf Ghanaians had challenges accessing information about their rights, and as a result had limited knowledge. The problem could be attributed to the lack of information available in sign language, a lack of education among deaf people, and the exclusion of deaf persons from information programmes on human rights. This finding is consistent with recent research on deaf rights under the CRPD in other African countries such as South Africa (Haricharan *et al.*, 2013; Holness, 2016).

Lessons for Moving Forward

In their recent edited collection, Grech and Soldatic called for more empirically grounded research involving the participation of PwDs in the Global South (Grech and Soldatic, 2016). The contributions in this volume show the possibilities of this approach, especially with respect to identifying priorities for moving forward. Our contributors offer many suggestions, including calls for better and more disaggregated national data on disability (Chapter 8) and the development of accessible information, especially for social groups such as deaf persons, in the interests of advocating for the translation of rights into entitlements (Chapter 9). Chapter 9 also speaks to the importance of removing environmental and transportation barriers in order to increase the chances that WwDs will be able to achieve their rights under the CRPD.

In addition to the above suggestions, our contributors identify two priority areas that are especially important: legislation and advocacy. Regarding legislation, Chapter 4 observes that it is very important for States to domesticate the CRPD, not just sign and ratify it. This would include, at a minimum, drafting national disability laws and/or amending constitutions. However, Chapter 2 argues that in addition to national laws, it is necessary for States to implement specific legislation surrounding disability rights. Focusing on ID, Capri illustrates her argument with very rich snapshots from two persons with IDs, to illustrate the picture from the grassroots. She argues convincingly that legislation for people with intellectual disabilities must include issues of legal capacity and supported decision-making. For South Africa, Capri argues that the government should implement specific legislation allowing supported decision-making for persons with IDs. In addition to equal access to justice, assisted voluntary decision-making could open up a world of possibilities, including increased participation in healthcare policy or public policy generally, or involvement on private sector boards. This chapter also recommends government legislation and policies to provide incentives to employers to increase employment opportunities for PwDs, especially women.

Perhaps the most significant contribution of Chapter 2 is the idea of the ethical State as necessary to the achievement of disability rights. A State that acts ethically will be more likely to implement the range of legislation necessary to achieve rights for PwIDs in South Africa. To achieve this, Capri makes the interesting argument that it will be necessary to publicize the government's complicity in exploiting persons with IDs. This could be done through naming and shaming, in the media and otherwise, or by exerting pressure on the State to change. Chapter 4 echoes this sentiment, although not within the framework of the ethical State. Muyinda and Whyte argue that the CRPD and national legislation might provide an enabling framework, but they will not in themselves produce fundamental change on the ground. The focus has to shift instead to resources and implementation, based on the real needs of PwDs at the community level.

Better data, more accessibility, and improved legislation will provide a foundation for achieving the rights enshrined in the CRPD in Africa. However, as Imafidon argues in his analysis of albinism in Chapter 10, implementing legislation can be very challenging. This is especially true when stigma and discrimination are pervasive among non-disabled society. In this circumstance, the implementation of disability rights legislation would require force and coercion on the part of governments. However, relying on conversion to enforce rights connected to democratic society is of course neither appropriate nor sustainable. For this reason, advocacy to reduce stigma and discrimination is essential to the achievement of disability rights in Africa.

The importance of advocacy is highlighted in many other chapters in this volume. Chapter 2 examines misconceptions about personhood and sexuality in relation to persons with ID. Advocacy to teach the population about their shared humanity and personhood is therefore very important for supporting persons with IDs, to teach the population at large about this issue and reduce erroneous beliefs and stigma. Chapter 3 connects IE to the need for advocacy to reduce stigma and discrimination.

Education can be a tool towards this goal. This includes IE, where students with disabilities are integrated into classrooms with students without disabilities. But in Zimbabwe, it has also taken the form of reverse inclusion, where students without disabilities are put into special schools for students with disabilities. In either case, integrating both groups of learners can lead to lower levels of stigma and discrimination in Zimbabwean society. Chapter 9 speaks of the importance of the sensitization of leaders at the grassroots level, including chiefs, to promote the right to IE. Chapter 10 argues that advocacy is very important in order to remove barriers to social inclusion such as stigma and discrimination. Rights do not automatically flow from the CRPD or national disability laws. They must be actively obtained by PwDs through proactive lobbying. This requires awareness-raising among PwDs themselves, as well as in non-disabled society. PwDs need to be empowered to fight for their rights.

Very importantly, PwDs must also develop the capacity to self-advocate. As Imafidon argues in the case of albinism (Chapter 10), stigma can be internalized and self-directed, where the individual with a disability absorbs the stigmatizing beliefs of non-disabled society. The first step towards group advocacy, therefore, is for individuals to overcome internalized negative cultural representations and to begin lobbying on behalf of themselves. As Mprah and Duorinaah argue in Chapter 7, it is not possible to achieve rights passively; PwDs must actively demand and lobby for their rights. Their research on deafness in Ghana shows that this can work, as with the example of deaf Ghanaians lobbying successfully for sign language interpretation services in the public sector. These kinds of efforts can open up possibilities for advocacy at the social level, supported by governments that – in Imafidon's formulation – actively pursue the enlightenment of their citizens through education campaigns that counter stigma and negative stereotypes.

In developing legislation, advocacy campaigns, and other disability initiatives, it is imperative for States to work in partnership with stakeholders in various sectors in order to advocate for disability rights and to develop appropriate and sustainable policies and programmes. Chapter 9 suggests that governments could work with CSOs, including DPOs, to provide training programmes to help WwDs become more competitive in the job market. Naami and Bekoe also recommend that governments should work with DPOs and other CSOs to develop leadership capacities among WwDs, to enhance their opportunities for political participation. CSOs could also lobby governments to appoint more WwDs to political positions and positions within the civil service.

Focusing on the needs and resources of PwDs at the community level raises further questions about DPOs. Chapter 4 speaks to the need to increase the capacity of DPOs to lobby for the rights of PwDs and to overcome barriers to the efficient operation of the DPOs themselves. The experience of Uganda shows that it might be necessary to disengage DPO leaders from patronage connections to government officials. Muyinda and Whyte also find hope in grassroots movements among PwDs that begin with initiatives to satisfy immediate needs, not disability rights as such. These community movements unfold beyond the scope of the formal disability associations and disabolitics, but perhaps they can link with DPOs and move their activities in a positive direction. Challenges facing DPOs are also present in Ethiopia, although under different circumstances. As noted above, Chapter 6 discusses CBR from the perspective of partnerships between the State and DPOs. At the present time, many of Ethiopia's DPOs lack the capacity to carry out CBR programmes effectively; therefore, the government prioritizes training sessions for DPO leaders. However, the formal DPO sector is hampered by the government's proclamation on the Organization of Civil Societies and Charities, which imposes an onerous process of official registration. As a result, many DPOs in Ethiopia are not formally registered. This limits their potential for capacity-building and action on CBR. More positive for the future is the fact that the Ethiopian government recently established a director for disability. In the wake of this development, the University of Gondar has been working on supporting DPOs to register with the government and carry out CBR programmes.

Chapter 4 speaks to a successful process of a government partnering with stakeholders at the policy level. Otundo describes an initiative by the Kenyan Ministry of Education in 2009 involving meetings with stakeholders and other partners to develop a policy framework for special needs education (SNE). It was a high-level policy initiative designed as a resource for staff with the Ministry of Education and other stakeholders to formulate IE policies consistent with the Salamanca Statement on education for all, which was developed in 1994 by the World Conference on special needs education (UN Educational,

Scientific and Cultural Organization [UNESCO], 1994). Notably, in 2018 Kenya revised the policy to align it with the CRPD's provisions on education. These initiatives established an important framework for IE in Kenya.

Considering the above priorities, education in its broadest sense is perhaps the most important goal moving forward. For PwDs, the achievement of the other rights in the CRPD flow from achieving the right to IE. Educational attainment can lead to employment, knowledge about healthcare options, increased participation in political and civil life, access to justice, and other disability rights. Education also prepares PwDs to lobby for their rights proactively. However, this education is not limited to PwDs. As noted above, arguably the most important foundational duty embedded in the CRPD is the mandate for States Parties and other stakeholders to advocate for disability rights. Advocacy is connected closely to education. This includes government-sponsored programmes to educate non-disabled society about disability issues and rights, targeting not only the general population but also the public sector, the health sector, and traditional leaders. It also includes government curricula in the school system, which can be developed to sensitize the population about the lived experience of disability.

Summing Up

The promulgation of the CRPD was an important moment for disability rights in Africa. However, there is a substantial gap between the adoption of the CRPD by African governments and its implementation on the ground. This collection illuminates important factors behind this gap, from a grassroots perspective based on the experiences of researchers and scholars based in Africa. The contributors identify a range of barriers to achieving the disability rights connected to the CRPD.

First, most of the chapters show that stigma is a significant barrier to achieving disability rights in Africa, as it is in many countries around the world. At a basic level, some of the authors observe that PwDs are not accepted by family or community members, or indeed employers, because they are considered non-productive. Chapter 9 presents evidence of serious stigma and discrimination in Cameroon which undermines the principle of equality and non-discrimination. This was connected to the idea among non-disabled family and friends that PwDs are not productive, which means that they cannot contribute to society. On a deeper level, several chapters raise the possibility that PwDs might be considered less than human in some African societies. Chapter 2 shows this to be the case for persons with ID in South Africa, where in some places the non-disabled population believes that persons with ID possess healing powers, including against attackers, or do not feel pain. Chapter 8 presents evidence that some chiefs in Ghana hold the belief that PwDs are not full members of their societies. Chapter 10 presents an important analysis of albinism, which has not been covered as much as it should be in studies of disability rights in Africa. Imafidon offers compelling evidence that many African societies believe that persons with albinism are not fully human, and that their condition is caused by spiritual forces. As such, they are not entitled to the same rights as others.

Mindful of unique African belief systems, Chapter 10 argues that the CRPD – based on a human rights model entrenched in the Global North – is culturally insensitive to the needs of the Global South, and as such will not produce results unless the rights are adapted to conditions in the Global South. This must be done on a case-by-case basis in different African countries, with the participation of PwDs in establishing policies and programmes to meet their needs within the broad framework of disability rights. This must involve dialogue between political leaders, policymakers, and PwDs. Policymakers must also be aware of the interdependence of the rights enshrined in the CRPD. As Ibhawoh argues in Chapter 1, social and economic rights are necessary for political rights, and political rights are necessary for social and economic rights (see also Falola and Hamel, 2021; Chataika 2019). This makes it important, especially in regions of the Global South such as Africa, for DPOs and stakeholders to advocate simultaneously for political participation, social inclusion and economic rights.

Just as importantly, the individual chapters in this volume point to a larger need for research that cuts across issues and categories, including types of disability. For example, when researching the CRPD's protections against violence and exploitation, there is a need for research that considers issues such as gender and ID. In examining political participation, researchers should incorporate a gendered perspective into their fieldwork. The contributors also point to the need for culturally appropriate research on disability rights in Africa. On this point, many of the chapters argue that it is vitally important to incorporate cultural beliefs about disability into advocacy and educational programmes, as a foundation for achieving specific disability rights. As Ibhawoh writes in Chapter 1, 'what is required is a holistic approach that grounds a rights-based model of disability within an indigenous cultural framework' (Chapter 1: XX). However, drawing on the work of Gebrekidan (2021), Ibhawoh also argues that real advancement on disability rights in Africa will require moving beyond cultural models of disability to focus on 'the overarching themes of economy, technology, and environment and their concomitant impact on marginalization, agency, and activism rather than culture' (Chapter 1: 36). If this transition can be accomplished, starting with building an understanding of cultural perspectives on disability in different African countries, then achieving the rights enshrined in the CRPD may become a reality in Africa.

Bibliography

Borg, J., Lindstrom, A., and Larsson, S., 'Assistive Technology in Developing Countries: A Review from the Perspective of the Convention on the Rights of PwDs', *Prosthetics and Orthotics International* 35(1): 20–29.

Chataika, T. 2019. *The Routledge Handbook of Disability in Southern Africa*. New York: Routledge.

Corsi, J.L. 2018. 'Article 5: Equality and Non-Discrimination'. In: I. Bantekas, M.A. Stein, and D. Anastasiou, *The UN Convention on the Rights of PwDs: A Commentary* (pp. 140–170). Oxford: Oxford University Press.

Dowse, L., Frohmader, C., and Didi, A. 2016. 'Violence Against Disabled Women in the Global South: Working Locally, Acting Globally'. In: S. Grech and K. Soldatic, *Disability in the Global South: The Critical Handbook* (pp. 323–36). Cham: Springer Nature.

Eide, A.H., and Loeb, M. 2016. 'Counting Disabled People: Historical Perspectives and the Challenges of Disability Statistics'. In: S. Grech and K. Soldatic, *Disability in the Global South: The Critical Handbook* (pp. 51–68). Cham: Springer Nature.

Falola, T., and Hamel, N. 2021. *Disability in Africa: Inclusion, Care, and the Ethics of Humanity*. Rochester: University of Rochester Press.

Gebrekidan, F. 2021. 'Rethinking African Disability History: From the Cultural Model to a Socio-Economic Perspective'. In T. Falola and N. Hamel, *Disability in Africa: Inclusion, Care, and the Ethics of*

Humanity. Rochester: University of Rochester Press.

Grech, S. and Soldatic, K. *2016. Disability in the Global South: The Critical Handbook*. Cham: Springer Nature.

Haricharan, H.J., Heap, M., Coomans, F., and London, L. 2013. 'Can We Talk about the Right to Healthcare Without Language? A Critique of Key International Human Rights Law, Drawing on the Experiences of A Deaf Woman in Cape Town, South Africa', *Disability and Society* 28(1): 54–66.

Harpur, P. 2012. 'Embracing the New Disability Rights Paradigm: The Importance of the Convention on the Rights of Persons with Disabilities', *Disability and Society* 27(1): 1–14.

Holness, W. 2016. 'The Development and Use of Sign Language in South African Schools: The Denial of Inclusive Education', *African Disability Rights Yearbook* 4: 141–89.

Hong, E., Zeeb, H., and Repacholi, M.H. 2006. 'Albinism in Africa as a Public Health Issue', *BMC Public Health* 6(212): 1–7.

Jerven, J. 2013. *Poor Numbers: How We Are Misled by African Development Statistics and What to Do about It*. Ithaca: Cornell University Press.

Kanter, A.S. 2014. *The Development of Disability Rights Under International Law: From Charity to Human Rights*. London: Routledge.

Mahomed, F., Lord, J.E., and Stein, M.A. 2019. 'Transposing the Convention on the Rights of PwDs in Africa: The Role of Disabled Peoples' Organizations', *African Journal of International and Comparative Law* 27(3): 335–58.

Mizunoya, S., and Mitra, S. 2013. 'Is There a Disability Gap in Employment Rates in Developing Countries?' *World Development* 42(C): 28–43.

Opoku, M.P., Huyser, N., Mprah, W.K., Badu, E., and Alupo, B.A. 2016. 'Sexual Violence against Women with Disabilities in Ghana: Accounts of Women with Disabilities from Ashanti Region', *Disability CBR and Inclusive Development* 27(2): 91–111.

Sackey, E. 2015. 'Disability and Political Participation in Ghana: An Alternative Perspective', *Scandinavian Journal of Disability Research* 17(4): 366–81.

United Nations Educational, Scientific and Cultural Organization (UNESCO). 1994. 'The UNESCO Salamanca Statement' <http://www.csie.org.uk/inclusion/unesco-salamanca.shtml> [accessed 10 April 2021].

Werner, S. 2012. 'Individuals with Intellectual Disabilities: A Review of the Literature on Decision-Making since the Convention on the Rights of People with Disabilities (CRPD)', *Public Health Reviews* 34(2): 1–27.

INDEX

For abbreviations and acronyms in entries and subentries, please see the Abbreviations list on pages xv–xvii.